Don't Call Me a Crook!

Dear Stewart,

I hope you enjoy the terrible life and times of Mr. Moore!

Best wishes,

Nicholas Towasser
Editor and Publisher
Dissident Books

CONTENTS

Don't Call Me a Classic:
The Mysterious Case of Bob Moore

1 oz. *Trainspotting.*
2 oz. Charles Bukowski.
1 oz. *Candide.*
Shake.
Add three shots of noir.
Stir.
Add enough Scotch whisky to kill a horse.
Pour over stolen diamonds.
Serve and enjoy.

BACK IN 2004, WHILE ON A TRIP TO HARTFORD, CONNECTICUT, I read the AK Press edition of *You Can't Win*, the vagabond memoir by Jack Black (the itinerant thief, not the Hollywood funnyman). It engrossed me. Like any powerful work of literature, it pulled me into a complete world, with its own language and culture.

When I finished it, I wanted more. Not more by Black, but another account of life on the road and outside the law. I would follow AK's example and unearth an outsider self-portrait, an autobiography by someone who lived on his/her own terms, a dissident in the truest sense of the word.

This quest led me to one of the most blessed places on Earth: the New York Public Library on Fifth Avenue and 42nd Street. I pulled books falling under the "Tramps" subject heading. They were worn, their pages yellow and crumbling. Forgotten words written by forgotten men. Nothing stood out and demanded the attention of a new generation. I wanted something bold and impudent, something that would take me for a walk on the wild side.

Then I came to *Don't Call Me a Crook!* The title was promising. Its opening sentence ("It is a pity there are getting to be so many places that I can never go back to . . .") caught my attention. By the first paragraph, I was hooked. "This is the book for me," I thought, "oh yes yes yes."

Don't Call Me is one of the greatest books I've ever read. It's picaresque, perverse, and darkly funny. With its unforgettable characters and strange plot twists, it reads more like a novel than a memoir.

Bob Moore, a Glaswegian, worked as a marine engineer, building superintendent, and moonshine runner. He traveled throughout the U.S., Australia, Egypt, South America, Japan, and China. He also conned women, fought with pirates on the Yangtze, and set a coffee shop ablaze. Clearly, this Scot loved life.

Moore might've appropriated things that belonged to others, but he was not—repeat, *not*—a crook. "I am not a crook at all, because a crook is a man who steals things from people, but I have only swiped things when I needed them or when it would be wasteful to let slip an opportunity." You got that?

And don't let the librarians fool you. Moore led a rootless and lawless existence, but he wasn't a tramp in the "homeless" sense of the word. His accommodations varied from Chicago's swankiest hotel to a Shanghai flophouse, but all the same, he always managed to sleep with a roof over his head, thank you very much.

The 1920s didn't roar for Moore: They *exploded*. And whether he was snatching jewelry or in the thick of a New York high-society orgy, he embraced the age with a bear hug. And nothing—not Prohibition, marriage, or the police—was going to stop him from having a good time.

Moore is charming and appalling, brutally honest and deceitful, clever and ignorant. Whether he's looking back at his brief stint in the military, his life on the sea, or the joys of dodging the police, he's always entertaining. Yes, he was a snollygoster, but he was a charismatic snollygoster.

Don't Call Me a Crook: My True Autobiography was released in 1935 by Hurst & Blackett, Ltd., a London publisher. (Two years earlier the firm offered readers the English translation of another untamed World War I vet's recollections . . . *Mein Kampf*.) Pat Spry is credited as its editor. Who Mr. or Ms. Spry was I've been unable to determine. Perhaps Moore told his stories to Spry, who transcribed and forged them into a cohesive tale.

Judging by the advertisements printed at the back of *Don't Call Me* of other books published by Hurst & Blackett, I suspect the publisher hoped it would be a worthy addition to its other world-travel and seafaring titles. The original edition included two brief introductory blurbs:

This is the log of a real rolling stone. The author, a Glaswegian, has roamed the world in many lands and on half the seas, and his stories of the underworld of America and the pirate-infested rivers of China are thrilling in the extreme. He has fought, starved, been in prison, shot men, deluded women, but he has never stolen—only "swiped" things as he puts it. From one who regards the law of "meum" and "tuum" in such [a] naive way, we can expect a very unconventional book, and whatever view we may take of the author's extraordinary activities, we are certainly given a glimpse of life that is definitely out of the usual.

And a "Publishers' Note":

In presenting this most unusual volume of personal experiences the Publishers have purposely preserved, or so far as possible, the unpolished yet often forceful and naive expressions of the Author's original style. As a result, a more real picture seems to emerge of the Author's personality and of those with whom in the many strange bypaths of his life [he] came into contact.

Don't Call Me never bores. Never. The book's tempo matches Moore's life. Like a ship, he is constantly moving, from job to job, scheme to scheme, land to land. Not even a marriage and a baby hold him down.

I've always been fascinated by rootlessness and Sadeian selfishness. What would it be like to go wherever and do whatever you desired, unrestrained by your conscience, the law, or convention? While this isn't the place for a discussion of values, it's often struck me notions of right and wrong are cultural norms that are instilled, not innate. To overcome learned ethics and construct your own values must be a truly heroic act.

That said, Moore doesn't make a conscious effort to unlearn anything. He's not a philosopher. He's just a guy out for a quick buck and good time.

Following my breakfast routine, one morning I lowered two eggs into a saucepan filled with boiling water. The phone rang, and I was dragged into a lengthy conversation. The eggs fled my mind. Later, smelling something funny, I lifted the pan's cover. The water had long since evaporated. The eggs were burnt black where they touched metal. That's how hard-boiled *Don't Call Me* is.

Moore's world is a terrible place. Around every corner wait disaster and death. It takes little to provoke a fight, or even a murder. Trust is met with swift and severe punishment. But as Jack Black puts it about his own tone, Moore tells his story "with a smile." His style is conversational. You don't so much read *Don't Call Me* as hear it in a broad Glaswegian accent. I can see Moore the raconteur telling his life story in a pub, peppering it with plenty of winks and nudges. And like any barroom bard, he's quick to impart his wit and wisdom.

Moore's humor leavens his story's darkness but also suits it in a strange way. *Don't Call Me* is both noir memoir and farce. I'm reminded of H. L. Mencken's admiring analysis of Joseph Conrad. The God of Conrad's universe, Mencken wrote, is "an extremely ingenious and humorous Improvisatore and Comedian, with a dab of red on His nose and maybe somewhat the worse for drink—a furious and far from amiable banjoist upon the human spine, and rattler of human bones."

I felt it was so important to emphasize *Don't Call Me* is composed of a trinity of distinct stories that I took it upon myself to divide the book into three parts: "Diamonds and Whisky," "Lobsters and Coleslaw," and "Mitchell and China."

I added an exclamation point to the title to give it some urgency. I also thought the book deserved a jazzier, more eye-catching subtitle. "My True Autobiography" just didn't cut it. "A Scotsman's Tale of World Travel, Whisky, and Crime" is a mouthful, but it sums it up.

I don't know why *Don't Call Me* didn't win recognition in its day. Maybe it was too honest and shocking for readers of the 1930s. Maybe there wasn't enough marketing and publicity done to promote it. I also can't tell why no one rediscovered it sooner.

I've found no reviews of *Don't Call Me*. A National Library of Scotland librarian told me she could only locate two advertisements for it in *The Times* of London. There mustn't have been many copies printed, because despite many Web searches, I've found no used-book dealers selling it. In fact, I've located only five owners of the original Hurst & Blackett edition: the New York Public Library; the National Library of Scotland; Cambridge University; Random House (years ago Random House acquired a publisher named Hutchinson, who had earlier merged with Hurst & Blackett); and a woman in Essex, England.

Joanne McEwen wrote to me after learning of my plans to reissue *Don't Call Me a Crook!* She told me she's Bob Moore's granddaughter. Moore's real name was Robert Macmillan Allison, Joanne wrote, and he was born February 22, 1899 at 706 Pollackshaws Road, Glasgow. His father was bricklayer named James Allison, and his mother was Agnes (née Martin), she said. His wife, Grace, passed away in 2000, and his son, John Allison, is still alive, Joanne wrote.

Robert used his wife's maiden name for his pseudonym, Joanne told me. He died November 24, 1937 of acute alcohol gastritis and was buried in a potter's field in London, she wrote. She also said that Pat Spry was an Australian woman. Unfortunately, there is no documentation linking Joanne's grandfather to *Don't Call Me a Crook!*, she said.

Joanne asked that I dedicate this edition to her son, Cameron McEwen, and I was happy to comply. Incidentally, that's not Joanne's grandfather on the cover: it's just a fellow my cover designer and I thought conveyed the book's cheekiness and roguishness.

The back cover of *You Can't Win* hails it as "a true lost classic." *Don't Call Me a Crook!* is a lost book that should've been, and I hope someday will be, considered a classic.

Nearly 75 years has passed since *Don't Call Me* hit bookstores. I wanted to do all I could to introduce this brilliant book to a new generation. And to facilitate that I couldn't just reprint it: I tried to anticipate questions readers outside of Moore's time and place would have about his vocabulary and allusions. It's my hope that the footnotes enhance the reader's experience.

Likewise, as an editor I'd be remiss if I didn't address inconsistencies and omissions in the original text. I also took the liberty of reworking what I felt were instances where the first edition's spelling and punctuation were distracting. For example, the original text spells out dollar amounts and street numbers. Except in cases where digits can't precisely convey what Moore wrote (e.g., "$1,000" can be read as "a thousand dollars" or "one-thousand dollars") I substituted numerals wherever possible. In cases were "dollars" might refer to Chinese dollars I've not used the U.S. currency symbol ("$").

The first edition also often uses colons and paragraph breaks to introduce brief quotations, which to my eyes is generally awkward and unnecessary. By today's standards the original text makes overabundant use of hyphens (e.g., "home-made," "state-room"). All edits were made in the spirit of humbly assisting Moore tell his story. Even Homer nods . . . especially after he polished off your whisky.

I wonder about the knock on the head Moore experiences early in his career. Could this account, at least partly, for his antisocial shenanigans?

In keeping with this book's general mystery, I've found only one mention of it in another work. In *Empire Made Me: An Englishman Adrift in Shanghai* (London: Allen Lane, 2003), Robert A. Bickers writes:

> But there was always an indigent Briton or two, seamen thrown up on the shore and the like. There is even one cheery account of drink-fuelled indigence in China, published in 1935. Bob Moore's *Don't Call Me a Crook* is a sensationalist and by no means reliable read, but it conveys the flavour of the fight, and the collapse. A Glaswegian seaman, Moore claimed to have worked for the Asiatic Petroleum Company on the Yangtsze in the 1920s and describes a six-month binge in Shanghai, before repatriation . . .

I don't see why Bickers finds *Don't Call Me* "unreliable." As with anything mined from memory, there's the possibility for distortion and exaggeration. I've detected a few minor inaccuracies, but the book feels true to me. It's scattered with the names of real ships, and even of one Scottish missionary. Moore gives a detailed account of an actual shipwreck off the Virginia Capes. Ironically, I'm ready to believe Moore, a liar and thief.

—NICHOLAS TOWASSER
Publisher
Dissident Books

ACKNOWLEDGMENTS

Bob Moore, a marine engineer, would be amused to know that this book, together with a new edition of H. L. Mencken's *Notes on Democracy*, is Dissident Books' maiden voyage. I would be remiss if I didn't thank the following for their invaluable help along the long, strange cruise: the staff of the New York Public Library's Humanities and Social Sciences Library; Tina Staples, deputy archivist, HSBC Holdings plc; Mark A. Berhow, the Coast Defense Study Group, Inc.; Susan Bellany, National Library of Scotland; Alison J. Lindsay, the National Archives of Scotland; Bernie Schleifer; Matt Avery; Christopher Smith; Norman Graham; Roger Rosenthal; David Mulrooney; everyone at Midpoint Trade Books, especially Ruth Esehak-Gillespie; the faculty of New York University, School of Continuing and Professional Studies, Center for Publishing, particularly Jan-Erik Guerth (BlueBridge Books) and George Davidson (GPD Publishing Associates, Inc.); and David Otis Fuller, Jr.

I am particularly grateful to James Kelman for his insightful afterword, and to Bob Moore, for this marvelous book.

PART ONE
Diamonds and Whisky

CHAPTER 1

1

I T is a pity there are getting to be so many places that I can never go back to, but all the same, I do not think it is much fun a man being respectable all his life.

I would like to go back to Hoboken, but if I did Heinz Billings might get me, because he said he would wait forever; though I think myself it is terribly mean of a man to say he will wait forever, when all you have done is to take some money out of the till in a speakeasy.[1] It is not even as if it was *his* money in the till, because I helped him myself to get it off the sailors when they were not thinking anything about their money, so you could rightly say that the money was half mine. I think it is mean of Heinz Billings, but then, of course, I always knew Heinz Billings was a mean man.

So, you see, I cannot go back to Hoboken while Heinz Billings is alive, and I cannot go back to the rest of New York[2] either, because there was the time the man was killed that held me up outside Kelly's Clam Broth House,[3] and the police came with the gun and asked me questions in my hotel. But they did not think I had killed him at the time, because they let me go away all right, but you never can tell when the New York police will come after you. And if they did they might find out about the diamonds and Mrs. Carr's ring.

So I do not think I can go back to New York, even if I make a lot of

1 *speakeasy* a place where liquor is sold illegally. There was a national prohibition against alcohol in the U.S. from 1920 until late 1933.

2 *rest of New York* although located just across the Hudson River from New York City, Hoboken is in northeastern New Jersey.

3 *Kelly's Clam Broth House* Opened in 1899, the Clam Broth House was a Hoboken institution. Its neon sign, shaped like a hand, pointed visitors to its location two blocks from the Hudson River waterfront. Frank Sinatra's mother ate there. From its balcony, President Woodrow Wilson during World War I said farewell to troops as they boarded ships and welcomed them upon their return. The building was torn down in 2005 because of structural instability. A local developer has plans to reopen the restaurant with its famed sign at the same site.

money out of writing my reminiscences, and though I would like to very much I do not think I can go back to Buenos Aires either. Because, though Buenos Aires is a nice place, there is the little old lady there that wore a silver chain round her leg and was going to set me up in business, only it was not what you would call a platonic arrangement, and I never did think much of a man who would sell himself for money, so I thought I would just have the money and I went to Atlantic City with it. So I do not think I can go back to Buenos Aires now.

It is a pity that it is so easy for a man to make himself famous, because now if I go to a place I often find that they know all about me, and though it is gratifying to feel that you have made a mark in the world, I sometimes find that when I come to a place, people misunderstand me because they have read things that make them think maybe I am a crook. And how is a man to have friends if everywhere he goes people are expecting him to be a crook? Though, really, I am not a crook at all, because a crook is a man who steals things from people, but I have only swiped things when I needed them or when it would be wasteful to let slip an opportunity.

Because I think it is very wrong for a man to waste his opportunities. But a crook is a man who does not wait for opportunities; a crook is a man who makes his own opportunities. I would never be a crook, because I would not choose to live by a life of crime.

If I make a lot of money out of writing my reminiscences I think I will go and settle on a farm in Australia, or, maybe, I will buy a house in Kobe in Japan, which is a very pretty place; because perhaps that would be better than Australia, as the people in Kobe do not know how to read English, so they will not have seen anything to make them think I might be a crook.

I would like to go back to China because it is easy to make money without doing a lot of work in China, and you can get boys to put on your socks for you. But they will not have my account anymore in the Hongkong and Shanghai Bank, and you never can tell if the captain off the ship that I blew up, away up the Yangtze Kiang, might not have come down the river and have told them to watch out for me. And I would not like to be caught and tortured by Chinese pirates, because I have seen what they do to women, and they have a lot of imagination about using torture in China.

So it seems that I will have to stay in London, or else go to Australia, because they will not bring the band out for me in my hometown, Glasgow, anymore.

Glasgow is a funny place because everybody there tries to be more respectable than everybody else, and it cannot be because they really want to be respectable, for I could tell you things about Glasgow that would make your hair stand on end. But there is no need to draw the curtains and hide this book under the mattress to read when there is no one looking, as I do not like to hurt people's feelings when I have known them from my childhood; besides, I would not like to lose all the money for my reminiscences by being drawn into a court case. But *I* do not think it is any fun being respectable, so I will tell you about myself.

When I was a little boy my mother made me eat a lot of soup. She said I must eat up my soup because it would stand by me in the future. And now that I am 36, and look back on all that I have been through I think it was through eating my soup that I have come through alive to this day. Because I have been round the world seven times, and I have been ship-wrecked three times, and I have spent £100,000.[4] I have had my hardships as well. But I have not died of starvation, or succumbed to disease, or given way to delirium tremens,[5] so I think I must owe the fact that I am alive and well today to the fact that my mother made me eat a lot of soup when I was a little boy. My mother always thought it was better to have homemade soup to give me, and though I like homemade soup myself, I sometimes think it is a pity that she did not buy someone's brand of soup, because then they would be able to put my picture on their labels and I would not have to write my reminiscences to make some money, but could live on the fat of the land for the rest of my days.

But perhaps you would rather read about my life than see my picture on a soup label, so I will now relate to you the major events of my career.

2

When I was a very little boy I used to like to have a lot of money, because, though I did not buy any drinks with it in those days, I think it is only when a man has plenty in his pocket that he feels able to cope

4 *£100,000* Beginning in 1925, Great Britain restored the gold standard, and the pound sterling was equivalent to \$4.86653. Hence, £100,000 equaled \$486,653. A U.S. dollar between 1925 and 1931 was equivalent to about \$12.74 in current terms: Using that as a metric, £100,000 was roughly 6.2 million contemporary dollars. However, in 1931 Britain dropped the gold standard. Four years later the pound experienced 43% depreciation.

5 *delirium tremens* A mental disorder marked by hallucinations and dis-orientation brought on by heavy and excessive alcohol consumption; also called "the D.T.'s."

with life. I mean it puts a man at a disadvantage not to have plenty of money, and I think it is because I feel this way that I have had to swipe a little money once or twice in my life. But at first I did not need to swipe money, because all I needed was a few shillings to buy sweeties and I used to get that from my mother, so it was not till I grew up that I found money is really very hard to come by in this world.

I used to win a lot of fights at school because I never think there is much sense in fighting anyone you know can beat you. When I had won a fight I used to buy my mother a present, and so my mother would like me very much. It is always a good idea to give a woman a present because often she will do things for you then. But I did not give my mother a present because I wanted her to do things for me. I liked to give my mother a present because she was very, very good to me. I am sorry now that there are things in my life that have made her unhappy, but a woman does not understand how a man has to battle for existence. A man could not get on at all if he was always thinking of his mother, because there are so many things that she does not want him to do.

My mother would have liked me to go to work every day and rear a family in Glasgow, but a woman does not understand how a man must have some excitement in his life.

So I decided I would go to sea and I started work as an apprentice; but I had only started just to work when the World War came along.

I wanted to go to the War, but my mother thought I would be killed so I told her I was going to a football match and I went away and enlisted. But my father got me out that time because I was only 16, but the next time I was more careful. They did not know what had become of me and I joined the Royal Flying Corps. I did not understand when I joined that a war is not all wearing uniforms and killing people. So when I found I had to wear overalls and grease aeroplanes[6] at a base near Boulogne,[7] and never kill anyone at all, but just work like an ordinary workman, only dirtier and harder, I began to be sorry that I had enlisted at all.

I asked to be transferred to the infantry so that I could have a bayonet, but the O.C.[8] said that I had better have my brain examined, and he kept me there greasing aeroplanes just the same.

The only good times I had in the War were when I came on leave to London, and I did not go home at all till I was hit on the head by

6 *grease aeroplanes* lubricate their machinery.
7 *Boulogne* port city in northern France on the English Channel.
8 O.C. Officer-in-Charge.

a propeller, and they did not know for three years where I had gone to from home. But when I was hit by the propeller I was so sick I nearly died, and the Government discharged me from the Army and gave me £150 gratuity, so I thought I would go home.

Now that I had been hit by a propeller and was still very sick through having served my King and Country, my father could not be angry with me for running away to join the Army, so they gave me a great welcome. And after I had had a holiday in the north I started to train to be an engineer all over again.

3

Because I had been serving in a mechanical unit in the Army I did not have to do five years' but only three years' training, so I was an engineer by the time I was 21.

I did not earn a lot of money while I was learning to be an engineer, but my mother used to give me some because I was a man now, not a boy, and you could not expect me to manage on a boy's wages.

The first job I got when I had finished my apprenticeship was junior engineer on a ship trading between Glasgow and Sweden, and it was when I got on that ship that my first adventures began.

I felt I was very important to have a job as junior engineer after having been only an apprentice, so I stuck out my chest and marched about that boat like I was Chief on the "534."[9] It did not worry me to think I was only getting £8 a month in wages, because I knew my mother would help me while I was only getting so little, and I had heard that you could make a lot of money by smuggling crystal through the customs, so I did not think financial matters were likely to worry me at all.

She was a little ship with only three engineers including the Chief, so, of course, I had to take the Chief's watch. And when I found I was going to be in charge of an engine room by myself I could have got down in the middle of the floor and stood on my head.

I kept looking at the time to see when it would be my turn, and when it was my turn I went marching down to the stokehold[10] and started yelling to the firemen[11] to get busy and shake up those fires. I

9 *534* The "534" was the order number and initial working name for the *Queen Mary*, the largest passenger liner of its time. The ship was built in Clydebank, a shipbuilding town to the west of Glasgow. John Masefield, Britain's poet laureate, penned "Number 534" to commemorate the *Queen Mary*'s launch on September 26, 1934.

10 *stokehold* the chamber on a ship where the furnaces are fueled.

11 *firemen* persons who maintain and fuel furnaces.

yelled very loud so that they would know that I meant it, but they did not do anything at all. They just leaned on their shovels and stared at me like as if I was something in a circus. So I thought they were trying to defy me because it was my first watch, so I yelled at them louder than ever, and I put in some swear words because I would not like them to think I did not know the right words to say.

But they still would not do what I told them—only one of them told me to go and take a look at the gauge.

So I did, and it was on the "Blood," which means if steam had gone any higher the safety valve would have blown off. So I saw why they would not obey me, and I made out to them I had been joking, because you have to keep up appearances or you would not have any discipline. But it was a pity I was in such a hurry at the beginning that I did not think to look at the gauge.

4

However, I was soon quite an old hand, and instead of ordering the firemen about when I was on watch I used to see everything was all right and then go away and have a bath.

I was having a bath when I was on watch the night the steering failed.

We were coming round the North of Scotland and it was one of those rough nights when you cannot see any thing past the rail if you happen to be up on deck, and there are plenty of things to hit along the coast of the North of Scotland. So I nearly jumped out of my skin when I was lying all cosy in the bath and I heard the engine-room telegraph[12] ring. It was not an ordinary quiet ring. It was loud and it kept on going, so I knew it must be something important and I jumped out of the bath and ran, just like I was. But the floor on the engine room was slippery and my wet feet went from under me and I crossed the engine room on my back—which is funnier to watch than experience, because there was only bare skin on my back, and when I had finished up sliding there was not any skin at all.

But I did not have any time to think of my sufferings because I remembered how it was my duty to be in the engine room, so I ran to the telegraph and it read, "Full speed astern."[13] Someone then told me that the steering chain broke.

12 *engine-room telegraph* a mechanism that relates orders from a ship's bridge down to the engine room.
13 *astern* in the direction of or at the ship's stern, its rear.

So I swung her into "Full speed astern" and then I grabbed up a hammer and a chisel and I ran for the deck to where he said the steering chain had parted, but it was only when I got on the deck where the wind was blowing icicles, that I realized I was wearing no clothes at all.

But I could not be bothered about my appearance at that moment because even in the dark you could make out that we were heading for some rocky cliffs. So I did not think about my back or how the cold wind might give me pneumonia, but I just ran to where the chain was parted, and it was not till a man came up and wrapped an oil-skin round me that I was fit for a public position at all.

We got the chain fixed, however, and the Skipper steered her safely off the rocks, and no one told him I had been in the bath when the engine-room telegraph rang. In fact he thought I had behaved with much credit, and he told the company about me, so they gave me £5 for a bonus, and I spent it on buying crystal to smuggle from Sweden into Glasgow because it was possible to make quite a lot of money that way.

You buy sets of it and take it ashore in your luggage and the dealers in Glasgow will give you twice what you paid for it. But every trip I did not have enough money to buy all the crystal I liked. So one time at Friedrickstad[14] where we had gone to load some timber, I made friends with a girl who had a tobacco kiosk, and I said if she would lend me some money to buy a set of crystal I wanted I would give her a present and would pay her back before we sailed on Wednesday. So she gave me the money.

But we did not sail on Wednesday. We sailed on Monday so I could not give her her money and then that girl played a very dirty trick on me.

She wrote a letter to the company and said how I had deceived her, so I would have got into serious trouble, only I went ashore at Gothenburg[15] and sold some whisky that I had swiped from the Chief's cabin, and I sent the money to her. So that is an example of how sometimes you have to swipe things, because I had no money to pay her; and if I had not paid her I might have lost my job on that ship.

---

14 *Friedrickstad* Fredrikstad, a city in southeastern Norway
15 *Gothenburg* a city in southwestern Sweden; also known as Göteborg.

5

I don't know how long I would have stayed on that ship if I had not got arguing with the Chief Officer about the War. But I find that it is fatal to argue about the War, and the Chief Officer was one of those people who think that they know everything.

He seemed to think that he could come in and sit down in our mess room and stuff us with any stuff he liked and not be laughed at; but what would you have done if a man had tried to fill you with a story like this:

He started telling us about being on a ship that was torpedoed, and he said she was sinking and he jumped overboard wearing a greatcoat[16] and with a lighted cigar in his mouth. He said he remembered coming up and taking off the greatcoat, and swimming. Then he knew nothing till he woke up in a ship's cabin with a photo of himself hanging on the wall facing him! And he looked round and recognized the cabin, and it was one he had been in years before!

He said that he had been picked up by this different ship that he used to be on and carried down to his own cabin.

"When I woke," he said, "I thought I had been dreaming!" And he looked round as if he expected us all to be goggle-eyed.[17]

So instead of being goggle-eyed I winked at the others and I said, "Yes, I think you must have been dreaming."

And he flushed up all red and jumped to his feet and yelled out, "Are you trying to call me a liar?"

So I winked again at the others and just went on giggling.

"Answer me!" he said, but I couldn't talk for giggling, so he up with a glass of milk and threw it all over me.

Well, it is a horrible feeling to have milk running down your face and making all your chest wet, so I grabbed the first thing that was handy and it happened to be a big dish of potatoes. I let fly with them, dish and all, and he had to duck, or I'd have killed him.

The rest of them grabbed hold me then and threw me out of the mess room. The Chief Officer did not come after me but he never could stand me from that day.

He used to pick on me. When he required water on deck he would yell down to the engine room, though an officer really has no business to give orders to the engineers.

16 *greatcoat* a weighty overcoat.
17 *goggle-eyed* with eyes that project out or roll.

When an officer wants anything he is supposed to come down the companionway[18] and ask for it, but one day when I was in the engine room he yelled down for water and I took no notice.

"D'you hear me?" he yelled.

"When you want something," I yelled back, "you can come down here and ask for it."

Well, of course, though I was within my rights, that was really cheek[19] from me—being only junior engineer—so he yelled out he'd come down all right and put my bloody head through the bulkhead.[20]

And down he came, clamping down the ladder, breathing so hard that you could hear him above the engines. He was about three times as big as me and his eyes were staring with anger. I did not feel happy at all when he got me round the throat. I was powerless to struggle, and he began to force me back against the bulkhead. I was frightened because I couldn't do a thing and it felt as if he really meant to kill me, so I reached out along the wall with one hand to where I felt the spanners[21] in the rack. My hand closed round a big spanner, I pulled it out, and lifted it, and brought it down across his head.

It was the first time I had crowned a man and I didn't like the way he let go and crumpled up just like a sack, because I began to think that maybe I had done a murder, and if you do a murder on a ship there is not any place at all where you can get away and hide.

So I dropped the spanner and started feeling for life in him, and I was still trying to find if he was dead when the Skipper came down and saw me, and he started an alarm, and then they all came.

When they all came tumbling down the ladder and there was that body lying with me not knowing whether it still breathed, I really felt that I got myself into trouble, and I would not have been at all surprised if they had taken me and put me in irons.

It was not as bad as that though, because I had not committed a murder, only crowned a man in self-defence, and he came round all right after treatment. But they seemed to think perhaps I made a practice of hitting people with spanners, so they had me confined to my cabin, and if I had not run away at Gothenburg I would have been like that all rest of my time on that ship.

18 *companionway* a stairway connecting one deck to another; also known as a "companion."

19 *cheek* sassy.

20 *bulkhead* a partition within a vessel.

21 *spanners* wrenches.

But at Gothenburg they all went ashore and left only one sailor to watch me, so I just had to wait till he went to make his tea in the galley[22] and then I picked up my bag and just walked away on to the wharf.

It was easy.

But I did not find it so easy to make my way in a strange country, because there is the language difficulty, and I had to watch out for the police. I had just managed to find myself a job in a brass foundry when I was found by the Swedish authorities.

They said they had been combing all Gothenburg for a fortnight,[23] and as my ship had gone they would deport me. I did not mind being deported as I did not have to pay for it, and that was how I came home to Glasgow.

22 *galley* a ship's kitchen.
23 *fortnight* two weeks.

CHAPTER II

1

MY next adventure describes how I worked as a deck engineer on a ship that was going to America. She was a passenger ship and I thought I would leave her for Hollywood, but you will nearly die when you hear what happened to me on that ship because it was a chance that does not happen to a man more than once in his life.[1]

There was a man on this ship where I worked as deck engineer who came up to me on the deck one night and we got talking. He leaned against the rail and kept looking at me, and he gave me a cigarette.

"I been watching you, kid," he said to me, "since I came aboard this ship, and I've took a sort of fancy for you. In fact I would like to give you a chance to better yourself. Maybe I could put you in the way of something good if you would let me."

But when I asked him what he meant he would not say anymore that night, but went away and left me, only next time we met he asked me into his stateroom[2] to have a drink with him. I wondered what his game was, but I waited because I thought that whatever it was it did not really matter very much so long as he was very anxious to ask me into his stateroom to have a drink with him.

Well, I did not have to wait very long because the night before we reached New York he started to get confidential and he asked me if I would like an easy way to earn a hundred dollars, so I did not say yes, but instead I asked what there was he wanted me to do.

"Nothing, kid," he said, "nothing . . . or as good as nothing. You see this little parcel here?" and he fished out a little parcel about as big as a tube of toothpaste.

"Well, when you go ashore tomorrow just slip that into your pocket—no one will ask you anything—and when you come out past the wharf get into a tube[3] to Hoboken and meet me at the Shellman

1 In the original edition this paragraph appears in Chapter I at the end of section 4. Given its content it makes far more sense as the opening to Chaprter II.
2 *stateroom* cabin.
3 *tube* underground train system.

Hotel. When you give me that packet I will give you a hundred dollars. Is that easy? I'll say, kid, you never got a hundred dollars as easy as that before," and he put the parcel in my hands so it seemed that everything was settled.

I looked at him and I looked at the parcel and I did not see why I should not do it, for after all you do not make a hundred dollars as easy as that every day. So I said to him all right I would do it, but I asked him what was in the parcel, and he winked at me and snuffed the palm of his hand against his nose, so I guessed when he did that it was drugs.

Well, I know that it is dangerous smuggling drugs, but if you are employed on a ship you do not get searched by the customs, so I thought I would be silly not to risk it and I put the parcel in my pocket. Then the man gave me another drink and we shook hands and I went below.

2

But it was when I got ashore next day that I really started thinking of that parcel, because a hundred dollars seemed a lot of money to pay for a few drugs like that, and I thought I would just look inside to make sure I was not being fooled.

I went into a cheap café where there were not very many people and I made for a table in the corner where no one could see what I was doing. When the girl came I ordered a coffee and as soon as she had gone I slipped the parcel out, keeping it covered with my hand, ripped it open, and looked inside.

At first I couldn't see anything because there were more wrappings, but in the end I tipped a little roll of cloth into my hand and when I unwound that I had to blink because I could hardly believe my eyes. It was not drugs he had given me at all . . . it was *diamonds*.

I had never seen so many diamonds all at once in my life. Even in that dark café they were dazzling there in my palm. I separated them with a pin and counted them. There were fifteen. When the girl came back with the coffee she nearly caught me counting them, but I closed my fingers over my palm just in time and she didn't see anything.

But now I was thinking so hard that I didn't want to drink my coffee, for right here in my hand was what might be worth thousands of pounds. I kept thinking and thinking of all that I could do with that money. And then I thought of the guy waiting in the Shellman Hotel for me, and I thought how he had meant to fool me nicely by making me take all the risk, and then paying me off with a paltry hundred dollars while he made thousands of pounds.

I began to decide that whoever was going to be the mug[4] in this deal it was not going to be me. I reckon he deserved to lose those diamonds for trying to put me off[5] with a paltry hundred dollars.

But I had a lot of things to think of first before my way was clear. Because I was supposed to have a job on that liner, and all my gear was aboard; but if I stayed in my job he would come down to the ship looking for me when I did not deliver the diamonds, so I decided the only thing to do was not to go back to the ship but to make straight out of New York.

This was the first time that I had ever swiped anything big, and I do not mind admitting I was worried as I paid for my coffee and walked right out of that café; but I do not think you could blame a man for being worried when he was as young as I was and had never had such a big opportunity come his way before.

But I did not waver except once when I thought I saw a man in the crowd who was like the guy who was waiting for me in the Shellman Hotel. That did give me quite a turn and nearly shook my resolution, but then I turned into an archway and had one more peep at those diamonds, and they looked so good sparkling there that I knew whatever might come I just had not the heart to part with them. So I did not waver again, but put the diamonds in my pocket and made straight for the Central Depot,[6] New York.

3

I had enough money in my pocket to pay for a ticket to Chicago and I had the clothes I stood up in, so I thought Chicago would be a good place to go to because I had heard they did not ask any questions there.

I went by that famous train, the Twentieth Century Limited,[7] and it took me to Chicago inside 20 hours.

When I landed in Chicago I had not any money at all, so the first thing I had to do was to sell one of my diamonds. I walked around

4 *mug* an easily deceived individual.

5 *put me off* to make a fraudulent exchange.

6 *Central Depot* Opened in 1871, Grand Central Depot was the first name and incarnation of the famed railroad and subway station on East 42nd Street. After renovations and expansions completed between 1898 and 1900 it was renamed Grand Central Station. The completely new Grand Central Terminal debuted in 1913.

7 *Twentieth Century Limited* an express train that ran between New York and Chicago from 1902 to 1967.

till I found where the grandest-looking shops were and I found that they were in a part that is called the Loop.[8] I went into a shop there and when a boy came I asked for his boss because this was not a matter that one could conclude with a mere boy.

So the boy fetched his boss who was a big greasy Jew and he was not at all respectful to me at first, but you should have seen him change when I brought out one of my diamonds.

"I want to know what this is worth," I said, and I said it as if I had been handling diamonds all my life.

So he screwed a little glass in his eye and squinted at it very closely and I think I would have died if he had told me it was a fake. But he did not say it was a fake, he only went on looking at it, and then instead of telling me what the diamond was worth he said, "How much you vant for it?"

So I did not know what to say at all, but I had to say something, so I gave a sort of guess and said, "Make it $500."

And then he said "O.K." so quickly that I could have kicked myself for being silly, because I knew when he agreed right off like that that it must really be worth much more.

But I could not go back on my bargain, so I let it go for $500, though I have often wondered how much that Jew did me down for that day.

That one was the best of my diamonds, but there were fourteen quite good ones left so I made up my mind I would not be taken down again.

I now had $500 so I went and bought some swell clothes and then I drove in a taxi to the Drake which the taximan told me was about the best hotel in town.

I tell you I felt grand when I walked into that hotel because I had never been able to afford a swell hotel before in my life. But I had always known that this was the kind of place where I really belonged, and I tell you I just felt right at home when I walked into the Drake with all that money and diamonds in my pocket.

I made them give me a swell room and a boy in uniform conducted me and said my luggage would be along later, so I decided to go out and buy some as soon as ever I had time.

---

8 *Loop* Chicago's downtown business district. The name is derived from the circuit formed around its borders by the city's elevated trains, named the "El."

4

When the boy had left me in my room I looked round and felt everything and turned on all the gadgets and tried the bed and the chairs, and believe me they had done me well. But when I had finished all that I sat down and took out my diamonds and rolled them around so that they winked in the light. They looked so pretty sitting there that it seemed a shame to have to sell them; but I knew that it would not be wise to keep them longer than I need.

I took up the telephone book and started to look for jewel merchants and when I found one that looked sufficiently important I put through a call to him and asked for the manager at once.

When the manager came I told him to come right round to my hotel because I had some very big business to propose to him and I must have impressed him a lot because he said he would come right away.

When the boy brought him up there were *two* of them, but one was an escort, so I knew he must have been impressed with what I said on the 'phone, and I was pleased and told the boy to show them in.

After they were sitting down and the boy had brought them some refreshment we approached the object of their visit and I brought out just one of my little diamonds to show them.

"What is that worth to you?" I asked, as if I had had dozens of offers.

So as soon as he had had a look he said straight off, "$400."

And when he said that I laughed right out at him, because I was not going to make the same sort of mistake that I had made previously. I said was he making a joke with me?

"I might consider $700," I said.

But I could see from the face he drew that $700 was going to hurt, so I guessed this one was not as good as the other and I quickly fished out all the rest and poured them out on the table.

That startled him a bit and I followed up my advantage. "Look there," I said, "there are fourteen, all as good as the one you have. They're not mine, I am selling them for four men. It's a chance you won't get again. You can have the whole lot for ten grand!"

And though he tried to pretend that he was not interested I knew from that moment that I had him by the look that came into his eye. But he would not agree to anything until he had examined each diamond separately, and then he pretended to think a bit, but his mind was made up already and at last he said straight out, "Will you have a cheque now?"

But I was not having any cheques, it was cash that I was after.

So he said it was not usual to pay cash, but I told him those were my instructions, so he sent his escort out to fetch the money, and while we waited I seemed to get tighter and tighter inside me till I thought that I would simply burst.

But I did not show anything because I had to act like I was only an agent, and when the money is somebody else's £2000[9] is neither here nor there. But at last we heard the escort coming back, and then all at once I got an awful sinking feeling because I thought, supposing the jeweller had got suspicious at me asking for cash and had tipped the escort to bring back not money but the cops!

When that idea got hold of me I nearly had to go out of the room and not wait for the escort, but I still did not show anything, and in a minute he was there and he was smiling and there were no cops with him at all.

So all my fear had been for nothing and there the two of them were packing away my diamonds and counting me out £2000 in fifty-dollar bills.

I could hardly wait till they were gone before grabbing hold of all that money and stuffing it into my pockets, because I had never seen so much money in all my life before, and as I was stuffing it in my pockets I could not help stopping to laugh when I thought of that guy still waiting for me in the Shellman Hotel.

5

The first thing I thought of to do after I had got all that money was to run straight out to the Western Union Telegraph Office. I threw down one of my bills and said I wanted to cable Glasgow, because I knew my mother would be glad to think that I had made so much money, and I cabled her right off a draft for $500, but I told her I won it in a sweepstake, because I did not think she would understand about it being such an opportunity to have been given those stones to bring ashore for the man in the Shellman Hotel.

---

9 *somebody else's £2000* as discussed in note 4 to chapter 1, a pound sterling from 1926 to 1931 was almost $5. While the interchange between pounds and dollars is confusing, £2000 and $10,000 were about equal.

6

Well as soon as I had sent my wire I went and cancelled my room at the Drake and bought a lot of new luggage. Then I drove to Dearborn Station and boarded a train for Los Angeles because I thought the right thing to do now was to launch myself on Hollywood.

It seemed that all the hopes of my life had been fulfilled in about two days and now I did not see why everything should not go right forever. I told the porter to put my new luggage in the van, and I had just a small suitcase that I took into the carriage with me. I felt everybody must be looking at me, because I had all my money in my pockets in notes, and it was so new to me having a lot of money, that I began to feel as if I had no clothes to cover me at all, but just notes hanging all over me so that everyone could see. But though I felt rather conspicuous I still felt very happy and I walked right into an empty first-class compartment and sat down to think of all I would do with my money until the train was due to start.

But I had only been sitting there for a very few minutes when two other men came and sat down in my compartment.

It seemed to me they gave me a look before they sat down opposite me and the minute they did that the thought came to me: were they after my money?

To look at them you would just have thought they were ordinary well-dressed Yankees, but you cannot tell by looking at a man whether he is after your money, and the more I thought about those two the more suspicious I became. Because I was *sure* by now that the minute the train was properly started and I was alone with them the two of them would do me for my money, so I determined I would not wait but would outwit them right away. So I got up just as if I was going down the corridor for something. I did not take my hat or my suitcase so as not to rouse their suspicions, and just as I was walking down the corridor I heard the porter calling, "All aboard!"

So I knew that this was my chance to outwit them, and as the train began to move I jumped out on to the platform, nearly lost my balance, recovered, and started running for the barrier as hard as if I had left my money on the other side of it. The porters all shouted out, but I took no notice. I lost every bit of luggage and the men were left watching my hat. I didn't care about losing anything. I had the wind up[10] properly. I was glad to get off that train.

10 *had the wind up* made to be concerned, afraid.

I ran out of the station with everybody staring at me and I shouted for a taxi to come over and when one came I jumped in and told him to drive straight to Marshall Field's store.

I bought a new hat at Marshall Field's store but I did not get another train to Hollywood, because by now I kept thinking that everyone was after my money. It seemed to be turning my brain having so much money, so I walked down to the edge of Lake Michigan and tried not be so excited so that I could decide what to do.

But in the end I decided that I would have to leave America if I wanted to secure my peace of mind. So I went to a steamship company and asked for a ticket to London because I did not think I would go to Glasgow just yet a while. But the man at the steamship office said, "Have you got an income tax clearance?"

And when I found I could not get a ticket until I had an income tax clearance I felt just as if someone had put a gun against my stomach, but I did not show anything, I just told the man I would get one, and I went away . . . stumped.

Because how was I ever going to get an income tax clearance? So I thought I would get over into Canada and try again there. But I did not know if you could get over into Canada when you did not have a passport; so I went into a cheap café and when the waiter came I asked him, "Can you tell me how a guy gets to Canada without a passport?"

And when he said I did not need to have a passport I could have stood up on the table and cheered.

The waiter said all I had to do was to tell the people on the ferry that I was just going over for the day. He said they fall for it every time if you do not take any luggage, so I gave him a dollar for himself and went off and got on to a ferry. He was right. It was easy. As long as you don't have any luggage. I was over on Canadian soil in seven or eight minutes.

I landed at a town called Windsor and I drove straight to the best hotel and ordered a pot of tea. I was not what you would call a heavy drinker in those days and a pot of tea was all that I could think of to order, though it did not seem right when I had so much money in my pocket. So when I had drunk my tea I went out to a swell store and bought three bags and filled them full of new clothes.

When I had got all this luggage I took a ticket for Montreal. I saw in a paper that there was a ship sailing in three days for the Old Country and I found you did not have to have an income tax clearance in

Canada, so I took a ticket for Liverpool—a first-class ticket, and I asked them to see about a passport, so they got me one from Ottawa, and all the time while I was waiting I spent my time in picture shows.

7

You would not think a man would get into trouble through going to picture shows, but I nearly lost all my money through going to a picture show the night before I sailed.

It was because of a French girl that I was sitting next in the theatre, and then when it was all over she came up and spoke to me in the foyer.

Now I have not very much time for French girls because they are the kind who always like to know first whether you have got any money, but this was a rather pretty girl, so I thought I would buy her a drink and we went to a place where we could get some beer.

But after I had bought her the drink I was quite disillusioned about this girl because while my head was turned away in a mirror I saw her put something in my glass. But I did not show that I had seen anything. I just turned my head back again, and then I asked if she would get me some cigarettes. While she was getting the cigarettes I changed round our two glasses and when she came back she did not dream what I had done.

She lifted up her glass and said, "Cheers, *mon ami*," and she drank down the wrong one with her eyes fixed on me; but if she was expecting me to collapse she must have been disappointed.

As soon as she had had her drink I said, "Come on, let's get out of here," and I took her arm and got her into the street. We got along half a block before her legs began to sag, but then she went right out to it and lay down on the pavement.

I did not know what to do with her so I stood there and two men came running. Then a whole crowd began to gather and the best thing I could think of to do was to get myself mixed up with them. They all wanted to know what had happened, and I kept asking like the others, so nobody thought I had anything to do with her, and after a while when I got bored I went away and left them still arguing. In any case I thought it would be better not to stay long enough to give that girl a chance to come round.

I never heard what happened to that girl because the next day I sailed for Liverpool, and looking back I really think that that was the better way.

CHAPTER III

1

I T was grand having heaps of money to take with me back into England, and when I got to Liverpool I thought I would not go home but would go down and have a look at London for a while. London is one of those places that you need to have money for; but there are so many people in London who have no money of their own that you need to keep your eyes open or soon you will have none either. I had only been a few weeks in London when all I got from selling those diamonds was gone.

I had had a party though, and the fellow who was knocking round with me, who was a Glasgow boy who had a job in London, had not been near his work for two weeks and now he heard he was going to be fired. Well, I was sorry about that because it was really through me he lost his job, but as I had no more money I could only say that I was sorry, and then I remembered the £100 I had sent to my people, so I thought I would go home.

They thought at home that I was still in America, so they got quite a shock when my telegram arrived. But they sent me my fare all right and I came right away.

There was a great homecoming after my long absence, but I never told them anything about the diamonds.

2

When I was home that time I took the most serious step that a man can ever embark on. I got going about with a girl that had won a beauty competition and somehow it came about that she and I got married. My people were quite pleased to think that I was going to settle down and they gave me a house and furniture in a very respectable quarter of Glasgow; but what did I want with being a married man and having a house and furniture in a respectable part of Glasgow? I had never been married before so I thought I would try it, but pretty soon I decided that I was not suited to be a respectable married man. I began to think I would like to go back to America, so I kept saying to my wife how America was a wonderful place and that I knew she would love it, so at last she agreed that she would come.

We had £700 when we started out for America, and the first place we went to was Chicago. It seemed a pity to settle down while we still had a lot of money, so I said to my wife that we would buy a second-hand car and do a tour of the United States of America.

She thought she would like that, so we started off, but the first car we bought was no good, and it was cold, and the wind was like a blizzard. My wife started to say that she wished she had stayed in Scotland; so I said yes, I wished she had, too.

And though we got another car and in the end we covered quite a lot of country you could not have called that trip exactly a honeymoon tour. We came back to Chicago in the end and we had no money left at all so I thought I had better look around and find myself some work.

By this time my wife was going to have a baby, so I was really oppressed with the weight of being a married man. I started to look down the advertisement columns in the papers and she kept on saying that she would like to go home. But I hadn't any money to send her back to Scotland, so I took no notice of all that she was saying, and one day while I was talking to a guy in a speakeasy he said he might be able to get me started with the Surface Lines—people who run the street cars.

He took me along to see a man and this man said the only job he had was working in a street car "barn," which was no sort of work for a qualified engineer like me. But I remembered how my wife kept on being unhappy, and how we had no money for anything, so I said I thought I would try it, and he sent me away to get a suit of overalls.

Now a street car barn in America is one of those great big sheds with open ends that the wind blows through, and believe me, no wonder they call Chicago the Windy City. When the street cars come in they are run over a pit and you have to get down in this pit and screw the underneath parts of them so as to do an overhaul.

It is an awfully dirty job and not one for a man with my training, but this is what you are driven to once you let yourself be made a married man.

So I got down in the pit under one of these street cars and you had to work a box spanner[1] about as big as your arm to unscrew a lot of nuts. It was not the kind of work for a man of my physical stamina,

1 *box spanner* a wrench in the form of a tube, with sockets at either end. It is turned by inserting a rod, known as a T bar, through two openings in the wrench's middle.

although I am not puny, but I kept on pulling away with that spanner and pretty soon the nuts began to come loose. When the nuts came loose, however, hot oil began to run out. It was burning, and it ran all over me. I was scalded and the oil was all black with dirt, but I kept on working, although I was in some pain. As I worked I kept on thinking, "This kind of thing ought to make a man's wife proud of him."

But then I saw how dirty I was, and my arms and back were aching, so I began to think that a man's wife would more likely just be disgusted at him sinking to this kind of work, so when the lunch hour spell came I said to the foreman thank you very much but I was through.

When the foreman heard that though, he said he would try me on something different, so after the lunch hour they took me away from the dirty hot oil and set me working above ground. The fellow I was working with was some kind of a foreigner and I didn't take to him at all. He seemed to think he could give me orders, so I asked him what he thought he was coming at, and instead of replying he just gave me a sort of push.

At the time that he pushed me I was standing on the edge of one of the pits, and, as it turned out, that foreigner is lucky that he hasn't got my life on his conscience at this minute, because I lost my balance when he pushed me and fell down into the pit, and there was a live electric wire down there, and it was only by some sort of miracle that I ever came to miss it.

Well, I may have missed that wire, but I didn't miss that foreigner when I came up and went for him. I picked up a spanner and threw it. It got him on the head and he crumpled and went out for the count. I would have killed him, but I didn't wait. Everyone let out a yell and came running at me so I bolted for the manager's office with the whole shed after me.

I got in, and banged the door, and locked it, so no one could get in though they were all yelling outside. The manager looked a bit surprised at seeing me come in like that, and he seemed to think the best thing to do would be to blow the air whistle. So he did, and when the police outside heard the whistle blowing all out of time they came to see what was up. But when I told them all that had happened they decided not to arrest me, so I stayed in the manager's office, and he said he had come to the conclusion that I was suited for something different from street car work, so he gave me my four hours' pay.

I changed my clothes and went out into the street where a crowd was waiting to see me, and there was a little foreigner who ran across the road and made for me. I thought perhaps he was going to make trouble, but he had a dollar bill in his hand, and when he came close he held out this and started patting me the way you do a dog.

"Good boy, good boy," he said and kept on patting me and offering me the dollar bill. So I took it and put it in my pocket and then it seemed that he wanted me to go back and give that other foreigner some more!

But I thought it would be wiser if I went home to my wife, so I left him there standing in the street, because after all a dollar is not much if you have a grudge against a man and want someone to beat him up for you.

3

My wife did not seem very pleased with that first attempt of mine to get work in Chicago, and she used to cry so much that I found it very depressing, so I decided I would write to my people and ask them to pay her fare home. I said that I had had bad luck and lost my £700 in a deal, but that I would soon pull up and then she could come back, if I had only myself to fend for for a while.

So after I had written quite a lot of letters and told them how things were getting worse, and how she was looking ill, and the baby might have to be born in a charity hospital, they decided after all that it might be a good idea for them to pay her fare home.

So my wife went back to Scotland and then all I had to do was to find myself a good job. But I did not seem to be very lucky with my jobs right at the beginning. I had to come right down to being a lorry driver,[2] which is a difficult position for a qualified ship's engineer.

But I lost that job after a couple of weeks through trying to do a kind action, for there was a Greek bogged with a load of garden produce and when I went to pull him with my truck his lorry[3] came in half and buried him under the vegetables. So I left the truck in the street and did not go to collect my wages, for I thought he might go to my firm and sue me for compensation.

4

It was a nuisance about losing that job because now I had no money at all, but I kept walking along the streets wondering what would happen and thinking how it was in this very town that I had

2 *lorry driver* truck driver.
3 *lorry* aside from a truck, "lorry" can also mean a sizable wagon, drawn by horse and devoid of sides.

sold those diamonds and made all that money and now I had nothing. I kept looking at the cops too, and thinking how they would like to pinch me if they only knew the truth, but I never was scared of cops much—only those plain-clothes detectives.

Well, a week after that I was in New York and the way I got enough money was to work as a commission speed cop. I only stayed one day but I did well at it. The day I had to work was Sunday and I spent that day holding up people all the time. You are supposed to get a commission on everyone you pinch, but I didn't get any commission at all because you see when a person is pinched he will generally offer you a few dollars to be let go again, and I found I could make a lot more money that way. The way they offer you the money is not to hand it to you, because you might be seen taking it, but they ask you to hold their gloves, or a book, and there is always some money there for you.

I took about a hundred dollars that Sunday, and then I thought perhaps I had better not be a speed cop any more, so I left Chicago that night and took the train for New York where I had heard there was money to be made at all sorts of things.

5

My luck seemed to turn from that day when I got into New York, because nearly the first paper I picked up had an advertisement in it for a hydraulic engineer. The address was down near 48th Street and when I got there I found it was a big block of apartments of the kind that were starting to get old-fashioned although they still catered for well-to-do folks.

You went in through swing doors into a great wide foyer where there were marble slabs to sit on, and the place was crowded out with all kinds of people who had come along to get this job as engineer. You would think I would be lost in that crowd, but in America they always feel they have done the right thing when they give the engineer's job to a Scotchman, so the man picked me out as soon as he heard I was "frae Glasga'." He asked me what pressure I had worked at and I said at 10,000 pounds to the square inch, so he started to say, "Man, are you mad?" because he was thinking in terms of hydraulic pressure for working elevators, and I had worked in a shipyard launching ships.

So when I said that, he saw that elevators would be play to me, and he told me I was hired.

* * *

There were four elevators in that building and not one of them was working, which was an inconvenience to the tenants as it was nine storeys up to the top of the house.

So the manager said he would be pleased if I could get one working right away. The place where the elevators started was away down in the basement. It was all stone down there and awash with four inches of water so I had to put on gum boots.[4]

It took me nearly all day to get the first elevator working, but at last I decided it was right and I came up on to the ground floor to tell the boss and have a spell. I forgot to tell you that I was sleeping in on this job and I had been given a room towards the back on the ground floor.

Well, there was a coloured porter in the foyer when I told the boss No. 1 elevator was working, and when he heard what I said he didn't ask if he could test it, he simply went up to where it was on the third floor.

I was just coming out of my room when I heard him shout, "Hey, boss, A'm comin' down," and he got into the thing and I made a dive for the basement, because you never can tell if an elevator is good till you have tested it, and this one had not been tested at all.

I was halfway down to the basement when I heard a shriek fit to split your eardrums, and then that elevator came shooting down and struck the four big springs at the bottom as if she was trying to bunt[5] through them, and I just had a glimpse of that porter crouched away in a corner, when it bounced away up again nearly to the second floor. It was like a huge football, only more violent. The second time it came down it bounced again, but not quite so far; the third time it bounced a bit, but finally came down and stopped.

I ran over then and opened the gate and let that porter out, but he was so huddled up in his corner that he could hardly stand up and his eyes kept rolling round and round with fear. I reckon he will be cured of testing elevators for a long time, though there wasn't much wrong with it—only a lock in the valve.

6

Before I went to bed that night, Elevator No. 1 was working quite well, but that porter had lost faith. He would have climbed forty storeys rather than go in it again.

But I slept well that night and I spent all next day tinkering with No. 2. There was nothing wrong with her valves, and just as I was

4 *gum boots* rubber boots.
5 *bunt* to hit with the head; to butt.

coming off for the day a party of people came in and they asked me if any of the elevators were working. So I said, yes, No. 2 was. So they said if I would take them up to the Penthouse on the roof they would give me a drink when I got there.

Well, I never would have taken them into that elevator if I hadn't known it was working all right, but how was I to tell that the old-fashioned machinery inside that controlled her would jam?

It was a long-lever affair that you hardly ever see now, and when I pulled it across she started off like a lady, but the higher we went the more she gathered speed. It was an awful sensation shooting up that shaft like a rocket and finding when I tried to stop her that the thing was out of control. You'd have thought we were going to shoot out through the roof like a bullet, and I know those others thought so, but when we were near the top and I couldn't make her halt at all, I reversed the lever and she started to dive down again.

"Saved!—For the moment." I know that is what those others were thinking, but I was too busy trying to get the lever to grip so it would shut off the valve to bother about much else—except to reverse our direction before we struck the top or the bottom. We went up and down about three times before I managed it. Then I did bring it to a standstill up near the top, so that when I opened the door we were so far below the floor level that there was just about room for a person to crawl through.

I turned round to them and said I thought they had better get out now, and they looked at me, and at each other, and at that low space, and they were *green*.

"Come on," I said, "you'd better get while the going is good."

But they wanted to know if it wouldn't start moving and catch them when they were half out, so I said I hoped it wouldn't, but that if they didn't care to risk it I would climb out myself and they could camp where they were.

Well, they decided they would risk it when they thought they were going to be left; so they did, one after the other, but I never saw any people with the wind up so badly in my life.

They went off to the penthouse after they had all crawled through, and forgot everything about the drink they had promised me. That is the way, I find, with people. Though I was feeling mighty like a drink after the trying few minutes that I had been through.

So when I saw they were not going to give me any drink I went down the nine flights of stairs to my room and went to bed. But I fixed that elevator next morning and by midday I had three of them running, so he really was quite right to pick on a Scotch engineer.

It was the fourth elevator though that gave me the most trouble, for the cylinder in the basement was cracked and would have to be oxy-welded, so I went to the boss and said we would need to have a man.

Well, he was a terrible one for economizing, that boss was, and he said he thought he knew a man who would do the job for us cheap.

"He's a Dane," he said, "a real good man, mind you. But just you watch him and see that he keeps off the drink."

He sent for this Dane fellow and I waited till he came along. He was given a room next to mine, and when he came he was a little bald chap with awfully broad shoulders. His name was Ol Carsen, and the two of us worked on that cylinder all the afternoon. By the time we knocked off I could see Ol Carsen getting to feel awfully thirsty, and before he went to his room he called a boy and told to him to go to a place he knew for some gin.

He was going out that night to meet a woman but he thought we might as well have a drink before he left. So when the boy came back, he called me into his room where he was shaving, and we had a couple of drinks and then he went.

But there was more than half a bottle of stuff left behind in his room when he went out, and that is the kind of thing I call putting temptation in a man's way. Because having had a couple of drinks makes a fellow feel awfully thirsty, so I sat on my bed thinking out how I could get at that stuff in his room.

The trouble was that he had taken his key with him, so the only thing to do seemed to be to pick the lock with some wire.

I came out of my room and had a look to see no one was watching, then I started in to pick open that lock with wire. But I had just got properly started when I heard the entrance door close, and looked up, and there he was—home—and he had caught me at it.

Well, picking a person's lock is not the sort of thing you can explain, so I just straightened up and gave a sort of grin at him, and he gave one roar and came at me, so I thought the only thing to do was to retire to my room. It was only about two steps and I opened the door and slipped inside it, but I didn't get it closed quite quick enough, and he pushed against it and came in too. So I thought I would leave plenty of space about him, and I went right down the other end near the window, but the window was no good for a getaway as it only opened into a well.

I turned round and faced him and he started to swear like anything.

"You dirty son of a louse," he said, "I am going to murder you," and he turned the key in the lock, and threw it on the floor and came at me. Well, I told you he was a powerful man, *and he meant it* when he said he would murder me, so I had about a twelfth of a second to look round for something to grab. I must be a lucky man because there was a bottle handy and I just had time to lift it up and bring it down across his head. He went down like a pole-axed bullock, and that bottle certainly did make a mess of his face. But you cannot look where you are hitting when a man is going to murder you.

Well, he lay there like a dead man, and there was so much blood everywhere that I thought the best thing I could do was to get out of the place, quick.

So I picked up the key where he had dropped it, and I unlocked the door, and I bolted, just as I was.

I never heard what happened to him and I never went back for my wages, so the man that owns these apartments got four elevators fixed for nothing. But I don't think Ol Carsen can have died or there would have been something in the papers, and I never saw anything, though I looked quite a lot of times.

7

I never went to bed that night after I nearly killed Ol Carsen, and when morning came I was in a speakeasy in Hoboken, and I kept wondering what I was going to do for some money.

But it is strange the way something turns up when you are desperate, because that very day a man came into that speakeasy saying that he was looking for someone to drive a truck. So I said I could drive a truck and he told me he would give me a trial.

I let him know then that I was on the floor,[6] so he bought me something to eat and then he took me along to where the truck was that I had to drive.

It was a big truck, closed in all over, and I didn't have to be told that it was for carrying booze. We had to run between New York and Detroit, which is a goodish long distance, and far as we could we did our travelling by night. The booze used to be packed inside cases and four men used to travel with me in case we met trouble on the way.

6 *on the floor* impoverished. *A Dictionary of Slang* forwards two possible etymologies: Rhyming slang ("poor") or a variation with "down and out" and "on the deck."

It was not the cops we were specially afraid of, because most of them were squared[7] already, but the hijackers would watch out for us and try to shoot us up and take our stuff. The fellows that were with me were jumpy the whole time, and all the while we were on lonely deserted bits of road they kept thinking they saw things and heard things till I got fed up with their talk.

We had made about four trips without any trouble at all and I began to think this danger talk was all a lot of boloney.[8] But just as I was feeling secure there came a night when we struck it properly. We were about 60 miles out of New York, hoping to make it by morning and there was not a living soul in sight anywhere along the road. I was driving along quite gaily, chatting away with those others, when suddenly shots started to come crackling out of the hedges, and the best thing I could think of to do was to jam my foot on the accelerator and let that truck go for its life.

But we didn't get fifty yards, because those hijackers hidden in the hedge opened fire on our back tyres. When I heard them go I knew the game was up. I pulled up, jammed on the brakes, switched off our lights, took one jump for the roadway and dived in under the hedge.

The firing was still going on when I got away, and I heard one of the men in the truck yell that he had been hit. I was frightened to sneak away at first, in case I should run into them, so I just lay low under the hedge and waited to see what would happen. They kept on firing for a few minutes and then they started to close round. Some of them kept the truck covered while two others climbed up to have a look.

"There's three dead here, and one wounded," I heard them call back to their mates. Then, as everyone seemed to be busy, I decided that this would be a good time to get away.

I sneaked away across a field and made a detour back on the road. Then I started walking towards New York, and I was still walking next morning.

It seemed that I was always having to leave my jobs in too much of hurry to be able to collect my wages, and I began to think working for no money is rather hard on a man.

I hailed a man in a car when it was light, and after I had talked to him a bit he gave me a lift into New York, but he was frightened to at first, because he thought I might be one of those hijackers he

7 *squared* bribed.
8 *boloney* alterative spelling of "baloney"; nonsense.

had been hearing of. But I said I was a stranger in the country, just out "frae Glasga'," and after a while he got quite friendly and was warning me of the pitfalls in a new land.

So I thought that was very nice of him to be so kind to a stranger, but I laughed to think of the shock he would have got if he had known who I really was.

When we parted he shook me by the hand, and I went back to a place where I had left some of the new clothes I had bought out of the money I got for rum-running.

8

I had decided by now that I would not be the mug any longer. I had to have some money so I would find a mug for myself.

So I went and took a room at a house and got all dressed up and that evening I went along to Times Square.

It is a principle that I always stick to, never to take money from people that do not deserve to lose it, and that is why this night when I was hard up I decided to go to Times Square. Because there is a part of Times Square where you will always see a lot of "nancy boys,"[9] and when one came up and spoke to me I reckon it was only right that he should learn a lesson from a man like me.

So I looked at his painted face and said it was a very nice evening, and he said with a lisp, suppoth we went and had a drink. So I went along with him, and when he had bought me several drinks he began to ask if there was a place where we could go and have a talk. He wanted to know if I was living all by myself in New York, but I said no, I lived with some people, so he said I ought to come back where he was living, so I told him I would come with him but I asked him to take me outside to the cloakroom first.

I was laughing all the time to hear him because he thought he had got off with me, but when I had him alone in the cloakroom I shoved him up against the wall and I said, "Now I want your money."

So he squeaked like anything, "If you rob me I will call the polith." But I pointed out that if he brought the police into the place where we were there would be a raid and everyone would be arrested.

"Come on," I said, "I want your money."

9 *"nancy boys"* homosexuals.

So he gave me about $200, which will give him a lesson about picking up strange men in future, and when I had taken his money I told him to wash his face and learn to talk like a man, and I went out and left him and got the next train for Chicago.

I meant to keep out of trouble after lifting that fellow's two hundred, but I fell into temptation again with a woman I met on that train.

9

She was very nice-looking, but not really a young woman, and she was sitting in the seat on the other side, opposite me. She kept reading a magazine and I could see her looking at me every now and then, but I wasn't of a mind to get mixed up with any woman so I just went on reading and pretended she was not there.

It takes 24 hours to travel from New York to Chicago (except on the Twentieth Century) and this train had started in the morning so I had to get my meals all that day.

I had my breakfast and my lunch and my tea on that train, and every time I came back from the dining car that woman was still sitting there looking at her magazine. She would give one of those glances at me without lifting her head, and then pretend to go on reading, but I didn't say anything to her, so in the end she must have started to feel impatient because she reached over and handed me her magazine. But it was pretty clear she didn't want me to sit down and read it. She started patting the seat beside her for me to come over and talk, so I thought, in spite of my resolution not to get mixed up with women, that it would be impolite to disoblige a lady, so I went and sat beside her.

She gave me an awfully nice smile when I went and sat beside her and then she said, "Say, boy, I've not had one bite to eat all this day. I'm starving."

Well, that made me feel really sorry because it is an awful feeling not to have anything to eat. So I rang for the coloured waiter and told him to bring her something, and she ordered swordfish and buttered toast.

While he was fetching it she told me how she was really quite a well-to-do woman, but she had been staying in New York and spent all her money, so now she was going home to her mother.

"I spent everything," she said. "I've only got my engagement ring. But what would my husband say if he came home from abroad and found that that was missing?" She held out her hand and there was a big solitaire diamond on it, and I said I didn't know what her husband would be likely to say. But it only came to me later, after I had got drinking, that I was the very man to help her to find out.

After the waiter came along with her tray I asked her if she would like a little drink of real Scotch whisky, and she said, "Aw, you're kidding."

But I went over to the ice-water bucket, reached in the top, and felt amongst the four bottles I had there and fished one out and showed her. The ice-water bucket on trains was always a good place to stow drink you wanted to carry when Prohibition was on in America, because if the Prohibition officers happened to come on and search the train, it was the one place where they never thought of looking. I always carried my drink in the ice-water bucket when I went on a long train journey in America.

So anyway this lady proved very partial to real Scotch whisky, and after she had had a spot or two she began to get partial to me. It turned out that she was a Mrs. Carr. So I told her then that I was Mr. Ford, and that made her laugh like anything, because she was one of those ladies that are very easily amused when they have had a drink of whisky.

She started to giggle so hard that she nearly spilt her next drink of whisky, and she tried to make a joke by herself, but I do not think it was a very good joke myself . . . it was something about "high speed" and a "clutch" but she was giggling so hard that you couldn't hear most of it, which I think was perhaps just as well.

So, seeing that she seemed to be that kind of a lady, I said how about passing her station and coming on with me for a week in Chicago, and she took another drink of whisky and said that would be swell.

So we went on past the station where her mother was waiting to meet her, and we travelled all that night on the train.

I never saw such a woman for putting away whisky as that one, and in the morning she sat up in our sleeper and started at it again.

It was now quite light and we were just a few miles from Chicago. I looked at her, and the condition she was in, and I started to be seriously worried, because before I left New York I had wired friends of mine to come down and meet me at the station, and I didn't think it would look quite nice for me to get off the train with this woman in such a condition.

She was still thinking she was going to spend a week with me, but I started to look in my pocketbook[10] and say my money was nearly

10 *pocketbook* wallet.

all gone, so I was awfully sorry but I didn't see how I could manage it after all.

When she heard that she started to cry, which was very embarrassing for me because when a woman has been drinking whisky she forgets that there are any other people on the whole train, and when Mrs. Carr started to cry it made an awfully loud noise. But I didn't know what to do to stop her, except offer her some more whisky, and how could I do that, now that it was all gone?

It was very fortunate though that she stopped herself the next minute. It seems she had had an inspiration. She had thought of her diamond ring.

"We'll pop[11] this, Bobby," she said. "I'll do it for *you*, Bobby."

So I said I knew a place where we could get a good price for it and she gave me her diamond ring.

So I put it in my pocket and I said how some friends were coming down to meet me and that I would have to go away with them for half an hour. But I said if she would wait I would come back as quickly as I could, so she said she would do that, and when I got off the train at Chicago I was apparently alone.

They were two Yankee boys who had come down to meet me.

"Hallo, Bobby!" they said and held out their hands.

But I was too busy for handshakes.

"Let's get out of here, quick," I said.

"Why?" they said. "What's up, Bobby? Have you got the cops after you?"

But I said it was worse than the cops, though really I was in an awful hurry to get away and pop that diamond ring. I knew it was a good one all right, and the Jew I went to gave me $350 for it.

But when I went back to meet Mrs. Carr she was not on the station any longer, because you see things happened to delay me, and in the end it was a week later that I went back to the station. I often wondered though what her husband said to her when he found she had given away her diamond ring.

I suppose there are people that would say I should have got back quicker to meet her, but I really think she has learnt a valuable lesson, because now if she ever has a daughter that she has to warn about how dangerous it is to get talking to a strange man in a train she will be able to speak from personal experience.

11 *pop* pawn.

10

Well, now that I had come into some money I did not have to get a job all at once in Chicago, so I spent a little while enjoying myself with the boys. Chicago was a terribly wild sort of city at that time and you would get a shock if I told you the things I used to see in the streets.

One day I was walking in that part that is called the Loop when I saw three men going along the sidewalk. There were people passing all the time, and there was nothing special to make you notice these three, till presently two of them went on and one of them went round a corner, and the one that went round the corner suddenly started to yell out, "Murder!" Well, when people heard that it took about two seconds for a big mob to collect round him, and then it turned out that he had been held up and robbed, right in the middle of Chicago, and nobody knew because the two that were holding him up had guns pressed against his ribs as he walked along, and they said if he let out one yell they would shoot right away. So he walked along with people passing, and let them take all his money. Then they turned him down a side street, and the minute they were out of sight he started yelling as loud as he could.

But the cops never caught the two that had lifted his money, and in my opinion that was a very daring crime.

11

At this time what must I get but a letter from my wife telling me that now she had got the baby she thought she would come back to Chicago, so it seems it never rains but it pours.

She thought I was doing better through my having sent her a present when I got back from New York with all that money, so here she was on her way, and I had not a job or a penny, so what was I going to do? I had never had a baby before, at least not this kind of a baby, but I do not think we need go into that now. I was very worried because I could see that this baby and my wife at the same time were going to be a great drain on my resources, so it seemed that best thing I could do was to get some work without delay. I started to look down the columns in the daily papers and I must be a lucky man because the day before my wife arrived I started as a member of the technical staff of the University of Chicago, which is one of the largest universities in the world. My job at the beginning was to help lay some underground pipes for the new steam heating they were having, but I was on the technical staff of the University of Chicago just the same.

My wife was ever so pleased when she heard what a good job I had and I found her some lodgings with some people that had come out from Glasgow, and she used to look after the baby while I used to go off to my work every day.

I was quite like a family man. I used to bring home my wages. I never broke out at all, except sometimes on a Saturday night.

It is quite a big job laying pipes under buildings as big as the buildings of the University of Chicago, and we used to be crouched underground in the duct, hammering away all day. While you were away down there you couldn't tell what was happening up above, and one day while we were working, gangsters drove into the place in a flivver[12] that had two machine guns mounted on it, and two guys held everybody off with the machine guns, while the others went in and robbed the bank of the University—because they had their own bank there—and it wasn't till we came up for lunch an hour after they had gone that any of us knew a single thing about it!

The police in Chicago were no good at catching gangsters. They never caught those men who held up the University and believe me in the city of Chicago you could get away with almost any crime. It may be different now that Capone is finished, but at the time that I was in Chicago I could easily have become a crook and made a good living at it, but I do not think my wife would have quite approved if I had.

Do you know what I saw one day when I was walking in the street in Chicago? This will just show you how easily a man could get away with crime. It was in the Italian quarter and there was a man sitting outside his shop.

It was a barber's shop, and I heard that man give the raspberry to another man who went past. And the man who had gone past turned and out with a knife and grabbed that Italian barber, and slit him up so that most of him spilled out on the pavement. Yet nothing happened to the man that did it, because I watched the papers to see and he was never caught. I bolted when I saw what was happening, partly because it is inclined to turn my stomach to see a man killed like that and partly because, as I told you before, there are reasons why I do not care to get mixed up with cops who might inquire into my past life.

12 *flivver* a low-priced, little, and often old car.

But I just told you that instance to show how crime could be committed in broad daylight at that time in Chicago, with no fear of retribution. So I really think it was quite to my credit that I did not take to being a crook all the time that I was living there.

12

That was a good job while it lasted, but it was a strain living up to it all and being a respectable married man as well. I started to feel quite old what with one thing and another, and every now and then I would have to break out a little.

My wife could not go out much because she had the baby to look after, and in any case Chicago was no place to take a child about in. Do you know, one Sunday afternoon when my wife and I were going visiting, we got down on to a sidewalk, and were waiting for a street car, when I found I had no change, only a five-dollar bill, so I went into a men's haberdasher's to ask them to change it for me, but before I could open my mouth the guy behind the counter shoved a sawn-off shotgun in my stomach and shouted, "You get out of here!" So I went, and the wife and kid with me.

That will show you how jumpy they were, for I couldn't have looked much like a gangster seeing that I had brought a wife and baby along.

It was that very same week that I had my first sight of Al Capone, at least I saw the car that he was in. It was great big armoured car, closed in all over, with a machine gun mounted on the front and it came shooting down the street with two speed cops going ahead to clear away the traffic for him! That was how much Capone had the cops bluffed in those days.

The very same month the Italian toughs in Cicero[13] were dropping bombs on each other, but the police just let them go ahead, thinking, I suppose, that one lot was as bad as the others, and working on the principle that it made a clearance. Of course you didn't see much of the tough side of Chicago so long as you kept over in the respectable suburbs.

That business about the sawn-off shotgun put the wind up my wife properly and she began to think now that we might be killed any minute, so what with me breaking out occasionally and the gangsters shooting the place up she began to talk again about going back home again.

13 *Cicero* a suburb west of Chicago.

Things came to a head one night over me going out to a roadhouse in Gary, Indiana, and coming home round about morning with one leg all torn off my trousers. I wouldn't tell her how it had happened and she swore I had been up to no good, though as a matter of fact I had bolted when the shooting started, otherwise I would not have torn my trousers at all.

This was a roadhouse that was built right on the boundary line between Indiana and Illinois. It is a good idea to build a roadhouse like that because then when one half is raided you can open up in the other half and the police that have raided you cannot do anything to stop you.

Well, I went out to this roadhouse because I was feeling weighed down with the strain of being a respectable married man. It was a roadhouse where there was drink and girls, and there was an ex-pug[14] to chuck you out if you got rowdy. The drinking part was on the ground floor, and the girls were upstairs. There was a dance floor on the ground floor and there were slot machines round the wall where, if you put in a quarter and got the right number you won money, but of course they always had it fixed so you put in a lot of quarters before you won any money.

Well, the ex-pug in this roadhouse was sweet on the girl that served the drinks and you could hardly get her to give you anything because she was always so busy smooging[15] with him across the counter. But I was not interested in the girl who served the drinks. I found that there was one whom I liked much better upstairs.

Now to make this story clear I will have to explain to you that earlier in the day before I came out there a fellow had come in and been caught using slugs instead of quarters in the slot machines. So the ex-pug had thrown him out.

But it seems that later on this guy had come back to the roadhouse, and while I was upstairs he walked in with a woman. The first thing I knew about this was when I heard two shots ring out, and suddenly every person in the place started screaming. The girls ran out into the corridors with only half their clothes on, yelling and crying, and it got to be pretty clear that the cops would arrive.

So I thought about me being a respectable married man, and how I had my position at the University to think of, and I thought I had better get away while the going was good. So I ran to the nearest

14 *ex-pug* former boxer.
15 *smooging* exhibiting loving feelings.

window and threw it up and jumped, because I knew I was only on the second storey. But what I did not know was that there was a rotten bit of corrugated iron right below and I came on to it the way you do on a stair that you aren't expecting, only in this case it was much worse than a stair.

I landed on to that roof as if I had been shot there and it was so rotten that I crashed through and tore all my trousers. But I didn't stop to think about the damage I had suffered. I just took to my heels and ran till that roadhouse and all the screaming people were over a mile behind.

Well, I admit that it was not very dignified for a man with a position to keep up to arrive home in the small hours with half his trousers torn off, but my wife should have been glad really, because when the papers came out next morning they were full of the murder that had happened there and the names of people who had been caught, and we were saved all the disgrace because my name was not there at all.

It had been a double murder and as usual they had got away.

The trouble had come about through the ex-pug saying to the man that he had thrown out earlier in the day, "Come along now, I've told you once. Get along out of here."

And then the man who had come in with the girl did something with the coat that he had had hung over his arm so that he uncovered a gun he was carrying, and he shot the ex-pug, just like that! That was the first shot I heard. The second shot was when the girl behind the bar saw her sweetie fall and gave a scream and jumped over the counter and ran to him. But as she stooped over him the woman that was with the man brought out a gun of her own and let fly too.

The ex-pug and his sweetie both died within a few minutes. All the others were so busy screaming that the murderers got clean away. It was really a very cold-blooded murder, and though I am glad I got away so as not to be mixed up in it, I do not think anyone ought to come in and shoot a man over a little grudge like that.

13

It was after this that my wife went back again to Glasgow, and after that break we did not come together again. But I did not worry very much because I really think I am cut out for a single life. I did not keep my job after my wife left and now the scene of my adventures shifts away from Chicago. But first I will have to tell you about my getting the Shriner's sword.

There was one evening when I went with a Canadian to a dance hall in Cottage Grove[16] and Rudolph Valentino[17] was there dancing a tango called "La Paloma."[18] It was a big modern dance hall where there were four bands playing at once, because that is the way to make a dance hall go in America. And in the middle of the hall there was Rudolph Valentino dancing, and all the women at the tables were swooning with their emotion as they watched that fellow dancing and wished that they were his partner. But I never could see anything in Rudolph Valentino myself.

But what I was really going to tell you about us going to that dance hall was how the Canadian and I got tight[19] towards the end of the evening and the chuckers[20] out came up to the gallery[21] where we were and threw us out into the street, which was not any joke because it was snowing blue murder.

So I was angry with that Canadian for getting me thrown out just as if I had been a rough guy, and I left him to look after himself and went along to find another place I knew, but when I got there I found a whole crowd collected outside, and the cops were pitching tear-gas bombs in the windows, because it was being raided for being a disorderly house, so I just stayed in the crowd and watched and did not go inside.

All the windows and the doors had been barricaded through the cops trying to get in, but at the top you could see some girls looking out, and they looked terribly scared, because they knew the police were going to get them.

16 *Cottage Grove* Although there is a Chicago neighborhood named Cottage Grove Heights, Moore is probably referring to Woodlawn, a community on the city's South Side. "By the 1920s, Woodlawn had become one of Chicago's premier retail and entertainment centers," reports *chicago-l.org*, a web site devoted to the city's rapid transit system, "due in large part to popular theaters like the Tivoli, dance halls and cabarets such as the Trianon Ballroom. . . . *Cottage Grove station* was at the center of this popular business and recreational district." (Italics added.) Other sources confirm the area around the station, located at the intersection of Cottage Grove Avenue and East 63rd Street, was a spot for shopping and diversion.

17 *Rudolph Valentino* Film actor (1895-1926).

18 *La Paloma* "La Paloma" was composed and written by Sebastián Iradier, inspired by a trip to Cuba in 1861. It eventually gained popularity around the world. Singers as diverse as Maria Callas and Elvis Presley performed the song. "La Paloma" may have been recorded more often than the Beatles's "Yesterday."

19 *tight* drunk.

20 *chuckers* bouncers.

21 *gallery* an upper section of a theater or auditorium.

Well, as I stood there watching the cops breaking in I felt a hand come down on my shoulder, and I must say I never do like that feeling because it puts me in mind of detectives, so I stiffened and looked straight in front of me, but in a minute there was a voice that said, "Well, if it isn't Bobby!" and I turned round and there was a lad named Angus I used to go to school with in Glasgow, so I grabbed him by the hand and pumped at it because it was such a relief to know that it was not detectives.

Then I asked him what he was doing and he said he had a job driving a delivery truck for a firm that supplied plumbers porcelain fittings, washbasins and bowls, etcetera; which he said was a very paying proposition because you would be surprised how many things you could lift in that job and dispose of for private profit. In fact it seemed that he was doing pretty well.

He took me home to his apartment, which was luxurious for a young boy, and brought out drinks for me. And then he told me how he was a Shriner, which is a high society of Masons, and that next week was going to be their annual ball.

He said he could take me to it if I would like to come. So when my work was over the following Saturday night I joined Angus at his place and we went along to the ball.

You would have thought when you walked into that place that it was somewhere in the middle of Turkey instead of in Chicago city because there were dozens and dozens of these Shriners marching about in fezes, with long robes like the Great Panjandrum, and big curved swords.

The beginning of the ball was just a march round in costume, but presently the dancing started, and as they could not dance without getting their legs mixed with their swords, they all marched into a little room and put them in a big box. There was a bar and padlock on this box. I found that out afterwards when I went along to see.

I just thought in the beginning that I would have a better look at those swords, because everyone was busy dancing, and there was nobody close enough to say anything to me. So I went into the little room and found the padlock on the box.

I had to hammer off the padlock to get the box open, but everyone was making so much noise that I was not heard. And when I opened the box and saw what lovely swords they were, I thought it would be a shame not to have one as a souvenir.

So I chose one that had a long curved blade and jewels imbedded in the handle. I do not think all the jewels were real, but there was one ruby that was, and that sword had the initials J.D.R. on it. So for all I know it may have belonged to John D. Rockefeller himself.

When I had chosen my sword I shut up the box again, and I pushed the sword down my trouser leg so that no one would notice it. But being curved it stuck out in front as though my leg had grown crooked, and I found it awfully hard to walk out of that dance hall with a curved sword stuck in my trouser leg, and at the same time preserve what you might call a nonchalant air.

I think it was a good job everyone was enjoying the party because no one seemed to notice me at all, and when I got outside I just looked along the street and called a taxi and got it to drive me home. When I got home I hid the sword in the bottom of my trunk and I thought no more about it until after I had left Chicago.

I packed up all my things and wrote my mother I was coming, and took a passage home on a ship that was leaving from Montreal.

This ship that I travelled on had 400 doctors on board her who were going to a conference in Vienna. And as they had had not had a decent drink for a good many years in America they were drunk all the time now that they could get good stuff and not have to pay through the nose for it.

Well, when we were well out to sea I unpacked that sword that I had taken from the Shriners, and I showed it to the steward[22] and his eyes nearly dropped out of his head.

I asked him what was the matter and he came over all stuttery, but I found out in the end that the whole trouble was that he was one of those Shriners himself.

"Did you steal that?" he said to me, but I said No, I had not stolen it. I had *swiped* it, because I would not like him to have thought I was a thief.

So when he heard that he said, "Cripes! Put it out of the porthole. They'd never rest till they'd got you if they knew you had swiped that."

But I made out I thought he was talking a lot of boloney though I decided I would get some money instead of keeping that sword as soon as ever I could. It would be a nuisance to think that the Shriners

22 *steward* someone employed by a ship to manage the food supply and deal with passengers.

were always trying to chase after you, but I did not put that sword out of the porthole all the same.

I got talking to one of the doctors. And when I found he was not a Shriner I asked him if he would like to see a very valuable ruby, so I brought him down to my cabin, and when he saw that sword he said he would give me a hundred dollars for it right away. I said that the ruby alone was worth more than a hundred dollars. But he said I could take it or leave it, so I decided I would take it if he made it cash in dollars.

I don't know if the Shriners got him, but it seemed to me it was a better idea than throwing it out of the porthole because nobody would get any benefit that way.

And now you are going to hear about a woman that I met in Glasgow, because that is the most interesting part of this visit that I paid to my home.

CHAPTER IV

1

THIS woman was a Mrs. Flight, and looking back I think that that was a very good name for her to have, for the first thing she did when she saw me was to come up and ask was I a crook. Now if she had not meant it for a compliment I would not have liked that at all, but it seemed she did mean it for a compliment because she told me that she liked crooks.

She said, "You may look respectable, but *I* think you are a crook."

So when she had said that she asked me to have a drink with her. Now this was in one of the biggest hotels in Glasgow. But I did not mind having a drink with her because she was a very good-looking woman with expensive clothes and diamonds.

She was not young, however, and she told me she came from Liverpool, but that her husband had a house for some months on the outskirts of Glasgow, and after we had some more drinks she said I must come to her home.

So she called a car and there was a chauffeur and we got in and drove to her home.

It was a very big house that she took me to, and inside the house there was a butler and a whole lot of maids. So she took me inside the house to a place that she called the music room, and then she sat down and sang to me, and she said I was a nice boy so I thought that I had made quite a hit.

But we did not do anything that time, only she held my hand before I went away, and said I must come again because she had a lot of things to show me. So I said I would come again, because at this time I had not any money at all.

2

So I used to go often to her house and she showed me all the things she had promised, only sometimes her husband was there. So when her husband was there the maid would bring in tea and she would sing songs on the piano. But all the same I do not think her husband was so stuck on me really, although I will say that he was a very nice man.

She had a little boy too, who was 10, but she did not like him round too much because she said it made her feel her age.

Sometimes I would go there in the morning and then she would have the car out and I would drive with her into town. So one morning when I was there she asked me to go to her desk and get a fiver out of it for her, and that was the rock she perished on because I had never known where she kept her money before.

But when I opened that drawer in her desk there was a roll of notes that would keep a man in comfort for a year. So I did not say anything, but just took the fiver and closed the drawer up again; but all the same I could not get the memory of that sight out of my mind.

So when she had finished dressing she took some keys out of her handbag and locked up the drawer in the desk and then we went into town. We went to a hotel and had some drinks, but all the time I could not keep listening properly to the things that she was saying because the thought of those notes in the drawer would not go out of my mind. But suddenly I heard she was saying, "Bobby, my husband suspects you. He says he believes you have kissed me. If you had any guts, Bobby, you would go and make him apologize."

Well, I did listen when she said that because it gave me the idea I had been looking for. Because if I went away to look for her husband maybe I could go back to the house and take those notes out of the drawer. So I said she had no right to say I had not got any guts, and just to prove she was wrong I would go away right now and find her husband and make him apologize.

Well, she was pleased when I said that because she had not thought that I would do it. So she went over to the wall to press the bell for some more drinks, and while she was pressing the bell I snibbed open[1] her handbag and took out the bunch of keys that were inside.

But she did not notice I had done that because she was now getting to the stage when one does not notice little things. And after we had the drinks she said she would wait there for me and I went away to find her husband to make him apologize.

1 *snibbed* Moore misuses the chiefly British verb "snib," which means to close an opening with a catch or snib. He probably meant to write "I popped open her handbag's snib."

3

I thought after all her house would be the best place to look for her husband and I got a taxi back there. And when I rang the bell at the house I did not ask for her husband but I asked if Mrs. Flight was in, only she was not in so I said that I would wait inside.

The maid was used to me coming so she said I could wait in the music room, and I was glad when she said that because that is where the desk was.

So the maid went away to get tea and I was left in the music room. Well, as soon as the maid had gone I thought I would not waste any time so I went over to Mrs. Flight's desk and started trying the lock with her keys. But it seemed that there must be some mistake because none of these keys would turn the lock as far as I could see.

I was just trying them again to make sure I had not missed a key when the maid came in quietly with a tray and I had to drop under the desk and pretend I was feeling for the top off the whisky bottle, because if she had known I was trying to open Mrs. Flight's desk it would really have been very embarrassing.

When the maid had gone I sat and drank my tea and kept thinking what I could do next, because to be stumped like this when victory was just within my grasp was enough to exasperate any man, even a man like me, who has got quite a lot of patience.

Because it really was very tantalizing to be so near and yet so far. And I was just starting to feel quite depressed over having my hopes dashed to the ground, when suddenly I heard footsteps walking along the passage and who should come into the room but Mrs. Flight's little boy.

So as soon as he came into the room I had a kind of inspiration, because there is nothing a boy likes so much as to have a pistol, and I remembered that I was carrying a wee pistol in my pocket.

I did not take it out and give it to him because he might have got the idea from that I was giving it to him for a bribe, but I took it out and started to examine it just as if he was not there and I was the only person in the room, and pretty soon he came over and asked me straight out what I was doing.

So I said I was just examining my little gun.

"How does it work, Bob?" the kid said to me, so I showed him how it worked, and then he asked to hold it in his hand.

"Gee," said the kid, when he was holding it in his hand, "I would like to have a gun like that."

"Would you?" I said. "Well, maybe I can let you have it. I don't mind really. I can get another one."

So when the kid thought he was really going to have a gun, though I did not give him any ammunition, he was so pleased he would have done anything for me.

But I just said, "Oh, that's all right, only don't you tell your Daddy or Mummy because maybe they would take it away from you." So I did not ask him to do any thing for me at all, only when he was going out of the room to hide the gun where no one would find it I just asked him to do something to please his Mummy. Because I said his Mummy wanted £5 out of the drawer, only I did not know how to open it with the keys she had given me. So the kid said, "Oh, that's easy. You watch me."

And he came back into the room and took the keys, and lo and behold! it was of those reversed locks that you have to turn the other way to get open. So if I had not thought of that I might have been trying till doomsday without meeting with success at all.

The kid took out a fiver and locked the desk and gave me back the keys. But as soon as he had gone away to hide his gun I opened the desk again, and this time it was easy. So I succeeded after all in getting Mrs. Flight's money, though I think a lot of fellows would not have been so persevering and would not have thought of ways to overcome the difficulties that beset me.

But I must not take all the credit because it is really quite true that fortune was with me that day. I had only just got the money properly away in my pocket when I heard footsteps again and this time it was her husband himself who walked in.

So think if he had just been two minutes earlier—everything I planned to do would have been frustrated.

4

Well, he cannot have been pleased with me that day, because when he saw me in the music room he did not seem to see me at all, but just sat down and started reading his paper as if he had been alone, which I do not think was very courteous to a guest in his own house. So I went right up to him and I said. "Say, Mr. Flight, what is all this about?"

But he would not respond to my advances, but just went on with his reading, so I was forced to take the bull by the horns myself.

So I said, "Well, you needn't tell me because I know, Mr. Flight.

You wife has already told me, and your wife is very upset, and I think you should apologize to me."

"What's that?" he said, looking up quick. "Apologize to *you*?"

But I was not to be diverted by such uncouth tactics, so I just said, "Yes, I think you should, because it is all wrong to say I was seen kissing your wife, Mr. Flight. I was seen doing no such thing. I would not dream of being seen kissing your wife, Mr. Flight." (And neither I would for that matter, for where is the sense in being seen?) But he thought I meant I had not been kissing her at all so he said, "Well, I'm sorry Bobby." And I said, "Aw, that's all right," so we parted quite good friends.

But I did not go back to their house anymore after that because Mrs. Flight and I went away until all her money was spent.

But she did not know that it was her money we were spending, or she would have been mad at me, but I told her I had been lucky and won some money at the dogs.

She thought I was taking her for a holiday on my money, and that will show you what a funny woman she was. For why should I have taken her for a holiday with my money, when she was not really young anymore and she had a house where I could go without spending any money at all?

But I think really I was not so bad taking her for that holiday because after all I need not have taken her at all, but I could have gone away and spent all that money on myself.

But instead I took her to London and we stayed at a smart[2] hotel. And as she was a woman who liked to go to smart places we went to all the restaurants and night clubs that generally you only read about in the newspapers, so you cannot say that I did not do my best to give her a good time.

I did my best to give her a good time so much that sometimes in the morning I would be feeling quite faint with fatigue, and I would not be fit for anything until I had been massaged on my temples and over the heart with a electro-vibrant machine that she had to send away her wrinkles. Only I think it was more use for reviving me in the morning really.

5

But after a while Mrs. Flight's money began to get finished up, only she did not know yet that it was her money, so she wrote to her husband for some more because he was thinking all this time that she

2 *smart* fashionable.

was staying with a woman friend. But her husband did not answer her letter asking for some more money so we got to be very hard up, and the only thing we could think of to do was to pawn her fur coat and her rings.

A very funny thing happened to me the morning I was going out to pawn Mrs. Flight's coat and her rings, because though I have been mistaken for a lot of things in my life, nobody has ever taken me for royalty before. But this morning as I was going out of the hotel a man came up to me and asked if I was a *Hohenzollern*.[3] Which just goes to show that we do not see ourselves as others see us because it had never occurred to me before that I looked like a Hohenzollern. But I had to tell him that he had made a mistake because I was not a Hohenzollern. In fact, I said, when I had looked at him, "I am just the same as you are." So he asked what that was.

"A crook!" I said, because I did not mind saying just for a joke that I was a crook. But I was right when I guessed that he was because he just touched his forehead then and said, "Bye!" and gave a grin and went off. So he was easily finished with. But wasn't it funny him mistaking me for a Hohenzollern?

So after that little experience I went out and popped Mrs. Flight's things. But when I got back a dreadful thing had happened because she had got the D.T.'s and there she was sitting on the bed catching things that she thought were flying round her, so I really felt things were getting too much for my stamina so I said that perhaps now we had better go home.

But when she found I got some money she would not agree to going home because by now she was afraid of her husband because she thought he might not believe that she had been staying with a woman friend all this time.

So I had to stay with her in London till we had no money at all. But there was nothing to pawn this time when all her money was gone, so the hotel would not have us any longer, and I pointed out to Mrs. Flight that if we did not want to go and sleep in the streets we would just have to go home. So we could not buy railway tickets, but we got a man that had a taxi and I told him who Mrs. Flight was so he said he would drive us to Scotland. We set out for Scotland together and it was when we got as far as Newcastle that I told her it had been her money we had been spending all the time.

3 *Hohenzollern* the royal family who ruled Germany from 1871 to 1918.

Well, it really was very embarrassing, the scene she made in Newcastle when she heard it was her money we had been spending. And the first thing she said she would do was to put the police after me, but then she remembered she could not because if she did that how was she to stop her husband knowing that she had not been away in London stopping[4] with a woman friend?

"You've got me," she said. "My God! You've got me!" And she seemed to think I was to blame because she could not put the police after me, but really it was not my fault because *I* did not make her come to London and stay with me at a smart hotel. But that is the way with a woman, they will never see where they are wrong. A man must always take the blame. So I did not say anything to her because she was not looking very well by now, but I took her back to the taxi and we did not talk very much more all the rest of the way to her home.

4 *stopping* staying.

CHAPTER V

1

AFTER that time with Mrs. Flight my people thought it would be better if I went somewhere different from Glasgow, and the farthest away place that they could think of was Australia. So I got a job on a grain ship that was going there.

God! That was a trip to Australia. When you travel on a grain ship you never know where you will finish because your cargo gets sold again while you are on your way to one place, and you are wirelessed[1] in the middle of the ocean to face about and go somewhere else. I was the third engineer on this ship and she was an old tub if ever a ship was. There was no ice box on board her although we spent weeks in the tropics, so we started on salt junk[2] when we were only two days out. We only had eggs twice a week, except for the Chief who brought his own, and all the porridge had weevils[3] in it, and the apprentices got so hungry that they ate the ship's biscuits out of the lifeboats. If you have ever tried to eat a ship's biscuit you will know that they taste like wood and it takes a man half an hour to get his teeth into one, so you will now have some idea of how hungry those apprentices were.

The first place that we called at on this ship was Alexandria, and we had hardly tied up to the wharf before a whole lot of those Egyptian hawkers began to tumble on board. They spread their stuff all over the deck so that you could hardly walk for[4] it, but I did not look at any of it because I was busy working in the engine room at the time. I did not come up on deck for some time after we had berthed, but when I did there was a smart Egyptian waiting for me. He had on good blue clothes and one of those red fezes, and when he saw me he beamed all over his face.

---

1 *wirelessed* radioed.
2 *salt junk* tough and salted beef consumed while at a sea.
3 *weevil* a type of beetle that causes injury to grain.
4 *for* because of.

The next minute I heard a voice asking, "Hoo are ye the noo?" and I looked around, blinking, for the Scotsman, but there was no one in sight but this Egyptian so it seemed that the Scotsman must be him. So I blinked and had another look at him and he said, "Are ye the third engineer? Don't you know me? I'm Spud Tamson."

And I was more puzzled than ever because I knew quite well that Spud Tamson[5] was a book. At first I thought someone must be having a loan of me, but I could see quite well that his colour was not the kind that rubs off, so I said to him, "Why do you talk like that when you are an Egyptian?"

So he said it was because he had been brought up like that.

"Do you know Glasgow then?" I asked him, but he said he had never been there in his life.

"I was brocht up to be a Scotsman though," he said. "I was brocht up by a Scotch regiment in the War."

So it seems he had learnt to speak good Glasga' in Egypt, and it turned out it was the only English he could speak. Well, I thought I would go on calling him Spud Tamson and I decided that I would go ashore with him.

2

It was a Sunday so I could not get any money changed, but Spud said that if I stuck to him he would see that I had plenty of money. So I told him I would pay him back and something over as soon as I had my advance from the Skipper.

So Spud waited while I went below and got all dressed up and then I went ashore with him and he showed me Alexandria. Alexandria is like all those Eastern cities—you can have anything you want if you like to pay money for it. But this day Spud and I just drove about in a gharry[6] and looked at things. He wanted to take me to meet a nice Armenian girl, but I said I thought maybe that would cost too much money, so we just drove up Sisters' Street instead and when it got dark I decided to go back to the ship.

Spud was walking beside me on our way back to the ship and a ragged-looking Egyptian suddenly pushed right in front and then

5 *Spud Tamson* The book is *Private Spud Tamson*, a novel about a Scottish soldier during World War I and his fictitious regiment, "The Glesca Mileeshy." It was written by Captain R.W. Campbell and published by William Blackwood and Sons (Edinburgh and London) in 1915.

6 *gharry*: a horse-drawn carriage, particularly used in Egypt and India.

stooped down on the pavement and pretended to pick something up. He gave Spud a look and held out to me what he had picked up, and I could see it was a ring with a stone as big as a pea and like a diamond in it.

But I shook my head when I had had a look at it and said, "No good, no good," making out it was only glass, and I could see Spud and the other Egyptian looking at each other. So I decided this must be a put-up job between them. They thought they would make me spend a whole lot more money but I had made up my mind that I would do nothing of the kind. So I asked to have one more look at the ring. And when the man handed it out I took it in my hand but instead of looking at it I swung my arm round as quick as I could and pretended to throw it fifty yards down the alley, but really I had it still in my hand all the time. That Egyptian thought I had thrown it though, and he went scuttling down the alley like a dog after a bone. I put my hand in my pocket and said, "Come on, Spud, it's getting late."

So we went on down the road and presently we came to a café. I had put the ring on my finger by now, but I kept my hand in my pocket until Spud had gone away and left me. Then I decided that I would go back to the ship.

It was very late when I got back and the ship was not very well lighted, so somehow I did not see that part you have to step over when you come into an alleyway from the deck. I caught my foot against it and I shot right along into the alleyway with as much noise as if I had been a sack of coals. And everyone came running from the saloon[7] to see what had happened to me.

I was not feeling very well by now so they carried me into the bathroom and sat me up in the bath, and then somebody noticed the ring that was on my finger. I tried to pull it off to show them but my finger had swelled up so that nothing you could do would bring it off. In the end they went and got a vice and screwed it on to the side of the bath and I had to have my finger held in that while they got the ring off with a file. It hurt getting it off, and when all that trouble was over I had a look at it under a strong light. It turned out then to be no diamond ring at all, but brass with some imitation stone stuck in it . . . so I had gone to all the bother of getting it for nothing. It made me angry to think of all my bother for nothing for after all there is enough to spend your energy on in this world without wasting it on getting a ring that is not even gold, let alone a real diamond.

7 *saloon* the officers mess on a cargo ship.

3

Well, we stayed three days in Alexandria and by this time Spud Tamson said that I owed him £5. But I only gave him £4 because that was all I could get from the Skipper. He would not be quiet with £4 though and he kept coming down to the ship and crying that his wife was hungry, so that all the fellows got looking at me and I did not know what I could do.

So while I was thinking what I could do to get Spud Tamson the £1 that I owed him an old hawker came down to the ship with a lot of Spanish shawls.

My cabin was the one that he picked on, and he came down and started spreading them all about the place. But I was just going to say I couldn't buy any when someone came to my door and called him out into the alleyway, so I thought of poor Spud Tamson and the £1 I owed him, and I made a swipe at two of those shawls and hid them under my bunk.

The old hawker must have had so many that he didn't know how to count them, because when he came back he never seemed to notice that anything was missing, and when I told him that I found I didn't want any shawls after all he just packed them all up and went away.

Well, as soon as he was off the ship I pulled out the shawls that I had swiped and went looking for Chippy—the carpenter—because he was not a married man, but he was mean[8] and therefore I thought he would have the money to buy two shawls that were going to be a bargain. So I found Chippy and I asked £1 for the two shawls, which was dirt cheap really, because I told him £1 was what I needed to pay Spud Tamson with.

But after I had got the £1 I thought that it would be a pity to give it all to Spud Tamson so I went ashore with it in my pocket. I meant to keep some of it for Spud but somehow when I came back to the ship every penny of it had gone. And when Spud came along next morning crying for his money I was no nearer getting it for him than ever.

4

Well, it worried me to think about Spud Tamson because all the fellows on the ship were treating me as if his being poor was my fault.

So I thought I would have to do something to make them see I was not to blame for being in a position where I could not give Spud his

8 *mean* stingy.

money. So the morning before we were to sail, when I was down in the engine room by myself, I suddenly lay down on the floor and started screaming blue murder. Now this is a thing which I had never done before in my life, but I really was in a predicament over Spud Tamson and his crying, and I did not see what else I could do to escape from it.

So when they all came running to the engine room and found me lying there groaning as if I was in mortal agony they decided that I must have fallen off the top of the boilers, because I was in far too much pain to collect myself and tell them what had happened. So they all picked me up, and I yelled in torment when they touched me, but they told me it was all for my good so I tried to be brave while they carried me to my cabin.

They ran up the yellow flag then and a French doctor with a beard came hurrying from Alexandria. He was just the sort of doctor I was looking for, for after he had examined me and I had yelled to show him where the pain was he decided that I would have to be put in a plaster cast because I had three broken ribs! Well, it was news to me that I had three broken ribs but I thought a doctor ought to know what with all his experience, so I did not contradict him, but just lay there trying to have courage, while he took off all my clothes and bound me up in plaster of paris.

He seemed to think I was so bad that I ought to go ashore to the hospital, but I said I did not want to leave the Skipper in a hole over getting a new engineer, because I thought how Spud Tamson would be sure to find where I was if I stayed in Alexandria, and it would delay my convalescence very much if he kept coming and crying about how I owed him money and his wife and children were starving.

Well, the Skipper did not want me to go ashore at Alexandria either, because the company would make a fuss about having to pay the expense, so he was pleased when I said I would come on with the ship to Piraeus,[9] and that is the only thing the skipper and I agreed about on the whole of that long voyage.

When the French doctor had bound me up he went away and left me in my cabin, and when I felt the ship get under way I began to be very pleased about how things were turning out, because here I was with no work to do till my broken ribs had mended and now I would

9 *Piraeus* also known as Piraiévs; the port of Athens, Greece.

never have to see Spud Tamson anymore. But I found that things were not so good when the time came round to have dinner, because it turned out that that French doctor had ordered me to have nothing to eat: only barley water! So I decided I would have to feel faint and then they would bring me brandy. But a man cannot live all the time on barley water and brandy, and there were not any symptoms I could think of that would make them bring me steak and eggs.

By the time we got to Piraeus in Greece I was nearly fit to eat the blankets, and after we had berthed at the wharf I told the Skipper that I did not like giving so much trouble on the ship, so if I could have two sticks I would try to hobble about so I would not need to be a burden on them any more.

At first the Skipper thought I was not strong enough to go ashore, but I said I just wanted to cross the wharf to get two fresh eggs, so he let me hobble down the gangway, and I went into a restaurant on the other side of the wharf; when nighttime came I was still eating and drinking there.

5

Bunbury, where we went from Piraeus, is a little town on the coast of Western Australia. They have a jetty nearly two miles long there and the ships come in to load grain. We were twice at Bunbury while I was on that ship so we got to know all the people in the town pretty well. In a little place when there is just one ship in, all the people make a fuss of you. The girls used to come walking along the wharf in the evenings and you would get talking to them then, and if you liked one you would ask her if she would like to see the engines. There was one girl who afterwards used to take me riding in her sedan car. But the first time I asked if she would like to see the engines she laughed like anything because she said she had seen the engines before. She did come to look at them one day, however, and after that she used to bring me homemade scones and cakes down to the boat. So I was really quite a success at Bunbury. But the first time I was in Bunbury I spent a lot of time fishing in the water as well.

Bunbury is the place where they tell you you can catch kingfish by sprinkling pepper on the water and knocking them on the head with a mallet when they come up to sneeze! But I did not see anyone catching kingfish like that.

I used to use a line and bait, and one night I left my line set and went away to play the gramophone, and I was still playing the gramophone when there was a whole commotion on the deck. I went up and saw that everyone had run to have a look at my line. All the people on the wharf were crowding round too, and my line had gone tight in the water and it was hardly moving at all, except very slowly from right to left.

I went up to it and grabbed hold of it, but whatever was on the other end was something that felt exactly like a piece of rock. So I thought they had been playing a joke on me, but they were all as serious as I was, so we decided the best thing to do was to haul to the surface and see what on earth had got on. So we started up one of the winches,[10] because nothing that we could do ourselves would bring in an inch of that line.

It was evening, but it was still light, and as the winch slowly brought this young mountain to the surface I began to get all excited, so I jumped on the wharf and climbed down to the edge of the water to take a good look at what on earth was coming up.

At first it came up like a great black lump. It was nearly as wide as it was long, and as it came up near the surface a little tail like an elephant's tail, only barbed, began to lash above the water and everyone on the wharf yelled out to me to come up quick out of the way of that tail.

So I did because it was a poisonous stinging ray—a giant one—and its tail would just about kill you. But once we had got a knife on a long pole and cut its tail off it could not do any more harm.

So we got a rope round it and hauled it up on deck with the winch and it was like the side of a house hanging up there above the deck. When it was dead we had it weighed and it weighed 800 pounds. It was the biggest fish that I ever saw in my life.

The Skipper was wild though that I had caught it instead of him, and he kept saying, "Yes, they're all along the beach. Anyone can catch them."

But everyone else thought I was very lucky to have caught it, so I felt quite pleased.

The Chinese crew, because all the seamen on this boat were Chinese, came crowding round to look at it; and their Chief Steward who used to feed them in his own way, wanted to buy the fish from me, so I said he could have it for £2. He thought that was a great bargain, and he left it hanging there all that voyage, all the way back to Piraeus and then round by the Cape to Australia again. After a few

10 *winch* a mechanism with one or more drums that coil a chain or rope for raising or drawing.

weeks you could hardly go on deck when the wind was with us, but none of the Chinese seemed to mind.

6

By the time we got to Bunbury the second time the Skipper hated me like poison and I had not grown to love him anything extra myself.

The first people we met when we pulled into the wharf this time were three Pommies.[11] They came to ask the Skipper if they could work their passages home because it seemed that Australia was no longer their land of promise, but the Skipper said he would see them hanged first, and he said it in such a discourteous way that they all up and said to him, all right then, they would jolly well stow away.

"If you stow away on my ship," he roared at them, "I'll have you all put in the cooler!"

But they just laughed and said that was O.K., they were going to stow away.

So all the time we were in Bunbury that trip the Skipper kept watching those Pommies and if they disappeared for an hour or two he was as jumpy as a cat on hot bricks until they turned up again.

We were loading grain as usual that trip and everything went all right till we came to No. 4 hold. But soon after this hold was started those three Pommies came along the wharf and I happened to be leaning on the rail, so I went down the gangway and sat on the jetty and talked to them.

They were trying to think of a way to get aboard into No. 4 hold, and not being any too partial to our Skipper myself I thought it would be a good idea if I offered to give them some assistance. So we talked for a long time down there in the dark on the jetty and I told them if they came alongside in a boat the next night I would help them to get in the hold.

The next night I happened to be on duty in the engine room. The old man was ashore enjoying himself with his ladies, but a whole lot of the others were on the ship. I did not want them to know that I was going to help these stowaways aboard, so I sent an apprentice for'ard[12] with six bottles of wine and after that no one paid any attention to what I was doing at all.

But just as I was getting everything nicely set I heard the Chief come aboard, so now something would be done to keep him off the scent too.

11 *Pommies* Australian for "Englishmen." [Original Edition]
12 *for'ard* the ship's bow—its forward section—or in its direction.

The Pommies were alongside by now in their little dinghy and they were just getting a rope ladder fixed to the side. I was scared in case the Chief should walk along that side of the deck and see them, but instead there was a sizzle and a lot of flashing in the engine room and he came running down swearing like blazes to know if I was trying to blow the ship up. But I wasn't trying to blow the ship up, I was trying to keep the Chief busy. It took him a couple of hours to locate and fix the fuse I had made. In the meantime the three Pommies were climbing up their rope ladder and getting themselves fixed in the hold. I kept squinting along to see if everything was all right, and making sure no one else had come back to the ship.

The decks were absolutely deserted, and there was more than enough noise for'ard, where they were finishing the bottles of wine, to drown any sounds the Pommies were making as they dragged their things over the side.

One way and another they had quite a lot of things. For instance, there was food for four days and then a whole lot of planks for them to make a sort of dugout under the wheat bags. The wheat was already 15 feet deep in the hold and they had to have another 14 feet put in on top of them. The only way to prevent their being squashed was to put planks across over their heads and make a hollow amongst the sacks against one side of the hold. By the time they were snug in this hollow they had made, the Chief had fixed the fuse and the wine was all finished, but when they began to come aft along the decks the rope ladder and the dinghy were gone and there was no way at all of telling that there were three men hiding in the hold.

So I walked round the decks with the others to have a smoke, and I was whistling. And as I got into bed that night I kept stopping to have a laugh when I thought of how the Skipper would look when we were four days out to sea and he had to open up that hold.

7

Next day the wharf lumpers[13] filled up No. 4 hold. It was funny to watch them doing it because they could see those three hidden in their dugout under the bags all the time, but they didn't breathe a word, only they were laughing like anything every time they came to put down some more bags.

13 *lumpers* dockworkers.

The bags got higher and higher and at last those three Pommies were buried away down out of sight. They would have been squashed as flat as pancakes if the planks over them had collapsed and let the weight of the bags down on them, but it was the only way they could be sure of not being found by the Skipper, and it would be their funeral, not ours, if anything happened.

I was thinking particularly about it being their funeral when I saw the last sacks go into the hold and the hatches battened down. Because when that was finished the crew went round covering up all the ventilators with bags!

I decided that I would rather be where I was than down in that hold under 14 feet of wheat sacks. But there is no accounting for tastes, and there is one thing about it—they would not be cold anyway.

Well, the hatches were just down and the crew just finished with the ventilators when the Skipper came striding on board and you could see by the look on his face that something was preying on his mind.

"Those fellows aren't in the village," he said, and then he looked straight at me. "Do *you* know anything about them?"

But I didn't see why I should know anything about them when I had scarcely been ashore for the last two days. But he looked at me just as if he thought I must be telling him a lie and gave orders for the whole ship to be searched.

So they searched her from bow to stern but they did not find anything because they never thought of taking out all the cargo in No. 4 hold.

The Skipper was still suspicious, but he did not see where they could be hiding, so he just threw me a look, and then we started out to sea.

8

It was a Wednesday when we started out to sea and for two days we sailed right into the Indian Ocean, and all the time no one heard a word from those fellows down in the hold. I knew they were all right though, because at night when I came off duty I used to walk around the deck for a smoke before I went to bed, and when I came near the ventilators I would bend over and call down to them, and when I listened hard I could hear an answer. So for two days I knew they were all right.

But the third night I went round and called down I heard nothing at all. I listened very carefully but there wasn't the slightest sound, so I started wondering if they had been squashed or suffocated, but then I thought perhaps they were just asleep. So I went down to my cabin and didn't think anymore.

But on Saturday night there was not any answer either, and when I tried to call louder down the ventilators to wake them if they were only asleep, I thought I heard somebody coming, so I bolted down below quickly, because if someone came along and saw a man talking to a ventilator they would only think that he was daft.

But I was worried in my bunk that night to know how I could find out whether they were dead or not, but by next morning everyone on the ship knew.

The next morning was Sunday and, it being a cargo ship, everyone had to do his "dobying" (that's nautical for washing) on Sunday morning, so Chippy had got down early and he was busy scrubbing his shirt when suddenly he heard a noise like knocking coming from No. 4 hold, which was just through the wall.

So at first he thought he must be daft, but he listened and the knocking came again.

"Cripes!" said Chippy. "There's someone in there." So he dropped his shirt and knocked back, and when the answer came he turned round and bolted up to tell the Old Man.

The Old Man went livid round the gills when he heard there were noises in the holds.

"It's stowaways!" he said. "This is that Third's doing."

So there he was blaming me when he had no evidence against me at all.

But all the time this was happening I was working in the engine room not knowing a thing about it, so I got quite a shock when two apprentices came pelting down to me. "Third, there's three stowaways laid out up there on the deck and the Old Man wants to speak to you."

So I waited just a minute to collect my air of nonchalance, and then I strolled up on the deck. The whole ship was crowded round where they had opened up the hold, and in the middle of the crowd there was Chippy who had heard them knocking, and the Old Man, and the three stowaways. The latter had passed right out owing to the strain of their privations, but by looking into the hold you could see that they had managed to accomplish a tidy bit of damage first.

It must have got uncomfortable down there in their dugout for apparently they had set to work to cut their way out with knives. If you had been a tidy person you would have wept to see those wheat sacks, for they were tumbled, and ripped, and spilling wheat not in bucketfuls but in tons.

"You've had a hand in this, Scotty?" the Skipper roared as soon as he saw me, and he wouldn't believe what I said for all my nonchalant air. But I kept thinking how he had no sort of evidence against me, when suddenly they started coming round and the beastly bunch of twisters[14] sat up and split on the spot.

"What?" roared the Skipper. "*What?* I'll lose him his engineer's ticket,[15] I will," he said, "I mean it," he turned on me again.

But that was the rock he perished on, saying he would lose me my ticket, because I knew then that I had been right to keep the addresses of the houses he had slept at and I was glad about that because I never like to expend my energies in vain.

"It'll be clink for the lot of you," the Skipper was yelling at the stowaways; and I hoped it would be clink, though clink was too good for a set of twisters like those three.

9

We went home via Durban,[16] and we were a long time there too, because it was while we were there that I found out there was something wrong with the engines. If it had not been for me there would have been a big explosion, because the crowns[17] of the boilers had dropped over an inch and if I had not happened to look in one day and see, no one would have known a thing until the big bang came.

At first the Second Engineer would not believe me because it is not a thing that you expect to happen to a seaworthy vessel, but when he found I was right he said, "'Struth!" and we cabled to Glasgow to know what to do, because it was certainly not safe to go on in that state.

The answer came from Glasgow to get marine engineers to put hydraulic presses on the boiler crowns and then there was a postscript at the bottom of the cable which shows you how it is

14 *twisters* untrustworthy individuals.
15 *ticket* license.
16 *Durban* a port city in South Africa.
17 *crowns* crown sheet; a plate that serves as the roof for a combustion chamber or an internally fired furnace.

that shipping magnates have sometimes £50 million to leave to people in their wills.

Stop the officers' afternoon teas, it said. Though it was hard to see how that was going to pay for the repairs to the boilers when all we got for afternoon tea was a cup of tea and a biscuit!

And they did not let me off having my afternoon tea stopped like the others even though it was due to me looking in the boilers that we were not all at the bottom of the sea.

10

It was a weary voyage back to England and we ended up at the head of the Manchester Canal. The Old Man was glad to get there because he had been nursing up his schemes for paying out me and those stowaways all the way home.

So as soon as ever we were berthed he had the police on board to arrest them and when they were brought up in court he had me there charged with assisting, and tried to lose me my engineer's ticket the very best he could. But he did not manage to lose me my engineer's ticket and if he had not tried he would have kept his reputation, because then I would never have gone back on board the ship after everything was over and walked into the chart room[18] where his wife and daughters were talking to him and told them how I could provide all the evidence if ever his wife was thinking of instituting divorce proceedings.

So I think that will teach him not to be vindictive again.

---

18 *chart room* a compartment beside the pilothouse where navigational gear and charts are kept.

CHAPTER VI

1

AFTER I came back from Australia I was engineer on a ship going to Montreal. I used to be in Glasgow once a month and that was how I got to know this fellow Arthur Fitch. You would think after my experience on that voyage to Australia that I would have been cured of going out of my way to help people, but it is a funny thing about me that I never seem to learn not to do a man a good turn. I do not think I am a man who is very lucky with his friends, but I still seem to go on thinking that they are not going to let me down.

This fellow Arthur Fitch is a very nice fellow really, but he is a terrible trial to his mother, and she a widow and he her only son. Arthur Fitch's mother has really got a lot of money, but sometimes when he makes trouble she will not have him at home anymore. He is very well-educated really, and he went to the University, but he had to leave the University, so though he has really been there he is not one of those fellows who can put a lot of letters after his name.

Most of the time Arthur Fitch does not have to do any work because his mother gives him money, so he just drives about the town in a taxi, and buys a lot of drinks. He always likes to carry a rolled-up umbrella because he says it is the mark of a gentleman to carry a rolled-up umbrella.

Even when he is drunk so that you would not introduce him to a lady he still likes to carry a rolled-up umbrella. In fact, when he is drunk he remembers about being a gentleman more than ever. When he is drunk like that he will tell you about it all the time. But the first time I met Arthur Fitch he was not really so very drunk.

We had all gone to a wedding, and it was a teetotal wedding, so we went across the road with the fellow who was the best man, who never took a drink as a rule, and we bought two bottles of whisky. When we had finished these we hid them under the bath in the house where the wedding reception was going on, and the old lady who was the aunt of the girl that was getting married found them and came into the room and asked in front of all the guests for the names of the people who had put the bottles under the bath; but no one was able to tell her because they had not seen us do it, so we would have been all right but for the fellow who was the best man.

He was getting to the stage where you feel like challenging the bridegroom to sock you one and see what happens, so as soon as the speeches were over and the toasts drunk in lemonade, we took him out of the house with us, because you never know how a fellow is going to behave when he does not take a drink as a rule.

But we said if he was feeling like that we would take him up the town with us, so he went and changed his dress suit[1] for some ordinary clothes, and came with us while we changed ours and then we all went up town together.

Well, we went into a café up the town and the first thing this best man fellow saw when he got there was a girl he liked the look of, and it turned out to be a girl that I knew named Flora. So I caught her eye and she came over. But soon she had no time for us because she and this best man fellow who never went with girls any more than he took drink as a rule, were getting on like a house on fire,[2] so Arthur Fitch and I thought we would get up and leave them. We took out our wedding buttonholes,[3] which we had changed from our dress suits, and gave them to the girl for a souvenir. Well, she took them and then she said to this best man that she was sitting with, "Why haven't you got a buttonhole, too?"

So he said he had left his at home, and then he said if she liked to come home with him she could get it, so Arthur and I thought he was not so slow after all, and we watched them go off together and said they would find us there if they liked to come back later.

Well, we stayed in that café, but we forgot all about those two, and it was a couple of hours later that the best man came running in. He was so excited that his tie was all crooked and he was swallowing with excitement. When he found us he came over to our table and sat down and he was trembling.

So we asked what was the matter, but he didn't seem to know what was the matter, so instead we asked him where was Flora, and he jumped when we said that just as if you had stuck something in him, but he didn't seem to know where Flora was, only he said that

1 *dress suit* men's formalwear.
2 *getting on like a house on fire* enjoying each other's company and fast becoming friends.
3 *buttonhole* a flower bouquet that fits into a lapel's buttonhole.

she was gone. So we asked him why she was gone and all he could do was swallow and mutter something about his mother.

So we thought perhaps his mother had not liked Flora, and when we said that he began to nod his head hard. So we asked what had happened that his mother had not liked Flora and Arthur wanted to know if his mother had thrown Flora out of the house.

But it seemed that his mother had not thrown Flora out of the house, and it seemed—because we thought of that—that she had not gone for him either. In fact he said that his mother had not said anything at all.

So we could not think how he was so sure that his mother had not liked Flora, because after all if you do not throw a person out of the house and you do not say anything to them, how is a person to know? But he kept on saying he *knew* his mother had not liked Flora, only we were getting tired by now so we said we thought he was just imagining it all.

But he said, "I was not imagining it. If you had seen the way she picked up Flora's clothes and threw them out in the garden . . ."

But when he got to there we did not hear anymore, because when we learnt how he had discovered his mother did not like Flora, Arthur and I had exploded.

So Arthur and I went away and left him after that and we decided that in future we would not give a drink to a man that does not take one as a rule because it seems you never can tell where it is going to land him. And after all if you are going to disillusion a man's mother about him it is rather a responsibility.

2

Well, after that evening with the best man who never took a drink as a rule, Arthur seemed to have a bond of sympathy with me and when I was off my ship we used to go about a lot together. So in the end Arthur said he would like to have a look at Canada, and how about me getting him on my ship as a steward? So I said I would try, and that was the rock I perished on, because it was due to my recommendation that they took Arthur Fitch on as steward. For Arthur was not really a success as a steward and when he was fired I was told to go with him, so you see it does not always pay to do a good turn to your friends.

When Arthur and I went ashore, having both lost our jobs, we found that all our people were away on a holiday, both our homes were closed up, so we decided to go into digs,[4] and it was while we were in digs that Arthur met a girl called Mary.

4 *go into digs* move into lodgings.

She was a nice girl, too, but she weighed about 14 stone,[5] and I was always sorry myself about the fate that overtook her.

For a few days Arthur was nuts about Mary and we went everywhere with her, but one day we left her at home and went out just by ourselves. Arthur said he would go back and get her later on in evening, but when he got out he told me that we would not bother her that evening at all.

So we started down the road to some other place we knew and when we got in there it was full of ship's stewards. There were about 20 in there that had been on our ship, and as—being an engineer—I did not get to know stewards, they all looked like strangers to me, but Arthur hailed them as old pals, and started shouting them drinks.

When we had been drinking awhile it came out how he had been telling them on board ship about what a grand house his mother had, so now they were twigging[6] him about it, and Arthur, who was getting to the "I am a gentleman" stage, said, "All right, if you don't believe me you can come along and see it."

So out of the bar he trailed, with about 20 ship's stewards following after him. I don't know if there were really 20, but it seemed like that because we crammed three taxis full, and they all pulled up outside his mother's house.

The house was all locked up, Arthur's mother being away, so he went round to the back and broke in through a window. Then he came striding down the hall and flung open the front door, switched on the lights, and the 20 stewards came marching in with their eyes as big as saucers, because I swear not one had ever been inside as grand a house as that before.

So Arthur took them all through everything, then he opened up his mother's liqueurs and they started to have a party, and the stewards began to think that Arthur was just swell. But when it began to be late we all left the house together, and Arthur said good night to them downtown, and the two of us climbed into our taxi and started off for our digs, but we had to make a couple of stops on the way.

It was about an hour after we had left that we drove past Arthur's mother's house and when we got within sight of it Arthur nearly collapsed on the floor of the cab.

5 *stone* a British weight unit equivalent to 14 pounds: fourteen stone equals 196 pounds.

6 *twigging* reproofing.

"My mother's home!" he started groaning, because the whole place was lit up, and the only thing he could think of was that his mother had come home unexpectedly, and found all the mess he had left through entertaining those stewards.

So we pulled up the taxi and I said I would sneak up and look.

Well, I got out of the taxi and crept up the garden path, and you never saw such a sight as I saw in that house. The whole 20 stewards had come back and were ransacking it!

They had on every light in the place, and their pockets were full of table silver, and they were pulling out all the drawers to see what was in them. The house was really very untidy. You never saw such a mess in your life.

So I bolted down the path to tell Arthur and when he heard me he was very upset.

"My mother'll kill me," he said. "Oh, what shall I do?" and he got out of the taxi and started running towards the river. I ran after him, and there he was up on the parapet. He still had his rolled-up umbrella and that went first, then his bowler hat, then his gloves, then he was going to dive himself; but I pulled him back and told him that this was no time for suicide because I said if we hurried maybe we could get the stewards out and his mother might never know. So we started running back down the street, and we got into his house that was still full of ship's stewards.

Well, it took the best part of the night to part them from their souvenirs and get them to leave quietly, because being in a big house seemed to go right to their heads, but at last we piled them into taxis and got them driven away, and Arthur and I sat and looked at each other through the wreckage.

But all Arthur could find to say to me was, "I am sorry I lost that umbrella," so apparently he did not remember that if it had not been for me he would have been a dead carcass at the bottom of the river by now. Only I was not angry with Arthur because I have learnt by now that it is no use expecting a man to be grateful when you have done him a good turn.

3

Well, we had got the stewards out of the place but it was still not very tidy because the silver was all spilt on the floor and it was mixed up with empty bottles; but the bottles were not all empty so Arthur thought the stewards might come back. So he said he thought we had better sleep there just to be on guard in case the stewards came back. But he said he thought Mary would be lonely if we did not go home all that night so he thought we had better go and fetch her, so we got a taxi and drove to our digs.

Mary was in bed by now and sound asleep; but there is one thing about fat girls they do not often get in a temper so Mary did not mind being woken up and she came with us right away.

I had to go on a message[7] and I did not get back to Arthur's place till after he had gone there with Mary, and when I came back I was in a taxi, so I thought it was so late and cold that I would ask the taximan in. He did not mind coming into Arthur's place because I said if he came there he would see some very interesting things. But he did not expect to see Mary standing up on a table, because she had forgotten to put any clothes on, so that he did not know where to look because Mary being 14 stone it was hard not to see that she was there, but the taximan had his reputation as a married man to think of so he said he thought perhaps he had better go away.

I was sorry about that because he had gone very red in the face and you could see that he was quite embarrassed, and I do not think Mary should have forgotten about putting any clothes on, but of course it is hard to remember everything when you are called out in the middle of the night.

We told Mary to go upstairs and cover herself with an eiderdown, but it seems she did not want to do that, so in the end we had to carry her. But she was fighting all the way and I must say she was a good fighter, but I think it would have been all right if Arthur had not given her that wee tap with the poker. But that wee tap made her so mad that she jumped up and went for Arthur and she gave him such a punch on the jaw that he fell and cut his head open against the lintel of the window. So then Arthur was mad too, and I did not know what I could do with them because it looked if the fight went on like this that there would be a murder done. So I thought the best thing I could do was to put myself in between them because I could not stand by and wait till they were both killed.

But when I put myself in between them I had to give Mary a push and she lost her balance when I pushed her, so that she fell and struck the jutting out piece of the mahogany bed with her face. It was like an ox being axed because she went down with a crash and did not

7 *message* errand.

move anymore, but soon there was blood everywhere so that it was difficult to tell whether Mary was dead or not.

But Arthur was sure she had been murdered so he let out one yell and bolted out of the house into the street, and there was I, left to cope with the situation without any moral support. The only thing I could think of was to run to the bathroom and get a wet towel and start wiping her face with it, but when she did not seem to come round I thought the best thing I could do was to go and see what had happened to Arthur.

So I went to the front window and there he was outside running up and down as if he did not know what to do next. I could see that if I did not save the situation nobody else would do it, so I ran out to speak to Arthur, but as I ran I heard awful screams coming from the house behind me, so it seemed that Mary was not dead but she was calling out "Murder!" like anything, so the best thing I could think of to do was to make Arthur come with me quickly to the police station.

Because I thought if he would come to the police station we could say there was a woman in our house making a disturbance, so they would not think we were to blame if we came to the police first.

But the police said they could not do anything unless we would charge the woman, but we did not want to charge Mary as we thought that would not be chivalrous, so we left the police station then and went back to the house.

But when we got to the house we could hardly believe our eyes because there was a big crowd there, and there were people and an ambulance, and there were policemen in pyjamas with their helmets on, so we began to think we must be suffering with the strain of the evening, only then Arthur remembered that right behind his house there was a police barracks, and Mary must have yelled so loud that they had all jumped out of bed and forgotten their clothes just like she did.

We pushed through the crowd to where the ambulance was waiting and lo and behold there was Mary being carried away on a stretcher and she was still shouting "Murder!" So Arthur and I were very worried to think that in her delirium she might accuse us of some crime.

We thought the best thing we could do was to tidy away all the evidence and we went into the house and climbed up the stairs once more.

I started to try and wash the blood off the wall in the bedroom but I got so excited that I washed the wallpaper off as well.

You would think it had been my murder, the trouble that I was taking, and all the time Arthur could not do anything but walk up and down and groan and tear his hair.

While this was going on the detectives walked in and at first I thought we were all going to be arrested, but it seemed they only wanted us to answer some questions, and they made us show our hands to see if there was blood on them, and in the end they decided they would not arrest us as we had come first to the police station and perhaps the woman had fallen, so they left us and went away.

But Arthur could not stop thinking that perhaps they were going to arrest him, though I told him I had put everything right by going first to the police station because I am a man that knows how to handle these things. But Arthur did not seem to have any confidence in my judgment so he packed a bag full of crystal out of his mother's house and as soon as it was morning he went into Glasgow and pawned it and he got £15 for it, so he went away to London and I did not see him any more for some time.

But I went to see Mary in the hospital and there was a lady detective there taking down her statement, but I told Mary how she had got confused and that it was all an accident because nobody had murdered her, so she stopped her statement to the detective and I was let alone.

But one day after this when I was in Sauchiehall Street[8] I saw a sight such as I had thought never to see in my life. Because there was Arthur in a bowler hat with holes in it so his hair was coming through, and his boots were nearly walked off his feet and his clothes were only fit for the incinerator, for it seems he had spent all his money and had walked home from London. He said to me, "How do I look, Bobby?"

But I thought that was a question only his mother ought to answer, so I put him in a taxi and I drove him to his home.

8 *Sauchiehall Street* an upscale retail boulevard in Glasgow.

CHAPTER VII

1

AND now once again I had to pack my bags for America. This time I was a passenger. I went second class on the *Melita*[1] but I roamed all over the ship.

There was a Dutch fellow on board who was travelling first class and he seemed to be spending a lot of money so I thought it would be a good idea to make friends with him.

He was not what you would call a very intellectual type, in fact if he had not been rich there may be folks that would have called him dumb, but I am always one to give a man the benefit of the doubt or how else could he have managed to make some money, so I did not put any intelligence tests on him and I thought maybe he was a crook who was giving out[2] that he was dumb.

I thought maybe he was a crook because he told me he had never been in America and the first time he opened a packet of Lucky Strike cigarettes he tore a hole in the end and knocked the packet against his finger in a way he could never have learnt outside the States. So I thought if he was a crook he was not a very clever one to give himself away like that.

When we had been at sea about two days he had me down having drinks in his stateroom, and I looked at his things down there and sure enough he had been in America whatever he might like to say. His hat was American and his shoes, you could tell his suits by the way they were half-lined, so taking off the labels hadn't done any good.

I kept wondering and wondering what game he was up to and one day in his stateroom I suddenly called his bluff.

1 *Melita* Built by Barclay, Curle & Co. of Glasgow. After 146 trips across the Atlantic, it was used briefly for cruises and then sold in April 1935 for scrapping in Genoa. However, the ship was not dismantled but bought by the Italia Line, renamed *Liguria*, and used for military transport. It was damaged in a 1940 air attack in Tobruk, a port city in northeast Libya, and scuttled the next year. The ship was scrapped in 1950.

2 *giving out* proclaiming.

"Come across," I said, "what's the big idea, never been in the States before?"

So he turned quite pale. He was a fat man and he could tremble like a jelly. He was frightened when he saw that I had spotted him and he came across easily.

He was not a crook at all. He did not have the brains to be a crook. He was a steward who had beat it off a ship in New York 10 years ago and he had made a pile out of real estate when making a pile was easier than getting tight on moonshine whisky. But after he had made his pile he thought he would go back home and settle down in Holland, only when he got back Holland seemed all different from what he had remembered and now he wanted to come back to America again. But he didn't know how he was going to get back into America because he had no right there in the first place and now the quota[3] was against him to prevent him going in at all.

So he was worried about his prospects, but he thought he might sneak in through Canada, because having been in America he knew money could buy you most things, but what he did not seem to know was that when a man is dumb people sometimes take your money and then do not give you the thing you think you are going to buy.

So I told him how he was not likely to get into America by himself, but would only lose all his money, so he looked upset and asked me what he ought to do.

Well, I never like to see a man looking all upset like Hans Kohn did, so I said if he stuck to me I would see what I could do to help him and he was so grateful for that that he pushed the bell for some more drinks right away.

2

Well, Hans and I landed in Canada and took a train at once for the border so that we got to Windsor in Ontario as quickly as ever we could. We got in a taxi from the train and drove straight to a big hotel, because Hans is one of those chaps who always like to be comfortable and I like to be comfortable too, if someone will pay for it for me.

So we took rooms at this hotel and then we went out to get some whisky. I do not know whether it is true that you can think better on

3 *quota* The vast flow of immigration to the U.S. in the 19th century was drastically reduced in the 1920s by the Immigration Quota Law which put an annual cap of 150,000 immigrants. There was also a limit on immigration according to nationality.

whisky, but thinking when you have been drinking whisky does not make you nearly so sad.

So we went out and got some whisky and after that we quite enjoyed thinking how we could sneak across the Canadian border into the United States.

All the trouble over getting into the United States was over Hans, not me, because when I was in Chicago I had become a naturalized citizen, but it was different for Hans, who had not any papers at all. So after we had drunk a lot of whisky we had still not thought of a way so we decided we would call the boots[4] and ask him what he thought we ought to do.

So we rang the bell for the boots and the first thing we did when he came was to fill up a glass for him.

I think that is what you call setting a sprat to catch a mackerel[5] and when the boots had swallowed his sprat, hook, line, and sinker, I said for him to sit down on the carpet and open his ears because here was a chance for him to make a few dollars.

So when I had explained the position about me having a passport but Hans having none, but how Hans was anxious to get back into the States, the boots said he knew just the fellow we were looking for, so he sent us out and told us to hail a particular taxi.

We had to tell the taximan he had sent us and then the taximan would know where we wanted to go to, so we went out and did just what the boots had said.

The taximan understood all right, so he must have been getting a rake-off[6] on the job too. I think getting rake-offs must be a major industry in America, and it is a very good way to make money once you get to know how.

Well, this taximan that was getting a rake-off drove us all through back streets in Windsor on a very roundabout route, but at last he brought up at some arches along by the river, and suddenly when we got there he turned in down a sort of subway[7] and there we were, in a big underground room that was lined with more guns than I had ever seen before in my life. It was clear that this was a proper tough joint, and as when we drove in there Hans and I had £8,000 on us—

4 *boots* an employee charged with shining shoes, particularly in a hotel.
5 *sprat, mackerel* a sprat is a small herring, while a mackerel is roughly 18-inches long.
6 *a rake-off* a percentage off of; a cut.
7 *subway* an underground tunnel.

half of it in each of our shoes—I did not think we would be stopping long at all.

When the taximan pulled up a guy got up off a seat and came slouching over, and the taximan said, "Well, boys, here's two chaps that want to go across. How about it?" And while the taximan was talking to the guy I was looking the place over. I could see by now that it was a proper rumrunner's joint and I knew that if they guessed we had £8,000 under out feet it would be goodbye to our chances of getting anywhere but to the bottom of the river, so I nudged Hans to keep his mouth shut because he was a terrible one for saying the wrong thing, and I tackled the guy that had come slouching over.

"So you want to get across?" he said. "Well, brother, you will have to pay for it. Have you got one hundred bucks?"

So I trod on Hans' foot just in time to stop him saying something stupid and then I said no, we had not got one hundred bucks but maybe if we went away and looked we could get them. So the guy gave a look when I said that.

"That'll do me fine, brother," he said. "You come back with your hundred bucks at three o'clock in the morning. 'Slong," he said, and the taximan started up his engine, so he stood back when we swung round and headed out of that subway into the good fresh air. That was the last we saw of him, standing amongst his guns looking after us, because we did not go back there at three o'clock in the morning, nor any other time either. I did not want to frighten Hans so I told him they were too expensive.

That was really a narrow escape that we had from those gangsters by the river and after that I did not rely on the bootboy anymore.

I thought I would depend on my own brains instead, so I said to Hans that it ought to be easy to bluff our way in as ordinary day-trippers who are Canadians who go across from Windsor to Detroit on a ferry. On the other side of the river they have turnstiles and they draft you into three sections. One section is marked "American Citizens," one "Emigrants," and one "Naturalized Citizens." I thought we would go through the last one, and if anybody asked us any questions we would say we were now living in Canada and were coming into Detroit for the day. We would say we were going to a show, so I had Hans all coached up over which show we were going to, and where the theatre was, and what show was there the week before, because those are the kind of questions they ask you, to find out if you are really a stranger in disguise or not. I spent a whole week getting Hans to have his answers all perfect. We used to drive around in a taxi while I made him practice, and by the end of a week he said he thought he knew them properly. But I was not sure of him myself, though I had taken so much trouble, because Hans was the kind of person who could never keep an idea in his head for five minutes at a time. But Hans was getting worried at the way the bills were mounting up, so to please him I said we would risk it.

You would think a week would be long enough for a man to learn to answer questions in the way that he has been told, but Hans was not a man that you could judge by ordinary standards. He was so frightened that morning when we went to cross on the ferry that he took a whole lot of drinks just to keep his courage up. I told him it was silly to do that because he would be sure to get muddled, but he would not take any notice and the result was that all my week's work was wasted. When we got to the first turnstile before he had even been asked anything, Hans went rolling up to the officer as if he was going to slap him on the back and said, "I'm a Hollander over here on a holiday!" Then he started to reel off the answers I had taught him, but of course it was now too late, so the officer would not let him through and we had to go back on the same ferry we had come by.

On the way back on the ferry I called him a number of things, but he didn't seem to see what was wrong since he had given the answers I told him. So I told him I was through and when he heard that he started to cry, because he said he had spent so much money and he still was not over the border. So I said we would have another try on a different ferry after dinner. So he cheered up and we went along and had a good dinner.

But it was a pity that we had that dinner because he cheered up so much that he got proud over being a Hollander again, and when we got to the second turnstile he out with it the same as before. So I quite lost patience and I would not speak to him all the way home.

3

Well, after that experience I could see our whole week had been wasted so I started to think of another way to smuggle Hans into the States. He kept saying all his money was going and I asked whose fault was that, anyway? So he started to cry again. I don't know why I had such patience with a fellow who let me down and was always crying, but that night I could not stand him any longer so I went off by myself.

It was lucky I did that because I met a man that night who said he knew a way to get us over but it would cost five hundred bucks. Well, Hans would have jibbed[8] at five hundred bucks a week ago but it did not look much now after what all the rest had cost him. So when I told him he cheered up a lot and we decided we would try.

It was a Canadian cop that we went with to this place where they would get us across. He was helping us because he was going to get a rake-off on the deal. He took us down the river to a roadhouse that looked all shut up, but when we knocked on the door a window flew up and a "Polack" (Pole) looked out at us.

This Polack did not seem to be very hospitable at first, but when he heard we were going to pay five hundred bucks to get taken across the river he cheered up considerably and came down and let us in.

It seems we had to wait till we could be taken across the river so we had to buy some drinks from the Polack to pass away the time, and Hans began to get so stupid that there he was hauling out $20 bills and slapping that Polack on the face with them, so I had to keep taking them away and putting them in my pocket. But as fast as I did he hauled out some more. The Polack was quite jolly by now, but I did not see why he should be the one to have all Hans' $20 bills.

I do not think that Polack liked me very much, but if it had not been for me Hans would never have come out of that place with any money left at all.

Well, at last when it was nearly morning, two men came who were going to row us across the river, so we followed them down to the water and climbed into the dinghy that they had. It was nearly winter at this time and already the river was starting to freeze over. We got more than halfway across all right, but then we ran into an ice floe, and there we were stuck! It was fun, I can tell you. Day started to break and Hans was nearly crying again. We couldn't get the boat forward or back whatever we did to it.

As the light got better they could see us from the American bank, and it must have been snoopers[9] who saw us because right away they

8 *jibbed* balked.

9 *snooper* Someone authorized to inquire or watch nosily. As an example, the *Oxford English Dictionary* cites a sentence from a 1928 *Chicago Tribune* article: "Prohibition Commissioner Doran has warned dry snoopers to stop gunplay against innocent citizens."

started taking pot shots at us, and all that Hans could do was to crouch down and try to hide behind the boat. We made a pretty good target against the white ice, and we were lucky that the light was bad or I would probably not be writing this story at all.

All the time the snoopers were shooting I kept thinking what we could do and at last I decided that to run was the only thing. So I got hold of Hans and lugged him up from behind the boat and told him to run wherever I ran but to say nothing whatever. We took the rest of our whisky with us because I had an instinct that it might come in useful, because a man's instinct to hang on to his whisky very often proves right in this life. Well, so it proved in this case as I will demonstrate in due course, but in the meantime Hans and I had to carry it while we dodged across the ice floes in the dawn with the American cops potting at us from the bank. The bullets were chipping on the ice and Hans was shaking like jelly but I told him to keep his head down and double the way I was so we zigzagged down the river and in the end we shook the cops off.

We came ashore at last right opposite one of the smart suburbs of Detroit and we were marching up the middle of a great big boulevard congratulating ourselves that we had done it at last, when we ran bang into a big Yankee policeman.

This was such a shock to come just when victory seemed within our grasp that I could not think of anything to say, and even Hans forgot to come out with the bit about him being a Hollander on holiday. It is a funny thing but if we had not been so flabbergasted we should probably have been arrested then and there. But the cop did not get a chance to be suspicious of our story because he never even heard it.

"Well, boys," he said, and he winked at our whisky bottles, "been making whoopee?" That cop never thought two fellows would try to sneak across the border with no luggage but some whisky, so I hopped in quickly before Hans had time to drop a brick, and I said we had just been to a grand party over the river.

I offered the cop a drink then and I said he could keep the bottle.

"Thanks, boys," he said. "That's swell of you," and he went off with his bottle of whisky so happy and innocent that it seemed a shame to deceive him.

We were glad when we saw that cop go and we thought we had now better get the train out of Detroit without delay. So we went to the railway station and I wanted to book to New York, but Hans was so windy[10] that he made me take tickets right round by Chicago, which was an awful waste of money, because it is 700 miles further, but Hans seemed to have spent so much money by this time that he did not mind any more.

Well, I was not the one to complain when it was his money that was being spent so we went round by Chicago and came to New York in the end.

We went to Hoboken in New Jersey where all the Hollanders stay and where there are a lot of speakeasies, and we stayed in a boardinghouse there. Hans gave a party to everyone he was so glad to be back in New Jersey and he paid for all the drinks himself, and for two weeks there was nobody sober in that whole place because Hans was so glad to be back in New Jersey and to have met me so that I could help him to get across the border.

4

It is not often that you get a man as grateful as Hans was to me for getting him back into New Jersey. There was nothing that he would not do for me, and if I had wanted to, I do not think I need have worked anymore until all Hans' money was spent. But whatever people may say about me when I am not there I am not really that sort of a man, and after I had been in the boardinghouse with Hans for a fortnight I began to think I could not stand his conversation much longer. So I decided I would play fair by Hans and go out and get a job of work.

The job that I got was as a shift engineer in a big hotel in 72nd Street. It was a Saturday when I got the job and I was to start on the Monday. But on the Monday morning when I woke up meaning to start out for work, there was Hans sitting up in bed looking fatter than ever in pyjamas, and lo and behold he was blubbering.

"What's up with you?" I said because I thought he might be cut up at losing me, but it turned out then he was not thinking of me at all.

"Scotty," he says, right out of the blue, "I'm married!"

And this was the first I had heard of his having a wife at all. But now that he had got started he told me all about it and it seemed he had got married before he left New York the first time, and now his wife was in England and thought he was still in Holland. But she had £2,000 he had given her so now he had got the idea that he would like her to come back to him after all.

10 *windy* alarmed

Well, the upshot of it was that he wanted me to fetch her because he remembered how I had got him across the border and he seemed to think I was the only person who would be able to smuggle her through the customs. So I said I would do my best, and I went off and explained that I could not start work that morning at the Halton Hotel.

5

I told Hans the first thing he must do was to wire his wife and tell her to come to Montreal. As I had a passport that would take me in and out of Canada it was easy for me to go and meet her in Montreal, and if you ever want to bring a man's wife into America when she has not got a proper passport this is what you must do:

You take two return tickets in New York and you get on the train to the Canadian border. When you reach your destination you throw away the first half of the second ticket, as it has not really been used, and then the man's wife travels on second half of that ticket just as if she was your wife, and has been with you all the time. Nobody asks you any questions. It is a very easy way.

Hans' wife did not mind pretending she was my wife a bit, and we really had a very nice journey, but of course there was old Hans waiting on the platform at New York to meet us. He had a $1,000 bill for me and a big hug for his wife and before I could even say goodbye to her he whirled her off in a taxi. But I did not mind because after all I had that $1,000 bill.

I did not see Hans and his wife ever again after that, but spending that $1,000 bill was not really good for my health. I was not really fit for work after it was all finished, but as I could not find Hans and his wife I had to get another job as shift engineer in a hotel.

I was very shaky when I started on this job, and the first work I was given to do was to climb up 15 storeys to the top of the building and hang out over the street while I changed all the light globes on a big electric sign. I had a rope to hold on to but I was shaking all over with the thought of the drop that was below me and if I had looked down once it would have been the last act of my career. But I did not look down and when I got all the lights changed I was able to come back to solid earth. Though it may not sound very exciting to a person who has not been in my position I always consider that was one of the hardest things I did in my life.

Well, this hotel where I was working was really service apartments and most of the people who lived there were wealthy Jews. It was my job to see the iced water in the rooms stayed running, and the air draughts[11] in the bathrooms, and the plumbing, and the radiators. You had to answer rings from the tenants and be polite whatever they called you, but I cannot always be polite to a man who calls me something, so one day there was a complaint about me and the boss said I was fired.

But it was funny. Just after I was fired every tap in the place ran rusty, and nobody seemed to know what was causing it all. So the boss came and asked me if I knew anything about it, but I said it was none of my business seeing that I had been fired.

So they kept trying to find what was making the taps run rusty and they only got worse instead of better, and all the tenants were sending down complaints and 'phoning the boss's office, so at last he said that if I would fix it up he would see that I was not fired. So I stopped the taps running rusty as soon as I knew I was not going to be fired.

6

All my spare time on that job I would be over in Hoboken where I had made a lot of friends while I was living with Hans. The Dutch people over there don't know anything outside their own business, which at that time was running speakeasies and there were so many of those in Hoboken that the police could do nothing about them and they stood open day and night for the benefit of the public. There was one place where I used to go a lot that is called Kelly's Clam Broth House, but it was through going there that I nearly finished up in gaol.[12]

Maybe you don't know what a clam broth house is, but it is a place where you pay for your drinks, but anyone that buys one can go up and turn on a tap and get a good cupful of this stuff that is made from fresh clams, out of a big urn.

Well, one night when I was in there I got talking to a couple of fellows and they said that this was a pretty lousy joint. They said if I would go with them they would take me where the drinks were better and where there were some decent girls. Well, I was not really wise to the people in Hoboken in those days, so instead of saying, "Oh, yeah?!" and sitting tight where I was safe, I got up like a big boob and followed them out of the place.

The next thing I knew we were in a dark alley and there was a gun being stuck in my ribs and every dime I had was taken off me. They

11 *draughts* British variation spelling of "drafts," i.e., ventilation.
12 *gaol* British spelling of "jail."

cut and ran when they had my money and I was left without my carfare home. I was so angry that I nearly thought of going to the police about it, but then I remembered about those diamonds, and about Mrs. Carr's ring—though you could say that she gave it to me really—but you never know how the police will look at these things, or what will come out once you go talking to them, so I decided that I would not go to the police, but I kept thinking of all things that I would like to do to those fellows all the time I was walking home.

I was still thinking of the things I would like to do to those fellows when I was at work next morning, and you could have blown me over with a water pistol when the boss called me up on the 'phone and said the police would like to speak to me if I could spare the time.

I had been so busy thinking what I wanted to do to those fellows that it was as if I had really done it and I thought the police must have come to pinch me so that when I came up to speak to them I had a feeling like a man might feel who was trying to walk through hell with tallow[13] legs. You would have thought the suspicions that the police had were true ones if you had known what I felt like, and when I got there they told me such a story that I started wondering if I had been walking about in my sleep. Because they told me that one of the two who had robbed me had been found with his brains blown out, and the gun that was lying beside him had come from the hotel where I was working!

They took me to see the man and I said I had only known him in Kelly's Clam Broth House, because I thought if I told them he had robbed me they would call it a motive for the crime. So they said then did I know anything about the gun? because they had traced it through its number to the dealers who said it belonged to some people who had an apartment that was at present locked up empty in our hotel.

So the police cabled to these people in Europe and they said they had left the gun locked up in their apartment, and I had a key to that apartment, along with chambermaids and bootboys and porters, so that is why I was being questioned. But as they did not know I had been robbed they did not see why I more than any of the others should have taken the revolver and committed the crime.

When I realized that I was glad that my instinct had told me not to go near the police when I was robbed, because if I had done so where would I have been now?

13 *tallow* the animal fat used in soap, candles, and other products.

The police did not arrest me then because they had no evidence against me more than the others, but I kept remembering how I had been seen leaving Kelly's with those two fellows and I thought if that came out they might come back and start making accusations.

The more I thought about everything the more worried I was, because how was I to know that it would not all come out now about the diamonds and Mrs. Carr's ring? So I thought the best thing I could do was to leave my good job and go right away till the trouble had blown over. So I did not tell anyone but took a train from New York that night. I did not even collect my wages at the hotel. So when I got to Boston I had no money at all and I had to start looking for work right away.

7

I was hungry for two days in Boston and then I saw an ad in the paper for a fireman with engineering experience to start work in a hotel. So I went along to apply for the job and there was a queue stretching down two blocks and when I was so desperate that did not look good to me.

So I thought I would not wait in the queue but would go and ask to see the manager on personal business. The clerk said the manager was busy, but I said I had come straight from New York and would only take a minute so I made him let me in. When the manager heard I had only come about the job he said didn't I see the queue, so I said yes, that was why I wasn't in it, but that I was just the man for him because it was not every day that he would be offered a man with a marine engineer's ticket.

Well, he brightened up considerably when he heard I was really a marine engineer because he was really wanting an engineer, not a fireman, only he had not said so in his ad because he did not want the engineer who was working for him at present to know that he was going to be sacked. You see, this was an old hotel with one of those complicated, old-fashioned steam-heating systems and this "Squarehead" (Swedish) engineer that he had, who used to be always drunk, was the only person who knew where all the valves were. He could never be sacked because he would not show a new engineer the workings, so the boss was going to outwit him by putting on an engineer who was supposed to be a fireman.

Squarehead would show a fireman because he did not expect a fireman to know how to make use of his knowledge, so my job was to start by being dumb until I had found out all the workings. When I knew I was to tell the boss and then Squarehead would be fired.

Squarehead was pleased to think he was going to have a fireman to help him because that meant he would be able to go off drinking every night. I was to be on duty from 12 midday till 10 at night and then I had to turn everything off and go home. Squarehead showed me everything and then he went off on his spree. I gave the place a look over and thought I would get the workings of it in no time. It seemed I had fallen on my feet, but you can never tell what is round the corner, can you?

The first night there were no hitches. I switched things off just as I was told and went straight home to bed. Next morning I got up feeling quite pleased over everything and at midday I went along to report for further duty. But I never had any further duty. I never worked there again because when I got to the place the street was full of fire engines and flooded two blocks back with water!

You nearly had to swim to the hotel, and when I got there and found the boss all he could do was to pitch a heavy ruler at me. So it seemed something must have gone wrong and I was not wanted to work there anymore.

At first everyone was too excited to tell me what had gone wrong, but when I found out I could see it was not me who was to blame, but that drunken Squarehead, only the boss would not listen to any of my explanations because he had been stuffed up with lies.

You see, what had happened was this: When Squarehead dragged home drunk after I had left the hotel he forgot that this night there was a new man ahead of him who had already turned off the water, and being used to doing it himself, he rolled down to the basement and turned it back on again, thinking he was turning it off. Then he rolled off to bed, and by morning the pressure of water had become so great that the pipes in the boiler room burst and started to flood the whole place out. When Squarehead dragged himself out at six in the morning to start things going again, he stumbled down the steps that were supposed to go into the boiler room, and instead he found himself in several feet of water.

There was so much water spilt that when I turned up at midday the fire brigades were still busy pumping the place out.

So I had to leave that job and I worked painting houses in Boston, but at night my work was tarred and feathered because I had not joined the union so I was driven back to New York where I thought the cops might be on my trail.

8

I was now growing very tired of being at the mercy of fate and it did not seem, no matter what I did, that I could earn a just reward for my labours, so I was feeling very disheartened when I came back to New York. But it seems it is true how they say that life is always darkest before the dawn as I will now illustrate by telling you how it was just at this time that I came to get the best job that I have ever had in my life.

PART TWO
Lobsters and Coleslaw

CHAPTER VIII

1

NOW this day I was completely broke so I went down to Heinz Billings' speakeasy in Hoboken where there was a guy who used to give me a ham sandwich when I was on the floor. It was 10 o'clock in the morning and I picked up the paper and there was an advertisement for an engineer for a yacht. I put down the paper and I said, "I'm going after that job."

So I borrowed a dollar and I went right away. I went on a bus and it took me two hours to get to the place. It was 12 o'clock when the bus put me down in the street the advertisement had said, and when I asked the cop where the number was he said up the other end of the street, a nickel car ride away. So I told him I hadn't a cent and I was going after a job so he gave me a quarter and I jumped on a street car.

When I got outside the number I saw it was a big foundry and such a lot of men had come to apply for the job that some of the queue were still waiting outside. I knew they were applying for the job because they had newspapers under their arms, so I got off the street car and went and stood at the end of the queue.

2

There was a man about 40 who was interviewing us in ones, and it turned out he was the owner of the foundry. When my turn came I talked in my broadest Scotch and he seemed to like that because he asked me to come with him into another room.

"I suppose you've had all your experience on big ships," he said.

So I said, "Sur-r-r-e," and took out all my papers.

He went through those very carefully and seemed to like the look of them. Then he asked if I knew anything about Bessemer diesel engines.

"Lor-r-d!" I said. "I worked for them in Boston."

"You did?" he said. "You're hired!"

But really I had not worked for them at all but I knew something of other diesels so I reckoned it would be a safe thing to say and that I would use my intelligence to worry through all right.

So the man that owned the foundry hired me. His name was Mr. Lock. He was a multimillionaire and he had this yacht just to take parties of his friends out on trips. There were four of them altogether—the Old Man who had made the money and this fellow, and two young sons. This fellow that I will call the Boss—even though he was a millionaire—was a most terribly mean man. When he told me to go down to the place where the yacht was in dock he sent me by boat instead of by train, which was faster, just because the boat cost a dollar less.

It was a picnic on that yacht. The Skipper used to dance a Highland fling[1] every time he got her in sight of a point he had plotted on the chart. That is the sort of thing that I think is called naive behaviour, but I never had much opinion of that kind of stuff myself. I always think it is a better idea to preserve an air of sangfroid.[2]

There were only the two of us on board so she took quite a bit of handling, but in the end we got her safely up where the Boss had told us to come. I was relieved, I can tell you, but you never would have thought it to look at me; whereas there was that Skipper right in front of everyone, looking just as if he was going to start another Highland fling.

He managed to keep quiet when the Boss came aboard, though, and we lay for two days stocking her up with crockery and cutlery and stores.[3] I was sent ashore to get uniforms and a whole outfit. I bought six white suits. I was the best-dressed man on board.

The Boss's two sons had the money but they didn't know how to put on their clothes, whereas I always think that having your things on straight helps a man in this world.

I met the whole crowd while we were tied up in the Hudson. The Boss's two boys would have been good chaps but they never seemed to be sober. About the only thing they knew how to do was swim. The Old Man was a real hard case.[4] He used to walk about the yacht in his socks and with his tie under one ear. The Boss's wife was a first-rate woman. I went ashore with her the day we bought the crockery and I got my new clothes.

When everything was loaded up we took on the Steward and the crew. There were six of us altogether. The Steward had to do the cooking. They were paying him $300 a month—$50 more than me.

1 *fling* a playful jump.
2 *sangfroid* composure, particularly under stress.
3 *stores* food supply.
4 *hard case* one incapable of reform.

But I didn't grudge him it. He earned it. He didn't have a minute's peace from the time we put out to sea.

The trouble with people when they drink is that they have no sense of time. The Boss's two boys and his friends were real champions at having no sense of time. It was nothing for them to want meals cooked at two o'clock in the morning and that Steward had to shake them cocktails for most of the 24 hours.

We were making for City Island[5] where there was some yacht racing, and they were all just about out to it before we were halfway across.

3

If you have ever been in Long Island Sound you will know it is full of lobster pots and the fishermen have coloured sticks poking up so as they can tell where the pots have been let down. Well, we were sailing in and out of these and they were all drinking and taking no notice when I came up on deck and saw we were heading right for a spar buoy.[6] So I yelled out to the Skipper, "Hey, look where you're going!" The next minute he had run us right on to a sandbank.[7] We went on to it with a shudder and stuck fast.

Well, he didn't dance any Highland fling that time.

"Ye gods!" he yelled and grabbed his hair with both hands.

The yacht began to heel[8] over and I thought we were gone. I didn't wait for orders. I dashed down to the engine room and put her full speed astern, but it wasn't any manner of use. She just stuck tight and you couldn't get a move out of her.

So I tore to Joe—he was the elder of the two boys—and I started shaking him.

"Hey," I said, "you're losing the bottom[9] out of the ship."

But he made a swipe at me as if I was fly or something.

"Buy her another bottom!" he said. And that was all the sense I could get out of him. So I went back to the Skipper and we thought about what we could do.

5 *City Island* a small island at the western end of Long Island Sound. It is home to several yacht clubs, and a part of the Bronx, one of the five boroughs of New York City.

6 *spar buoy* a float in the form of a stout, vertical log that is moored to the seabed and is used to indicate a channel or something underwater.

7 *sandbank* a sizable sand accumulation that has developed into a mound or a shoal.

8 *heel* to tip to one side.

9 *bottom* the part of the hull that is underwater.

But we stuck there for a long time and just as we were beginning to think there was nothing for it but a tug, the Skipper cast his eyes over the water and all of a sudden he hops up and starts doing another Highland fling.

"What's bitten *you*?" I wanted to know, and he pointed out over the water to where there was a steamer coming.

"When she gets right close, Scotty," he said, "you be ready with those engines."

So I went down below and when he gave the word I shoved her over—"Full Speed Astern." The wash of the steamer gave us the lift we needed. So we backed gracefully off that sandbank and went on our way to City Island, and when we got there the Boss's boys never knew there had been a thing wrong.

4

They had drunk the place out though by the time we anchored off the shore, and they'd come down to drinking Worcester sauce to keep them going. They were lying all round the smoke room[10] looking like something washed in by the tide, when suddenly the Steward landed up with six bottles of brandy that he had been keeping planted. Did you ever see dead men come alive? When they'd got outside that brandy they felt fit for anything so they all went ashore to look for some more booze.

While they were away the Boss came down in his car that he had had brought across by steamer and I don't think he was any too pleased at the way they had been going on. But I was too busy to worry about what he was saying because I was trying on one of my new white suits to go ashore and order a new washbasin from the plumber.

Well, I'd just got nicely dressed and come out on deck when there was a shout from the shore and there were the Boss's two boys waving bottles and hailing us. You could see from right across the water that they were oiled up again and the Boss looked sort of sour when he realized their condition.

"Someone had better go over and fetch those two," he said. And when I didn't seem to hear that distinctly—not fancying rowing in my good clothes and the motorboat being inshore[11]—he put it straight: "You hop into that boat, Scotty."

So I had to, though there were plenty of others that could have gone and I reckon he must picked on me because I had my good clothes on.

10 *smoke room* a room set aside for smoking.
11 *inshore* by the shore.

The boat was a flat-bottomed dory[12] and the Boss's two boys laughed like anything to see me sitting there rowing in all my best clothes.

"What's this coming, the admiral?" they said.

But I thought it would be best to ignore them so I just rowed alongside and they climbed down to the edge.

"Get along in," I said, "and watch you don't tip the boat over."

But it seems they thought it was their turn to ignore me, because they landed down into it with whisky bottles in each pocket and never took a bit of notice when I told them not to rock the boat. They thought they were being funny making her tip, and putting the wind up me, but I just kept on rowing. They kept on rocking till we got about halfway across. Then there was an extra big lurch.[13] The dory turned turtle[14] and the next thing I knew we were all in the water. I came up near the dory so I grabbed hold of her and climbed up and sat on her upside down, but the Boss's two boys went off swimming to the yacht. Only one thing was worrying them and that was that something might happen to the whisky. So there they were, still drunk, each swimming with one arm while the other was stuck in the air keeping the bottles well out of the water!

After a while a boat came out from land and fished me off and then I had to go back to the yacht and change all my clothes.

All the crowd from the yacht went ashore then, and it was early morning before they turned up again. When I got up at dawn to switch off the anchor lights everyone was sound asleep so I thought I would go ashore for a stroll.

There were a couple of cars parked on the waterfront opposite our yacht that belonged to people who had gone aboard. So I had a look in the cars to see if they had left anything and one had a case in the dickie[15] full of dry ginger ale and the other had the pockets stuffed full of bottles of gin. I was just going on with my stroll when I saw something lying on the floor of one of the cars and when I picked it up it was a roll containing $2,000 in bills. So I put it in my pocket because I thought it was a pity to leave it lying there, and just

12 *dory* as Moore indicates, a dory is a flat-bottomed boat; it has tall sides that extend outward and its bow and stern end in thin, keen edges
13 *lurch* an abrupt sway of a boat to one side.
14 *turned turtle* capsized.
15 *dickie* an additional seat in an automobile's back that can be collapsed to yield storage space.

to show you what a party they had been having, that roll of bills was never missed.

They had no sense of money—the younger ones, that is. The Boss's boys used to bring me down rolls of notes to mind when they were oiled, and you could always peel off sixty or a hundred dollars. They never noticed any difference when you handed it back to them, and it all went the same way so I thought it would be a pity not to have my share.

5

Well, this time when they finished their party and we put out to sea, we were going to do some deep-sea fishing. It was a lovely day and I had the engine ticking over nicely so I was up on deck lying on my back right up at the bow.

It is about the best feeling that I ever had, to lie there with the sails spread above you, and a fresh breeze, and sunshine, and a blue sky, and the yacht just cutting through the water, with the swish-swish of the sea falling back on either side, the only noise you could hear.

I used to lie for hours like that when I was new to it.

But this time we ran down a yacht, so we had to put back[16] with the survivors and then we had to get a new skipper because this one was taking his failures so much to heart that he came up to take over the wheel when he was as tight as a sausage. So we had to put him back to bed and when we got to Martha's Vineyard Haven[17] they sacked him and wired the Boss that they wanted another skipper.

So the Boss came down to see what all the fuss was and he said he was fetching a first-rate skipper for us.

"He's a Russian naval officer who served under the Czar," he said. "He knows all the ins and outs of this business properly."

So we kept looking out to see what this grand new skipper would be like.

Next morning he turned up and he was one of those short broad-shouldered guys that like to have their own way in everything.

The first thing he did was to sack every manjack[18] of the crew. He wanted a pack of Russian refugees and he got them. After that I was left right out in the cold. He came to me in the morning and he had

16 *put back* to change a ship's course and return it to the port from where it departed.
17 *Martha's Vineyard Haven* Moore here confuses names. Martha's Vineyard is an island off the southern coast of Massachusetts; Vineyard Haven is a harbor village in Tisbury, one for the six towns of Martha's Vineyard.
18 *every manjack* every individual man.

a jersey[19] in his hand with the name of the yacht written right across the front of it.

"Come on," he said, "you're a combination man" (meaning I was to help on the deck when the engine wasn't going)—"put this on."

"Here," I said, "what are you coming at?" and I took the jersey and threw it over into the water. "I'm no combination man," I told him. "I'm the chief engineer."

And he looked murder at me and went off and complained to the Boss. But the Boss said to leave me alone. After that he hated me.

Well, I hated him too so there were a pair of us. He wanted to lose me my job and I wanted to lose him his. We used to watch each other all the time.

I wanted to lose him his job but I wouldn't have put over the dirty tricks that he tried on me. I was down in the engine room one night taking out the board that I had loosened between the engine room wall and the back of the store[20] where the whisky was, and I had just got out a pint of applejack brandy when I heard him talking to the Boss's wife up on deck.

He didn't know I was there or he wouldn't have said what he was saying. I could tell it was him by the accent he talked with. "I would not have a man like that on my yacht," he was saying, "he does things, Mrs. Lock, that I would not like to talk of with a lady." But then he started talking of them, and I swear I never did such a thing in all my life, so I dropped the bottle of brandy and up on deck and went for him.

His back was to me when I got up on deck and he was standing near the gangway so I gave one shout and lammed[21] him behind the ear. He was a heavy fellow too, but the blow being unexpected it knocked him clean off his balance. He gave a sort of gurgle, swayed, and went shooting head first over into the water.

"Don't you take any notice of him, Scotty," Mrs. Lock said. "He had no right to speak to me like that at all." And she went away to tell her husband.

Everyone started to come running when they heard the splash old Offski made when he fell in the water, and they hung over the rail and laughed like anything to see him paddling around there waiting for a boat to pick him up.

19 *jersey* a pullover shirt or sweater.
20 *store* stockroom.
21 *lammed* struck.

We sent two of the Russians in the dory to effect the rescue and when he came on board swearing and dripping he didn't like the way everybody laughed at all. The only one who sympathized with him was the youngest of the Boss's two boys—the one called George—who never seemed to take to me right from the beginning.

George fetched out some drinks and went down to his cabin with him and you didn't need to tell me that as far as I was concerned they were up to no good in there.

Next morning was the day we were going on a swordfishing expedition—the Old Man, the Boss's two boys, and a whole party of friends. We had laid in stocks of cold chicken and salad and ham and cases and cases of whisky. The only thing, in fact that we didn't have was lobsters.

So I said to the Steward, "You're a bright one not to have any lobsters when you know that is about the only thing they eat once they are well-oiled."[22]

But he said those were the Old Man's orders. So I kept wondering what it was that had put the Old Man off lobsters. But when we got past City Island out into Long Island Sound I found he hadn't been put off lobsters at all. There he was, with one of the crew crouching down at the side, and they had a hook on a long pole, and they were fishing up the fishermen's pots and taking out the fresh lobsters. They had a whole pile of them clawing about on the deck.

And this was a man who was a multimillionaire!

So I thought, "Well, there is no end to this world's surprises." But now I come to think of it again I suppose that is how he came to be a multimillionaire. He never paid for anything he could get for nothing, that fellow. But all the same he was a nice old man in other ways.

He got more kick out of that yacht than all the rest of them put together. He used to love her when the sails were up.

"Doesn't she look lovely, Scotty?" he would say to me, and then he would go and sit amongst the ropes and smile.

He was sitting up there one day when I was down below with the engines. We had a bit of sail up but the engines were going too. All of a sudden there was a shout from that Russian skipper, "Shut off that engine, *quick*!"

So I shoved her over into neutral and he ran to the hatch and yelled at me, "Shut her off! *Right* off!"

22 *well-oiled* drunk.

So I saw something had happened to make him lose his senses, because it is much better to put an engine into neutral but I thought I had better humour him, so I shut her right off and then hopped up the ladder on to the deck.

"What's up?" I said, but everyone seemed to be running. They were all running aft and the yacht was swinging right round so I ran aft myself to see what all the fuss was, and at first all I could see was something dragging through the water on a rope and spinning as fast as a propeller, just like those things you use to catch fish with.

Only this was too big to be a spinner,[23] it was as big as anything, and then all of a sudden I saw it was the Old Man!

He'd been sitting amongst the ropes smiling away at his yacht and the crew had been hauling away at the slack without seeing him. All of a sudden the ropes had caught round his legs, tightened and dragged him overboard, and there we were cutting through the water with him spinning on the end of a rope like a juicy bit of bait for the first shark to come along.

Maybe it was the thought of sharks that made the Skipper get so excited, anyway he had lost his head, telling me to shut off the engine, and we had to start it up again before we could swirl right round and heave to and get the Old Man aboard.

There was a regular cheer when he came up over the side. But he wasn't a bit pleased with being rescued. He turned round to the men that had fetched him in and said, "Where's me hat, blast you?!" And when he found they hadn't saved his hat he was glum for the rest of the day.

6

Next day we were out in the Sound where you go for swordfishing. Some of the fish you get there are six feet long and weigh 600 pounds. We had a lookout man watching up the mast.[24] His job was to keep an eye out over the water and to yell as soon as he saw a fin sticking up. You can tell a swordfish's fin from a shark's because a swordfish's curves back and a shark's stands straight up.

Everyone was up on deck early that morning and we had all the tackle out. You use a spear with a five-inch steel head fitted into

23 *spinner* an artificial bait that revolves when pulled through water.
24 *mast* a long shaft that extends up from the ship's deck that supports the booms, rigging, and yards.

an 18-foot wooden shaft. There is a barb on the steel head and an eye with a rope running through it.

There were 40 fathoms[25] of rope and most of it was coiled round a barrel back on deck.

When we went after a fish a man would stand in the boom[26] with his spear ready, the man up the mast would call directions and we'd slowly come up to it, so close in the end that you could look down on it in the water. We'd sheer[27] right alongside it and the man on the boom would take aim and throw his spear. If he struck, and he generally did, there'd be a commotion. The fish'd lash up and shoot through the water, everyone start shouting, and they'd grab the barrel with the rope round and pitch it overboard.

You'd see it spinning like mad as the rope unwound in the water and then the fish'd drag it after him as he cut for his life trying to get away from the spear that was stuck in him somewhere.

After that, we just waited. Sometimes it'd be half an hour, sometimes three. It depended how badly the fish was wounded. We'd just cruise along keeping the barrel in sight, and we could tell by the wash[28] it cut in the water when the fish was beginning to tire.

When he was really tired we'd come close and launch the flat-bottomed dory with about three men in it, and row over to get hold of the rope and tow him back to the ship. Generally they were quiet by this time and didn't give much trouble, but if they'd been speared in the spine they were savage.

One time a big fellow came plunging at us, dived under the boat and drove his sword clean through the half-inch boards. He was caught then. We broke off the bit of the sword that was sticking through and rowed back to the ship. His tail was lashing up the water all round us, but he couldn't tip us over and he couldn't get free.

Swordfish are worth money, but the Locks only hunted them for sport. The ones we got they gave to the crew, and the hold in the well deck was full of ice to bed them down with till we got back to port. They fetch 35 cents a pound dressed[29] from the dealers so we used to do quite well at it.

25 *fathoms* used to measure water depth, a fathom equals six feet; forty fathoms equates to 240 feet.
26 *boom* a long, stout and rounded pole that extends along a sail's lower edge.
27 *sheer* swerve.
28 *wash* surge of waves.
29 *dressed* prepared for sale.

Besides swordfish Long Island Sound is full of blue sharks. They're bigger than swordfish. You get them 18 feet long, but they look much the same in the water except for the line of the fin.

Well, one day I was up in the crow's nest[30] looking out for fish and I thought I spotted one, so I yelled out. We got close and they let fly the spear and he was caught, but instead of shooting away out like swordfish do he dived, so we guessed he was a shark.

He went away down, and we all hung on to the rope but no one could move him. No matter how we pulled we couldn't make any sort of headway against that shark. So we fixed up a block and tackle[31] and got all our weight against it and hauled again.

He stuck it out for a bit, but then we felt him coming. Ever so slowly, but steadily. He was a big heavy fellow all right. Well, we hauled and hauled till we got him up to the surface; and there he was, plunging and lashing, against the side of the ship. We all ran to the rail and looked over and you could see his white underside and his dark back as plainly as anything, and when he rolled you could see his teeth. He was 18 feet long if an inch and he looked pretty savage.

The Steward was all excited. He was a funny little guy and he seemed to go off his head. He went tearing down below and came back waving a carving knife and a broom. He fixed the knife on to the broom and started stabbing at the shark. There was no holding him. He got a big cut in it where its neck ought to be and was going to saw its head off, but he didn't have the chance to finish. As soon as the shark began to bleed into the water you never saw such a sight. *The water was boiling with sharks.* They came up in dozens and lit into[32] their big brother as if he was their worst enemy and they hadn't had a meal for 12 months. You never saw such a clean job as they made of him. Talk about cannibals. Well, I would rather have them than those sharks.

7

We stayed out in the Sound till the fish well was as full of swordfish as we could pack it and then we turned for home. The whisky held out well that trip and coming home there was a regular party. The

30 *crow's nest* a platform at the top of the mast.
31 *block and tackle* a device of pulley blocks and ropes for lifting or pulling.
32 *lit into* assaulted vigorously.

Skipper drank in with the others and remembering that sandbank I began to wonder what we might strike next. So I started to carry a life belt[33] about with me—down in the engine room and everywhere else I went. I used to hang it by my bunk at night, and when I came down to meals I would put it beside my chair.

Everyone seemed to think this was awfully funny. They'd say, "Where's your pal, Scotty?" and nick up and hide it while I wasn't looking. But I went on carrying it about with me just the same. I didn't think it was funny looking forward to being nearly drowned, and the Skipper didn't seem to think it was extra funny either. But he never was notable for his sense of humour, that Skipper, and he took my carrying a life belt round like that as a reflection on his seamanship. . . .

He used to look black at me every time I passed, and I got to waving the life belt under his nose just to see his face. So, to get his own back on me, he started telling young George that I wasn't getting enough pace[34] out of the engine. I found out he had been saying that, because the night before we got into port young George came into the engine room, pretty well-oiled, and started being rude to me.

It was sheer luck that night that he didn't end up as mincemeat.

"Can't you let her have some juice?" he started. "You Scotsmen, you're too mean to feed a bloody engine. Can't you . . ."

"Look here," I said to him. "Who's the engineer on this yacht, you or me?"

"I'm the engineer for tonight," he shouted back at me. "I'll give her some juice and *then* we'll see what she can do."

"You'll leave her alone unless you want to crack her up," I told him.

But because he'd spent a few months in his father's foundry he thought he knew everything. "You mind your own business," he said. "*I'm* taking over here."

"You're tight," I said to him.

"Get out of here," he yelled, and he took a swipe at me. But being pretty drunk he missed, lost his balance, and fell right over the trapdoor that covers the reversing gear. Christ! He was lucky that night, because, to make it easier for oiling, I always used to work with that trapdoor open. It was the first time for weeks I'd had it down, and if he'd fallen through that trapdoor into the

33 *life belt* life preserver.
34 *pace* performance, speed.

reverse-gear machinery he would have been mincemeat in about two minutes.

He was too drunk, though, to realize what an escape he'd had and he seemed to think it was my fault he'd fallen over.

"Get out of here," he yelled at me.

"All right," I said. "I'm going."

So I left him to it and went on deck. I walked round the deck to where that Russian skipper was.

"You did a bad day's work," I said, "when you put that boy up to this," but he just kept on looking out to sea and wouldn't take any notice.

"All right," I said. "You'll see." And I went below and got a bottle of whisky. The Old Man was already in bed and Joe and most of his pals had passed out in the saloon so I went on down to my cabin and sat there drinking the whisky, and when I had finished the whisky it seemed to me a good idea to get up and break all the light bulbs on that yacht. So I made up my mind that I would do so and nobody stopped me. Then I strolled on the deck. I had a look down when I got along by the engine room and I could see George fiddling round down there. He had the engine opened flat out and the pressure up to 5,000 pounds when what I used to drive her at was 2,500 pounds.

"Take a look at your exhaust," I called down to him, "unless you want to blow the place up." Because I could see from where I was that the pipes were white-hot.

"You mind your own business," he called back at me.

So I said, "O.K., Chief," and went back and had some more whisky. After that I didn't care much if he blew the ship up or not.

I don't know just what happened after I finished the whisky, but I must have lain down and had a wee bit of a sleep.

Anyway I had forgotten everything about that fool of a boy when suddenly there was a noise that you could only call a pandemonium, a clattery sort of bang, as if an aeroplane had dropped half a ton of tools on the deck.

"God!" I thought. "He's done for us this time." And I grabbed hold of my life belt and hopped out of the cabin just as I was. I ran through the saloon and up on deck and made for the engine room. I got there first. The others were still stupid with last night's party. All the noise had stopped by the time I got up on deck. I knew something pretty bad had happened because the engine wasn't going at all.

Well, I ran along the deck to the engine room and nearly fell right into it. There was just a gaping hole. The whole engine room hatch had been blown away!

George was standing by the rail looking a sickly sort of yellow in the grey light of the dawn and I hope he knew that he was jolly lucky to be alive at all.

"Well, you've done it this time," I said, and he looked sort of sick. "Can't we fix it?"

"Fix it?" I said. "Just come and look here." And I brought him over and pointed down to where two cylinders were blown right out and leaning over sideways. "Fix it?" I said. "You'll never fix that. You'll have to get a new engine."

The light was still not very good but it was easy to guess what had happened. The wind in the night had made the yacht heel over and the sea had got in through the exhaust pipe and burst two of the cylinders and twisted the crankshaft like a piece of cheese. I was right when I said he would need a new engine.

"Can't you fix it, Scotty?" he said to me.

"*Me*?" I said. "I'm fixing nothing. I'm leaving."

"Father'll be mad," he said, so I told him that was his funeral.

While we had been arguing like this the others began to appear. They wanted to find if we were sinking or had struck a mine, but when they saw it was only George who had blown up the engine they went back to bed again, all except the Old Man, who was really upset. He stood there in his pyjamas with his hair on end.

"If your father learns of this," he said to George, "we'll never hear the end of it." And he looked nearly fit to cry.

But I was looking out to sea and not taking any notice.

So the Old Man came over to me and said, "Scotty, can we fix this engine?"

"If you wired Boston," I told him, "and got men down, you might do it, but I'm not having a thing to do with it. I'm leaving."

But they knew that if I left the Boss would find out what had happened, so they kept at me to stop. "We'll get you a raise if you stop," they kept saying.

But I was wild and I said I wouldn't stop. But while I was saying that the Russian skipper came past.

He was looking as white as a sheet and he didn't want to talk to anyone because he knew it was his fault that George had blown up the engine. He went on past us and had the crew out busy with the sails, because we had to go with the sails now the engine was out of commission.

So I waited till he was out of the way and then I said to the two of them, "I'll stop and get the engine fixed on just one condition."

"What's that?" they asked.

"Sack that Russian," I told them.

So they said they would sack him. We went below then and had a drink and got into bed. But all the time till he was gone after that I kept clear of that Russian.

8

Well, we pulled into Dightman Street and took on the new Skipper and he was a "Bluenose"[35] from Newfoundland with a book full of newspaper cuttings about the brave things he had been doing. So he seemed to think we ought to be impressed. But we said if he could stick this yacht it would be the toughest thing he ever tackled. "Why?" he said. "What's up with her?" So we just laughed and told him to wait and see.

Well, he didn't have to wait long, for the very first thing that happened us while we had that skipper was for us all to get arrested out in the middle of the Long Island Sound.

It was nighttime and we were making for Oak Bluffs.[36]

I had the engine going "Full Speed Ahead" and I was sitting leaning over the engine-room hatch with my feet dangling down the companion, looking out to sea. It was so pitch-black that you couldn't see a thing, but suddenly a searchlight flashed on me right out of the dark. That dazzled me so that I couldn't do anything but blink, and a shout came over the sea for us to heave to.[37] But the Boss was aboard this night and he called out for us to keep right on. So I took no notice of the searchlight or whoever was giving us orders.

"Keep right on," the Boss said, so the Skipper steered right ahead and I kept my engine at full speed.

35 *"Bluenose" from Newfoundland* Moore misuses the term "Bluenose." It is slang for a native of Nova Scotia. *The Facts on File Dictionary of Nautical Terms* reports it's derived from a "purplish potato peculiar to Nova Scotia." *A Dictionary of Slang and Unconventional English* posits that it comes from the tremendous cold of Nova Scotia's winters. A "Bluenose" can also be someone who has traveled north of the Arctic Circle, according to *Facts on File.*

36 *Oak Bluffs* a town on the northeastern shore of Martha's Vineyard.

37 *heave to* to move in a direction indicated.

But that searchlight held us. We couldn't shake it off, and presently we heard a motor launch[38] come chugging through the dark.

"Don't stop," the Boss ordered. "We'll give them the slip."

But we couldn't. They held to us, got level, and three of them came aboard. We had to heave to then. They had on government uniforms. They were Prohibition officers, with orders to search the yacht.

We heaved to out there in the Sound and the patrol boat came alongside. The officers searched the ship and found the fish locker full of whisky, so they said we would have to come along with them to New Bedford.[39]

The idea of that made the Boss madder than ever.

"You can't do this," he said. "Don't you know who I am?"

"I know you've been caught with bootleg whisky," the patrol officer said to him.

"I'll explain," said the Boss, and he wanted to explain with dollar bills. But that seemed to shock the patrol officer like anything. He wasn't what I would call a very intelligent man.

"You can explain when we get to New Bedford," was all the sense you could get out of him.

"I will," said the Boss, "and I'll explain how it is that men like you never get on the world."

Oh, he was wild, the Boss was, but the patrolman took no notice. He had grappling ropes[40] thrown from his ship to ours and then he left us to keep beside him, like an old moke[41] in harness, for the rest of the night.

But that was too much for the Boss. As soon as the patrol officers had left us he made me put the engine in reverse. But we were still tied to the patrol boat and she was going full steam ahead, so the result was we pulled her out of her course and started going round in circles. The more the patrol boat protested the more the Boss kept shouting at me to keep the speed up and not let her out of reverse. You would have laughed to see us.

We kept dragging that patrol boat round in circles till they were livid, and the Boss's temper was nearly worked off.

At last he told the Skipper—who was thinking by now that he had

38 *motor launch* motorboat.
39 *New Bedford* a port city in southeastern Massachusetts. Contrary to what Moore writes, it is beyond Long Island Sound's eastern boundary.
40 *grappling ropes* a grapple is a metal shaft with claws, typically thrown by rope to draw in a ship and hold it parallel before coming aboard.
41 *moke* donkey.

come on a hooligan ship—that he could heave to if he liked, and when we did, and the patrol officers came aboard again, the Boss was in such an improved mood with the success of his joke that he agreed to go quietly wherever they liked.

So they left three men on board and we followed the patrol boat to New Bedford. We came alongside the wharf there about three or four in the morning and tied up to wait till it was light.

There was only one other ship tied up there and that was a fishing trawler that seemed to be full of mackerel. But when it got light and the patrol officers started to unload her it turned out that under the mackerel there were cases and cases of rum. You never could tell where drink would turn up next while Prohibition was in force in America.

No one came to unload *us*. But as soon as the Boss had had some breakfast he went ashore to "explain" to the officials. I always think it must be easy to explain when you are a multimillionaire. The Boss explained as easy as easy, and he came swinging down the wharf before midday with a smile about six inches wide spread across his face.

He sprang aboard and waved good-bye to the patrol officers. "Righto! Pull away, Skipper," he said. And we put out to sea with the patrol officers watching and every bottle of whisky still in the fish locker!

9

The Steward we took with us on this trip was a real old fellow. He couldn't cook for toffee. He only lasted about three days.

We went for a weekend cruise and all he could feed us on was "coldslaw," which is a sort of *hors d'œuvre* dish that they always have in America, but it gets boring if you have it every day. So we thought we would call him "Coldslaw" and he didn't like it one bit.

The Bluenose skipper used to growl too. He was a devil for growling. You could see he was fed up already, so what was the point in all those newspaper cuttings, when he couldn't stand a few weeks of a millionaire's yacht?

We came back from the weekend cruise and anchored up the Hudson. After a few days the Boss sent down word to lay in supplies for a cruise. So old Coldslaw went ashore to give his orders, and since stewards get a rake-off on food the way engineers do on oil he ordered enough for a deluxe world tour. You should have seen the stuff come aboard. . . . Chickens and turkeys and hams and lobsters (even though we *never* bought lobsters) and fruit and salads, and the Lord knows what. We had a big icebox on the yacht but there was nowhere to put all this, and when the Boss came aboard and saw it he got very wild. He had the Old Man with him this day, and the Old Man nearly had a stroke when he saw we had been buying lobsters.

"Sack this man," he said. "He's mad, he's mad. Sack him. He'll have us bankrupt."

So the Boss called old Coldslaw and said that he would have to go. Poor old Coldslaw was very cut up,[42] especially as he had to take half the things back where they came from and he didn't get nearly all the rake-off he had been expecting.

Well, he went, and we had no steward. They never could keep a steward on that yacht. So this time they said to me, "You go ashore, Scotty, and see if you can get us a steward." So I did, and I landed a beauty. He said he didn't know about yachts but he had been on liners and he had a wife and a parrot, so I thought that he would do.

His wife had fallen down a fire escape and was going to get $20,000 out of the insurance for it, but her leg was still bad at present and he said they were starving. They'd pawned the parrot once and got a lot of money on it because it was a clever parrot. It could sing the "Barcarolle."[43]

But they wouldn't sell that parrot; no, sir, not though they were starving.

So I got a whole lot of stuff to eat and we got in a taxi and went along to his place, where his wife was—a big fat woman—but she could walk though she had to use a stick.

So I said, why not come out to the yacht now because there was no one on board at present, and plenty to eat and drink so we could have a little party. So they said all right, and I put them in the taxi with the parrot and drove down to wharf. When we got on board I opened up the icebox and he started slicing cold chicken and I started mixing drinks, and soon we were so happy we just didn't care whether it was Christmas or Easter.

Well, the next thing I knew after that little party started was when I was lying in my bunk without a stitch on me, and the new Steward was there, snoring, and a sailor called Hansen as well. The first thing

42 *cut up* emotionally hurt.
43 *"Barcarolle"* the song of a Venetian gondolier with rhythm that suggests an oar's stroke, or music derivative of a gondolier's song.

I thought of was my money. I'd had a thousand dollars on me the night before. I jumped up quick and went over and shook Hansen.

"Where's my clothes?" I said.

"Up on deck," he said. "Drying."

"Drying?" I said.

"Yes," he said and then he started to laugh. But he wouldn't tell me why they were drying, but he said, "your money's all right. I've got it under the mattress."

He fished out a roll and I took it. It was all there right enough. But sopping wet.

Just then the Boss's voice came shouting down to the cabin, "You there, Scotty! Come out and get ashore. You're fired." Then there was a lot of swearing and I heard him call out. "God help this flaming parrot if you leave it here much longer."

But the Steward never heard him. He was too sound asleep and so there was a screech as the Boss pitched his parrot, cage and all, overboard. It was a shame when you remember that it was a bird that could sing the "Barcarolle."

But by the time the Steward came round the Boss had gone ashore, after saying I could wait until my clothes were dry, so carrying on didn't help him any. But I was worrying more about how I had come to be fired.

"See here," I said to Hansen, "what happened last night?"

So he sat up and put his hands on his hips and shook his head at me solemnly.

"You mean to say you can't remember? Well, boy," he said. "I'll tell you . . ."

So it seems I'd been well-oiled. And I never had been very much while I'd been on that yacht, but this time I had jumped overboard with all my clothes on, and the Boss's two boys, who'd been coming down to get aboard, stood on the edge looking over and got the shock of their lives. There was their chief engineer swimming like a great grampus[44] across the harbour with his best suit on! They'd never seen me that way before. I was making for the shallow part where all the speedboats were anchored so they let me swim for a while, then had me fished out and taken on board. And I never knew a thing till I woke up next morning. So when the Boss heard he fired me. I felt wild.

44 *grampus* a small cetacean, such as a killer whale or blackfish.

While my clothes were drying I found four bottles of whisky in a little bag in the cabin, and what with being fired and all the rest of it, I started again. This time I got so I wanted to smash the place up. The next thing I knew I was carted ashore and put in gaol. The boss just said, "Lock him up till he comes to his senses and then let him go."

So I wasn't treated like a prisoner and I got talking to the cops. There was a man brought in who'd been molesting an old woman and they threw him into a cell. You could see him in there because they have bars instead of a wall in those gaols, so presently one of the cops said, "Have you ever seen a real scrap?"[45] and he went in and beat that chap up till he was unconscious. The chap didn't try to hit back, and the cop picked him up and knocked him down so many times he passed right out. Then the cop came away and left him.

Well, the Steward landed down after that and he had some drinks with him, so soon we had the whole place drinking and we had a little party till I left. Then we drove to Hoboken and spent the night there. I must have been a bit "nuts" over being fired I think because I was oiled again that night, and when I woke up in the morning every dime of my thousand dollars had been stolen.

The Steward was cleaned out too, so we thought we'd go to N.J. where the Boss's home was, and draw my back pay. We must have been still a bit off because we got into a taxi and told the man to take us there—*it was 30 miles*! So there we sat, like a pair of lords, with the metre ticking up and up and not a dime between us.

When we arrived I got out and left the Steward sitting with the metre still ticking up, and I saw the Boss's boy Joe—the one that liked me.

"What's come over you, Scotty?" he said. "Have you gone off your head these last days?"

But I didn't know, only I wanted some money, and he wouldn't give it to me.

We got talking and had quite a yarn,[46] when suddenly he looked out the window and saw the taxi in the yard with the metre still ticking over.

"God!" he said, "have you come in that from New York? You're nuts all right, Scotty. My father's a millionaire, but *he* takes a train when the car isn't running."

45 *scrap* fight.
46 *yarn* talk (Australian and New Zealand).

Then he saw the Steward inside, and that started him, because they reckoned that Steward was to blame for my breaking out this way. So he got his brother and they went out to him. They hauled the Steward out of the taxi and knocked him unconscious. Then they shoved him in and banged the door and told the taxi man to drive him to the nearest police station.

They didn't pay the taxi either, and *I* didn't. It was the Steward that had hired it.

10

Well, when they'd finished with the Steward they came in and we talked some more. At last they took me to the Old Man's place for the weekend.

I was going to leave on the Monday, but the Boss 'phoned through from the yacht and he was wild. "Fetch that Scotty down to fix this flaming engine," he said.

It seemed they'd had two marine engineers since I left and neither of them could get a kick out of the engine.

"You've done something to it, Scotty," the Old Man said to me, but I swore I hadn't, and how could I when the Boss had locked the engine-room door the morning he fired me just in case I was taken that way?

Well, they took me down and got me on board. There was going to be a party and there were 20 millionaires' sons there. They were all going to the racing at City Island and they were pretty mad because no one could make that yacht go. I got down to the engine room thinking it was going to be easy. Then I found those fool engineers had messed up all the timing.[47] Well, it took a while to get her re-timed but at last I had everything set, started her up, one kick, and she backfired and stopped.

They'd all been hanging round watching. They looked at me and I looked at them. But I knew I could fix her. She wasn't getting the oil, that was the trouble. For the oil to go on feeding to an engine there's got to be an air pipe kept open. I fiddled round a bit and found the air pipe wasn't acting. Well, that had me beaten. Because I didn't see what on earth could have blocked the air pipe. It was a narrow half-inch pipe running from the oil tank up through the deck. There was no covering over it. Anyone could get at it. That gave me my idea. I hopped up on deck to where it was and the 20 mil-

47 *timing* an engine's synchronization.

lionaires' sons came after me. I turned round to them and said, "Any of you chaps got a corkscrew?"

You won't believe me if I say none of them had, so I'll tell you the truth. I got 20. But one was enough. I shoved it down the air pipe and brought up the cork of a Johnny Walker whisky bottle!

That was what had been causing all the trouble.

I don't remember doing it but it must have been me all right. When I was mad that morning and the Boss locked up the engine room I must have gone and plugged the air pipe.

It was a good idea, really. Sometimes your brain works better when you are oiled. They were so pleased at me starting up the yacht that they signed me on again after that and I took them out to City Island.

"You can't beat Scotch engineers." That's what they said to me.

11

After me choosing that steward with the parrot they didn't let me pick another. They got one themselves. He was a "limey" (that is an Englishman) called Baker. He was really a second mate, and he had a master's ticket, but his eyesight had gone wrong so he had to work as a steward.

We went off to the yacht racing on City Island and for several weeks there was no trouble on that yacht at all. There were parties, mind you, and all that; but nothing that you could call a major incident—except that the Bluenose skipper got more and more disapproving, and he seemed to think that if he stopped on this yacht he might be getting his name in the press again but not as a hero this time, so he took his book of cuttings and said that he was going to leave.

"As you like," the Boss said to him, but really he was very annoyed because it began to look as if he would never be able to keep anybody on this yacht at all.

We were all pleased that Bluenose was going, but the Steward, Baker, was particularly pleased. He went up on deck when he knew and asked the Boss if he could speak to him. So they went into the Boss's cabin and when he came out we found he was to be our new skipper.

Well, did we laugh?

It was the Old Man who had persuaded the Boss to make Baker skipper as well as steward because he pointed out how they would be able to save wages. So the Boss brightened up at that and said, all right, they would give him a trial.

The new "Skipper" got round all next day with his chest stuck out about a mile, and you couldn't get him away from the wheel for love or money, though we all laughed when he had to give over to the sailor, Hansen, while he came down and got everyone their meals.

That night he moved his things into the captain's cabin, and as soon as we got back to New York he went ashore. When he came back he had a blue suit with four bands of gold braid on it and he strutted down to the ship as if he was skipper of the "534."

"Christ!" we said, "what's this coming?" But he was so pleased with himself that sarcasm rolled off his back.

12

But he didn't like me because I wouldn't take his orders. I had a good excuse too, knowing that his eyesight was bad. If he rang the telegraph when we were coming into harbour I would pop my head up through the hatch and take a look to see if it was safe to do what he said. That used to make him mad. He was getting to hate me. I used to laugh when he had to leave his gold braid up in the cabin and go down to the galley and put on an apron, and one day when I walked through and found him there, mashing potatoes, I had to ask him what it felt like "Captain," so he called me something unrefined and pitched the potato masher right at me.

I grabbed the most handy thing, which happened to be a carving knife, and went for him. You should have seen him drop those potatoes and run. I chased him across the galley and up the ladder on to the deck. When he got across the deck he looked round to see where I was, and I was just behind him, still flourishing the knife. He shot his eye right and left and saw that I could cut him off.

"Look out, Captain!" I yelled. So he up on the rail and dived overboard.

He came up ten yards away and I leaned over the rail, and waved the knife at him.

"Put that knife down!" he yelled up to me. So I teased him for a while, till I thought he would be feeling cold. Then I put the knife away and let him scramble up the ladder on board.

Even if I had wanted to kill him when he came back on board looking like the morning's washing I couldn't have—I was so weak from laughing. But he gave me a look as he went below to change and I knew that sooner or later it would be him or me.

13

One of the first things he had to do after he became skipper was to take a party of girls for a picnic up the river. He fancied himself, escorting the ladies. He had a gold cigarette case that he pinched when it was left after a party, and he had it open on the chart rack in front of him, and there he was smoking away at gold-tipped cigarettes.

We got started some time in the afternoon and went for a crab picnic up the river. There were a lot of girls on board and they all got into bathing things and went swimming. Then they dressed and when we got a good way up they went ashore at a place they knew and got a woman to boil up a whole copperful[48] of water out in the open air. They filled that up with clams and lobsters, and while it was cooking they had us rowing backwards and forwards from the yacht bringing drinks for them. Once the stuff was cooked they set to.[49] The last I remember is it being dark and all of us shouting and laughing and laying into the clams and lobsters. That's the last I remember.

When I came round next morning I was in my cabin. I got up and went on deck and it was women's clothes from end to end—lying in heaps everywhere. But not a sign of a woman. I went up and felt them. They were sopping wet, every one of them, but what I wanted was to feel them for any money. But there was no money, so I began to figure out what had happened. They weren't drowned, that was a cinch, or their clothes would have gone down with them, and it was too soon for anyone to have been dragging for bodies.

So I went down to the big cabin. They were all there, lying in heaps. That's how good a party it was.

But that was mild to some of their parties.

14

Next day we went farther up the river and coming back we struck a storm. Squalls[50] come down on you like lightning on the Hudson

48 *copperful* a quantity filling a large pot for boiling (a copper).
49 *set to* began (eating) with gusto.
50 *squall* an extreme and unexpected wind, frequently accompanied by snow or rain.

and this was the worst I'd seen . . . wind enough to blow you over and then sheets of rain. You couldn't see a thing. This was where our Captain-Steward nearly let us in for trouble. The crowd were up under an awning thinking they were still on a picnic, but I knew different. Suddenly something sheered up out of the rain. I saw it was a small lighthouse opposite Sing Sing prison, and we were running right at it. If we'd hit, we'd have gone straight to the bottom. I *knew* his eyes would play him up. I gave a yell.

"God! Are you nuts?" He nearly jumped out of his skin, swung the wheel over and we just scraped by.

So I went along and told the crowd they were lucky they weren't all dead, but they just laughed and thought I was kidding. So I said, "Let's put in here. I want to fill her up with oil."

So we did. And I 'phoned the Boss.

"This skipper guy of yours just about drowned us all half an hour back," I said.

"Tell him I want to speak to him," said the Boss.

"You're fired," the Boss told him, when he came to the 'phone.

"This is your doing, Scotty," he said to me, when he put down the receiver.

"Look out you don't hurt your gold braid," I said to him. "You won't get another lot now."

And he looked murder at me, but he never should have been in charge of a yacht when he had defective eyesight.

He sulked and sat in his cabin and I took the yacht down the river. When we got back to Dightman Street he said he was going straight ashore. So we didn't try to stop him. He took three of the Boss's suits and two bottles of whisky and that was the last we saw of him.

So there we were, in one fell swoop, deprived once again of both captain and steward.

The party of girls all went ashore that night and for several days no one came near the yacht. Then a new fellow came down and said he was to be the steward. He was a little blond Yankee and he tried to make out he knew everything because he had a brother-in-law who was working on one of the New York papers, but we said we didn't need a reporter to tell us the truth about life.

We were still waiting down on the yacht with this new steward, when one night when we were all in bed we heard a shout:

"Ship ahoy!"

It was after midnight but we knew they didn't worry what time they got us out of bed.

So we swore a bit, because it is no fun being dragged out of your bed for one of those millionaire parties, but they kept on hailing us so we felt for our trousers and went up on deck.

When we got up on deck there was a boat there with 15 people in it and we had to help them all come aboard. They were all laughing and shouting and excited, and they scrambled up the gangway and started prancing round the deck. The girls had on evening dress and high-heeled shoes, and they were scratching all the decks that you are supposed to walk on only with rubber. But they didn't care, and when I went to George and complained he told me to mind my own business. So that is all the thanks you get for looking after a yacht.

Some of the girls ran to my air horn and started blowing away on this, and I was wild because I have to have that air for pressure to start up the engine. But it wasn't any good my talking. They were all crazy that night.

"Start up the dynamo,"[51] said George, "we want some fairy lights round the deck." And he turned on the radio and they all got dancing.

By the time I had the dynamo going and all the lights on two more boatloads of them had come out. More men and Ziegfeld Follies[52] girls. The first lot had been New York society girls. When they were all on board there were about 40 people. Some of the men had names that you would know if I told you.

After that party, if I had happened to be a crook, I could have made a lot of money out of blackmail.

When I got the lights going I thought maybe I could go back to bed, but they started the usual thing, making me stay up and help the Steward mix cocktails.

So I did stay and mix cocktails and just to keep myself awake I had a few myself, but I never got oiled that night, never at all.

When the party first started it was just an ordinary party but after the first hour it began to get wild.

They had us making a kind of cocktail that has raw egg in it. You crack the egg and throw away the yoke and just use a bit of the white.[53]

51 *dynamo* generator.

52 *Ziegfeld Follies* A famed revue that ran on Broadway annually from 1907 through 1931. The shows were known for their spectacular sets and comely chorus girls.

53 *a kind of cocktail that has raw egg in it . . . use a bit of the white* Possibly a Clover Club, a Pink Lady, or a Ramos Gin Fizz.

We used 30 dozen eggs that night. The floor was so covered with shells that you couldn't walk for them, but by this time no one was noticing a little thing like that.

All the time they were drinking they had the music going and were dancing and they were shouting and shrieking so much that you couldn't hear yourself speak. The girls were running and the men were chasing them. Some of them were lovely girls. The men were out for a good time, and after a while, seeing we weren't as tight as the rest, we began to feel it was getting a bit past a party. Not so many were dancing now, though the music was still going, and a lot of them had taken their drinks to other parts of the yacht. I went into one cabin to fetch something and there was a well-known judge with a girl of 15, and she was screaming. I threw a whisky bottle at him.

Then I went down to the galley. I gave one look in there. Then I came out and shut the door. There weren't many of them left dancing. I went down to my cabin. A girl followed me down.

She was a little bit of a thing with big eyes and dark hair and she was one of those girls that drinking makes excited. Some get stupid, and some get sentimental, but this one got wild.

She pushed open the door and nearly fell into my cabin. Then she stood there and waved her hand round her head and stamped her foot.

"Lend me one of your uniforms, Scotty," she said. "Go on," she said, "lend me one." And she came over close. So I lent her one.

She off with her dress and started putting it on. It was a bit large, but she managed. She hitched up the trousers and gave me a salute. Then she whooped and bolted for the deck. The music was still going upon deck and she got amongst the broken eggshells and started doing a wild kind of tango. She was mad all right. She was whooping and dancing there like a crazy woman and I started to go over to her to tell her to stay quiet, but she shrieked when she saw me coming and ran and started climbing up the rigging.

She could climb too, though she was somewhat hampered by the uniform. But she went up, till she was away up near the top. Then she hung and waved and shouted. You could see she was pleased with herself, till suddenly she looked down.

It *was* a good way to the deck from where she had climbed, and looking up watching her you could just *see* the life go out of her. She let out a sort of moan and turned and clung to the rigging with both hands.

"You're all right," I shouted up to her, but she didn't seem to hear me. She looked very small, away up there hanging to the rigging, and now that the night air was sobering her you could see she had the wind up completely.

Several of the crowd who weren't so occupied collected round the mast and called out advice to her.

"Come down," they said, "you're quite safe."

But she just looked and then shrank against the mast and clung to it. You could hear her whimpering.

We began to be frightened that if she hung there much longer she would fall.

"You'd better get the river police, to fetch her down," George said to me.

So I got in a boat and rowed across to the bank where the river police had their offices. When I came back with three of them she was still clinging up there, crying.

They had brought a cradle on a pulley, and one of them climbed up and rigged this. At first she screamed when anyone came near her, but at last they persuaded her to get into the cradle and be lowered safely to the deck.

Everyone was pleased that she had got down the mast safely so they started yelling for the Steward to fetch out more drinks, and they turned the music on louder, and soon the girl was drinking again, and the police all had some drinks before they rowed back to the bank.

That little interlude scarcely caused a break in the party. It went on, wilder than ever, and pretty soon that silly girl started losing her head again. She still had on my uniform, and her face, which had been white enough when they fetched her down from the mast, was flushed again with excitement.

"Whoopee! Scotty," she called to me and raised her glass and had another drink.

"Whoopee!" I said, and I was just raising my glass to have another drink myself, when I heard hers crash on the deck, and there she was running for the rail, up on it, shouting "Whoopee!" and with both arms spread out she plunged over! It was like a bang between the eyes when I saw her disappear. But the splash as she hit the water brought me round.

I rushed to the rail after her. It was quite black. You couldn't see anything, but I vaulted it and jumped well out. As I fell through the air I heard shouting break out behind me and guessed the rest on the yacht had seen. Then I struck that black water and in the shock I forgot everything else. Before I came up I felt the current catch me and suck at me. Then I was up, right aft, and there was a blob floating in front of me that I guessed was that girl. I couldn't see any face and she wasn't calling out or struggling so I guess she was unconscious already. I made a grab and missed. Something black loomed up beside me and I realized it was the dory adrift aft. Well, I'm not a strong swimmer at the best of times, and half tight and with all my clothes on, I was not even in my usual form. So I reached up one arm and grabbed hold of that dory and when I looked again the blob floating ahead of me had vanished. I hung there for a minute, looking into the blackness but there was no sign of anything, so I scrambled into the dory and pulled her along to the gangway where I got back on board.

A whole crowd was waiting for me at the head of the gangway and those that had enough sense left to grasp what had happened were sobered up to some extent.

"Have you lost her?" George said to me.

"She's gone down in the current," I told him.

"She may swim out," he said.

I felt like saying "Oh, yeah?!" because I couldn't see that girl doing anymore swimming.

But I thought if it eased his mind to suppose she might swim out I had better keep quiet.

"Is she *drowned*?" someone said in the tone of voice that made you want to say, "No, she's roasted alive," but I didn't say anything, I just pushed through them in my dripping clothes and followed George into his cabin. He was upset, you could see that.

He closed the cabin door and turned on me.

"Keep quiet about this, Scotty. Don't say a word to anyone."

"I can't do that," I said, "I'll have to report it to the police."

"Don't be a fool," he said. "If you do there'll be trouble."

But I said I would have to report it, and as soon as I had changed my clothes I went ashore in a boat. I was frightened not to say anything because of how black things would look if the story came out later. So I went to the police and said a girl had been lost overboard. I didn't say anything about her being tight or wearing my uniform, but since they had been out to the yacht once already that night I expect they guessed pretty well.

They got out a motor launch and we went down the river in it. We thought some barge or something might have seen her and picked her up. But there was no sign of her and no one had seen anything. Her body was never picked up from that day to this.

15

By the time we got back to the yacht it was pretty near morning and the party was still going on. Some of them were wilder than ever.

The police came aboard and asked a few questions, but no one could tell them much. They wouldn't have any drinks this time, and after a few minutes they went away.

The party kept going till daylight, and by the time daylight came they were very nearly too exhausted to go back on shore.

George was wild with me for having fetched the police into it, but I said it would be all right because the police were well in with us through me having given them lobsters when the Old Man fished too many out of the pots in Long Island Sound. I always think it is a good idea to give presents to policemen, because even when there is no immediate need, it is pretty sure sooner or later to come in useful. And so it proved in this instance because we never heard another word from them about the girl being lost, and the whole thing would have blown over if it hadn't been for that new Steward who had a brother-in-law a reporter, and who was fed up with the way he had been kept mixing drinks all night.

So when morning came he said he was packing up, and he took his gear and went ashore and got a train to the works to collect his wages.

When he got there he saw George and Joe, and before he had even got his money he walked into the place and said he wasn't staying on that yacht, it wasn't a yacht at all, it was a place that ought not to be mentioned in the presence of a lady. So George and Joe were offended and they started to beat him up.

They threw him out in the end without a penny of his wages. That is where I say he was silly. If it had been me I would have got my money first.

So when he came round enough to travel, he went back to New York and the first thing he did was to 'phone his brother-in-law, the reporter, and give him the whole story.

For 24 hours that story was the talk of New York.

He went to the New York police too, not the ones I used to give the lobsters to, and he made a lot of statements about our moral characters on oath.

The result was, a few days later, when we had taken the yacht round to dry dock for an overhaul, Hansen came down below and said, "Scotty, there's two men to see you."

Well, I knew those two men were detectives the minute I came up on deck. I think when you've had trouble with the police you get a sort of nose for detectives, and the first thing that came into my head when I saw them was that they were after me over those diamonds I took from the smuggler, or the shooting that happened when I was a shift engineer.

Funny how your mind works. I forgot all about that girl going over the side, I suppose because in the back of my mind I had been frightened for years that the police would get me over those diamonds or the bother in that hotel.

So I went up to those two detectives and before they could even open their mouths I said, "I don't know nothing."

But they wouldn't take any notice. They took me down to the cabin and they showed me the story in the paper and they started offering me money if I would talk. But I still said I knew nothing, though I was glad it was only the party and not the other things they wanted me to talk about.

When they found I wouldn't talk they brought out a warrant for my arrest as a material witness and they took me away and we went to an hotel.

It was quite a nice hotel and they took a good room for me, but a detective stayed by me all the time. All that day he never left me, and at night another man came and he stayed in my room all night.

Next morning there was a message from downstairs that the Boss wanted to see me, so we went down and he said to the detective, "That's all right, he can come along with me."

That seemed to worry the detective, but it was all right really because the Boss had been to the police station and given a $5,000 bond for me, and we got into his car and drove to his place, and on the way he said to me, "Now what have you been telling those cops?"

So I said I had told them nothing.

"O.K.," said the Boss, "you keep on the way you been going and everything will be all right."

So we went back to the Boss's place and he told me there was to be a case and the Steward and I were to be called as witnesses, but that I was free to do what I liked until the case came on so long as I didn't go away from New York.

16

I had lunch at the Boss's place and then he said I could go, so I went back to New York and did some hard thinking. I didn't want to lose the Boss his bond for $5,000, but it looked as if he was going to be unlucky because the more I thought about it the more sure I got that I wasn't going to be called as any witness. Because they have a way in American courts when they start to cross-examine a witness of bringing in all your past life, and I kept thinking about those diamonds and the shooting that time with the gun from the hotel, so I decided in the end that the farther I kept away from that court the better.

So I bought a newspaper and looked down the shipping news, and there was a boat leaving next day for South America. It wasn't a very big fare, and in any case I always had plenty of money when I was working on the yacht, so I went to the bank and drew out all the money I had and next day I was on the way to Buenos Aires.

17

Buenos Aires is a grand place to enjoy yourself if you have plenty of money and for seven weeks I had a right royal time, but by then I was getting down to my last few dollars.

I used to buy the American papers every day to see if the case had come on yet, and it still hadn't come on, so I knew it was no good my going back to New York.

So just as I was getting down to the end of my money I noticed a little old woman come into the bar where I was drinking, and as soon as I saw the rings she had on her fingers I realized that it might be a good idea to get to know her.

She must have been about 60 because she had white hair, and she had a silver chain round one ankle, and expensive-looking clothes. I knew that a lady who would come into a bar in Buenos Aires and buy a drink like a man was not the sort of lady that would call a policeman if you spoke to her, and even though this one was 60 you could see she was not so tired of life. So I went up to her and addressed her in Spanish, of which I had learnt a few words, but, thank goodness, it turned out she could talk

English, and she was one of those old ladies that are very fond of young men.

She seemed to quite like me coming up to speak to her because it turned out that she was a widow and very lonely, so she said she was touched that a nice young boy like me should want to be her friend. So I said I was lonely too, because I was a stranger in the country and she said why not come to her house and perhaps we could comfort each other.

Well, my money was nearly done, so I thought that was a good idea and I went out to her house that very night.

She had a big house in one of the suburbs, with no one in it but servants, and it did seem a pity for her to be there all alone. So I stayed in her house with her, and we got on very well together. I think she started to get quite fond of me.

She wanted to know how long I was stopping so I said I had work that might call me back to New York, but she said, "Leave your work in New York. I'll set you up in a business."

At first I thought she was just joking, but it seems that she really meant it because she started making up figures and she said in the end that she could afford £3,000.

It was to be a business connected with tobacco, and she introduced me to a Spaniard who was going to teach me all about it, but when I had been in her house a month I found the case in New York had been up for about the fifth time and put off because of my absence.

The day before I went to the bank to draw out her money for her I read in the paper that the judge had said it couldn't be put off any longer, and it had been quashed for lack of evidence, because the Steward was the only witness, so I knew it would be all right to go back to New York now.

I didn't say anything to that old lady, however, because I knew it would hurt her feelings if she thought I wanted to leave. The trouble with that sort of old lady is that they never seem to know that they aren't the same as a young one, but she never was quite the same as a young one to me.

So I went to the bank and drew out the three thousand like she had told me, and then I didn't go back to her house but I got a boat to New York. I would have said good-bye to her only I thought she might say I couldn't have the three thousand for a business if she knew that after all I found I had to go back to New York.

So I never saw her again, and I didn't put her three thousand in a business after all. I spent it at Atlantic City because it takes a lot of money to have a good time at Atlantic City, and the young girl that I got to know there was really very expensive, but I felt that I needed a change after being in the house with that old lady for so long.

18

So one day I came round and found I had no money, I thought I would go back to the yacht. I took a train out to the foundry and I went in to see the Boss. He was sitting in his office chair.

"Christ!" he said. "Do you know you have cost me $5,000?"

So I told him I was very sorry, but I found that I really couldn't go up in court not knowing what they would ask me about my past life.

He said, "Never mind, Scotty. It's all over now, and maybe it was for the best really." Which was true, because you never know what they might have twisted me round into saying about the yacht.

He said then I could go on as engineer. "We haven't had her out since you left, Scotty," he said. "You're the only engineer I've ever had that's stuck by us." So we shook hands and I went back to the yacht.

The yacht was lying up in dry dock in Brooklyn and we got her out and started the same old round again.

We had to get a new skipper and this time it was a Porto Rican[54]— a little fellow between 50 and 60, and dark, like a Spaniard. We had a new crew too, all except Hansen, the Swede, who was still with us, and a steward, who was an Irishman.

I will not weary you with a recital of the minor orgies that followed in the next two months but go on to the occasion when I severed my connection with these millionaires forever.

It came through us planning to go on a swordfishing expedition. The Boss and his two boys were there, but not the Old Man. They had a party of lads with them, but not any women, and the second day out we ran into a thick sea fog.

I had the engine set just nicely, and being a diesel you could go off and leave her without any harm happening, so I went along to the saloon where they were all drinking, and I got some drink myself and went down to my cabin.

It is sort of lonely drinking by yourself so I called out to Hansen to come in and have a drink with me, though I do not generally lower

54 *Porto Rican* an archaic spelling of "Puerto Rican."

my dignity before the sailors—but I must admit that this night was an exception and I did. Hansen was a good sort, and not one to presume. He came in and sat down in my cabin and we drank till we were blind.

After a while I forgot all about the engine and the last thing I can remember is her pounding away as nice as nice. Then there must have been a blank period, because I came to to find everything as still as death, and pitch-darkness, and I was lying on something hard.

I started to feel about and I found I was half out of my bunk and was lying up against the bulkhead. The yacht wasn't moving any more and she was heeling over at an angle of about 40 degrees!

I went to jump out of my bunk, and then I thought I would move gingerly because she was heeling at such an angle that it made you feel the least thing would send her over. I felt about for some shoes and I climbed up on deck.

Well, you never saw such a dejected sight as I found on deck. We were stuck—in the middle of a thick sea fog. There was a foghorn and a bell going somewhere in the distance but not a thing could you see. The whole party, that had been singing and drinking when I saw them last, were sitting propped in a row against the rail on the upper side of the deck. Their heads were drooping and they were staring in front of them and no one had a word to say. The opposite side of the deck was two feet under water at the edge, and on that side the Porto Rican skipper was standing, in water up to his knees, with his arms crossed in front of him, looking glummer than I ever saw a man, and doing nothing at all.

It really was a funny sight to see them all squatting round doing nothing.

"What's up?" I said, because I wasn't sure yet what it was that we had hit.

"We're on a rock," they said.

But it seemed that we weren't sinking. We were just heeling over with the receding tide, the way we had that time we got on a sandbank.

"We'll go right over this time," I said, and they just nodded and sat on there, looking glum. They were still stupid with drink and they seemed to have lost their initiative. As for that Porto Rican skipper, he went on standing there, lost in thought, and you could see that the trouble with him was having regrets at what had happened, but what good were his regrets going to be if we all heeled over and went into the water while he was having them?

So I crawled along the deck to the Boss—it was at such an angle that you couldn't stand up on it now—and as he had a bit more sense left in him than the others, he said he thought it would be a good idea if we took to the boats.

"Where are we, Skipper?" he shouted. "How far is it to land?"

But that Porto Rican skipper didn't seem to know anything. It appears he had lost us in the fog, and he didn't know now whether land was north, south, east or west.

"Well, we'd better get to the boats, anyway," said the Boss.

That seemed to wake the Skipper up because he said he would fetch his papers, and he started to splash through the water and climb along the deck to his cabin, but the Boss said, "You won't need your papers where you're probably going."

And at that he looked glummer than ever and came back and went with us into the boats.

We kept calling out till all the crew had come—there were 25 of us altogether, and we got away in two boats with nothing but what we stood up in. The yacht was heeling over worse, but she still hadn't quite gone by the time we lost her in the fog.

We took the oars and started to row—it didn't seem to matter where—we thought we were lost in the ocean, but we hadn't been rowing five minutes when the boat that was in front ran aground. We couldn't see, but it was land of some sort, and that was certainly a stroke of luck. The second boat grounded just afterwards and we all scrambled out and found we were on a strip of beach. You could only see about five yards at a time because of the fog, and there didn't seem to be any sign of habitations so we just sat down on the beach and waited for the fog to lift or for daylight to come.

It was about four o'clock in the morning and they all sat around looking like a lot of drowned ducks.

All except the Porto Rican skipper. He was worse. He stretched flat out and hid his face in his hands.

We hadn't anything to eat or drink and it was damp and cold. So I went over to Hansen and we said we would scout around, but when we got away from the others I said, "Let's take a boat and go back and get some stuff from the galley of the ship."

So we rowed back, and she was still heeling over, but not much worse than when we left. We climbed up on the deck and I opened the hatch over the galley, because I wasn't going down in there in case she turned turtle and caught me, but I thought we were safe enough so long as we stayed on the deck. So I reached down amongst the stores and got cans of beans and cans of pineapple, and I fished with a loop of string for pots and pans and hauled them up, and all the time Hansen was packing the stuff in the boat for me.

When we had got enough we climbed back into the boat and pushed off through the fog. We struck the beach again pretty close to where we had left it, and when the others saw what we had brought back with us they started to get quite excited and cheered up a whole lot. It is wonderful what food will do to a man in that situation, and when we had scratched about and made a bit of a fire they all woke up and you'd have thought they were different men. All except the Porto Rican skipper. You couldn't cheer him up with just tinned pineapple or a hunk of bread and sardines.

I had brought a lot of tinned stuff but it hadn't struck me how we would need a tin opener, so it is a good thing they wrap up keys with tins of sardines. The Boss broke the bread up in chunks and smeared on sardines with his fingers, and we had to just sit and look at the pineapple and the beans.

But in the end we all had chunks of bread and sardines. We were sitting round the fire having this bite of breakfast when suddenly a voice came out of the fog:

"Halt!"

And we turned, and there was a soldier pointing a bayonet at us.

So we told him not to charge because we weren't doing any damage, and he came over and asked who we were, and we told him how we had come off a wrecked yacht.

"Where is this place, anyway?" we asked him.

So he said we were on Fishers Island,[55] which is a little island where there is a naval fort, and he said there was an officer back in the fog in a flivver, who had seen our fire and sent him to see who we were.

When the Boss heard about the naval fort and the flivver he finished his sardines and got up and called out to me.

"Come on, Scotty," he said, "we'll go along and see the commander."

---

55 *Fishers Island* Fishers Island is located at the eastern tip of Long Island Sound. Although closer to Connecticut, it is part of Suffolk County, New York. The small island was home from 1900 to 1950 to Fort H.G. Wright. It was an Army Coast Artillery fort, not a navy installation as Moore writes. It was closed in 1958 and its land sold off.

So I went with him to the flivver and we drove round the island to the fort.

19

It was daylight by now and the fog was starting to lift. We got to the headquarters of the station and told the commander all our troubles.

He said we had better send for a Coast Guard cutter, and he proceeded to do so, though the Boss looked a trifle upset because he thought that if the yacht was still afloat they might search her and find out about there being a lot of whisky on board. But he couldn't explain that, so he let them send for the cutter.

We went back to the beach when we had talked to the commander, and the fog had lifted so much by now that you could see the yacht where she was stuck. She hadn't gone right over, and she was straightened up more than she had been because now the tide was rising again and the water was righting her.

So the whole lot of us got into the boats and rowed back.

When we climbed on board we found a lot of water in her, but as there didn't appear to be any hole it must have seeped in through the boards of the deck. All my batteries in the engine room had fallen down on the floor with the angle she had been leaning at, and I had to get those straight and pump the water out of the bilges[56] before I could do anything.

By the time I had done that the Coast Guard cutter was alongside. She was a big, powerful affair, nearly as big as a torpedo boat, and when they had discussed our plight they said they would try to haul us off.

So the cutter drew away aft and they fixed a rope hawser[57] to us and we were supposed to go full speed astern when they went full speed ahead. I had my engine started up and the Porto Rican skipper, though he was really sacked, was in command of our yacht till we got back to port. When the cutter gave the word he told me to let her have it. So I did. And the hawser tightened till you could feel our boat shivering with the strain. The strain got tighter and tighter. Then suddenly there was a bang and everything slackened off.

The rope hawser had broken.

So the cutter came alongside and fixed a steel hawser to us instead. This time it was a different matter. I was standing with my feet

56 *bilges* an enclosed space where seepage gathers.
57 *hawser* a sizable rope used in mooring and towing a vessel.

down the engine-room ladder and my head up level with the deck. I watched everything that was happening, and I heard the men on the cutter call, "All clear?"

And we answered "All clear!"

Both engines were right out . . . I saw that hawser tighten . . . I saw our stern go up in the air . . . then it dropped . . . there was a crash amidships[58] . . . the yacht slid stern first under the water . . . and there was I swimming about . . . before I had even time to register in my mind that we had struck a rock properly this time. It must have come right through her and made a hole as big as a house for the yacht to go down in a matter of seconds like that.

So that was the end of the yacht. Everything I owned was on her. The 25 of us swimming round were mostly in the same plight. Fortunately no one was lost. I was hauled into a lifeboat by a boathook in the back of my collar, and in quite a short time they had got us all on board that cutter.

She turned round then and made for home.

We were put ashore at New London[59] and took a train back to New York. I went on from there with the Boss and the boys to the works, and the Boss paid me my wages and said I could have a job in the works if I liked.

But it is very dirty work working in a brass foundry, and I never was one who liked to get my hands dirty, so I thanked him very much but I said I would try to get a ship.

I went back to Hoboken with $500 in my pocket and I stayed at an hotel and hung my trousers over the bed. All my money was in those trousers and when I woke up next morning they had vanished. I hadn't any other trousers, so I had to borrow some to go out and fetch the detectives. But they weren't any good of detectives because they never got my money back . . . So there I was broke already, after seven months working with multimillionaires.

58 *amidships* the midpoint of the ship between the bow and the stern.
59 *New London* a Connecticut harbor city on Long Island Sound, near Fishers Island.

CHAPTER IX

1

I T was a public holiday that time I woke up and found my trousers had been stolen, but after I had told the police about it I had to try and get some work, so I went down to a wharf where I knew the superintendent engineer was a Scotsman but I found everything closed up except for a watchman.

So I got talking to the watchman and after a while he told me where the superintendent engineer was living.

"But he'll chase you off the place if you go to his private house," he told me.

However, I decided I would go.

It was a place on Rhode Island and I started out on the road. I got one lift in a car but I walked most of the way. It was afternoon when I got there and Mr. McCall's house that I had come to look for was standing back by itself amongst a lot of trees.

By the time I got to the gate after all the distance I had walked, and with no food since morning,[1] I started to feel discouraged and I remembered what the watchman had told me so I nearly turned away. But then I thought how that would be a waste of all my energy so I plucked up my courage and went in up the drive, and I walked to where there were a lot of men and women having tea under some trees.

The man who stood up when he saw me coming I guessed would be Mr. McCall, so I asked his pardon for intruding, but I said I was an engineer and that I had walked most of the way from his offices because my money had all been stolen and I wanted some work to do.

Well, at first he was not pleased, but he asked me to come into the house, and then I said I had known him in Glasgow which perhaps he would not remember, though, as a matter of fact I had not known him at all. Well, he seemed pleased to think I had known him and it

---

1 *since morning* The distance from Hoboken to Rhode Island is too great for Moore to have covered it over the course of morning to afternoon. It's possible he confused Rhode Island with other places closer to Hoboken, such as Long Island and Staten Island.

turned out he knew about my father, so then I said it was not money but work I was wanting, and he asked to see my papers, and then he 'phoned up the police to see if what I had said about losing my trousers with my money in was true.

When he found that I had really lost my money and had really been on the yacht, he called his wife to get me some food, and he gave me a $5 bill and told me to come to his office down at the wharf in the morning.

So I went back to Hoboken more quickly than I had come.

But next morning I was at his office just as he had told me to be, and when I had fetched my bag he called a taxi for us and we drove over to Brooklyn where one of their ships was in dock. I will not tell you the name of that line of ships because they are known in every port as the "lousy and hungry" line, but in spite of that I cannot but say that Mr. McCall was good to me. Their ships were very old ships, however, and it is not Mr. McCall's fault that the majority of them are not fit to put to sea. The one that I was put on always sailed with a list[2] to port[3] whatever you did to her, and the plates in the engine room were so rotten that there were planks over holes where the engineers had gone through.

I was three days aboard this ship before she started, and I very nearly didn't get away at all, because as soon as I was signed on I got an advance note from the purser,[4] and I went to an Italian who had a speakeasy that I used to go to when I was on the yacht, and after he had cashed it I got him to let me have some other money as well.

It would have been quite all right if I had not given him that advance note from the purser, but it was silly of me to do that because it had the name of my ship on it, and when I did not give back the other money I had had from him, he went and got two detectives and came down to the boat. You see it very difficult about owing people money in America. It is not like it is in England, where if you cannot pay it back all a man can do is to issue a summons against you. In America a man can come right at you with *two detectives*, and if you do not find the money at once they take you away to gaol. That is one respect in which I do not think America is as good a country as England, because how is a man to get on if he cannot borrow money when he is hard up, and it is silly to arrest him for not paying back,

2 *list* tilt to a side.
3 *port* a vessel's left side when facing forward.
4 *purser* a ship's officer in charge of documents and handling accounts.

because if he had enough to pay back he would not need to borrow any. So you see how they do not reason things out properly in the United States.

Well, I was in a terrible fix when this Italian came down to my ship with two detectives.

The only thing I could think of to do was to go and explain to the purser. But the purser would not give me much more, because he said I had had too much advance already, so I went along the alleyways and took up a collection and altogether I got about half what I owed the Italian, so he had to be content with that, and I told him he could have the rest when I came back from my voyage, so he went away and took the two detectives with him, and I must say I felt better when they were off the ship.

2

My job on that ship to begin with was deck engineer. That means I had to look after all the winches. She was quite a big ship with a whole crowd of engineers and she carried as well about 300 passengers.

She was on the run between New York, West Indies, and South America and all the greasers[5] and firemen, who were black, were signed on at Barbados. Barbados is a little island down near South America where you can buy good rum for a shilling a bottle, but we never used to buy any rum because the crew always brought some aboard for us. Later, when I was made fourth engineer, all the crew on my watch used to bring me two bottles of rum every time they were signed on at Barbados, and that used to make 20 bottles, so I would then have nearly enough drink to last me a whole voyage.

But the Second Engineer was the one who did best on that ship.

It was his job to sign on all extra hands, and as there are a lot of "Spikes"[6] (that is, Spaniards) in the West Indies who are ready to pay money for getting into America, he used to do well out of signing on these Spikes, making out he wanted them for chipping[7] and painting. They always deserted when we got into port in

5 *greasers* workers responsible for lubricating machinery.
6 *"Spikes"* Moore almost certainly means "spics," a derogatory term for Latinos.
7 *chipping* Either carpentry or work literally involving chipping, such as the scrapping away of old paint.

Hoboken, but he always used to say he didn't see how that was his fault.

I did four or five trips on this ship that we will call the *Veronica*, and then one day we got two days out from New York when we struck a terrible storm. The storm was so bad that we hove to,[8] with the ship's bow facing into it, and almost as soon as we stopped the ship's list began to get worse. We knew what that was. We had a cargo of heavy machinery and it had shifted out of position. We that knew the sea could tell that things were going to be serious, but at first the passengers thought it was nothing at all.

It was in the middle of the afternoon and they were all in the saloons drinking and playing cards, except the ones that kept getting seasick, because she was pitching[9] like a rowboat, now that she was going dead slow into such a terrific sea.

After we had been hove to for about three hours, with the list getting worse all the time, the Captain ordered every pump to action, because the seas were now breaking over her so badly that no one could go out on deck and water was pouring into her through the open alleyways.

If the pumps had been any good we might have held her, but they had not been properly inspected for the last three or four voyages and when they got going it was found that they could not hold back the water that was coming in.

It was when the engineers found that the pumps could not hold back the water that everyone began to get excited, and by now the passengers had begun to get worried by that list, so that groups of them were running up and down the alleyways screaming, and catching hold of anyone they saw in a uniform to ask if it was true that the ship was going to the bottom of the sea.

Of course we said she was not going anywhere near the bottom of the sea, but the way she kept listing over it was soon pretty clear that there was no hope of that lie turning out to be the truth, short of the ship growing wings and flying into New York harbour. By nighttime we began to wonder why the Skipper did not order us to take to the boats. But it seems he had an idea that another ship was due along this route, and that she would help us, so he did not order us to the boats or send out an SOS message.

8 *hove to* heaved to.
9 *pitching* the bow's steep dipping and ascending.

That was a terrible afternoon. There was nothing anyone could do except work the pumps and wait, and watch the passengers having hysterics and the officers getting more and more excited. In the end our Chief lost his head and started giving orders one minute and retracting them the next, and they were silly orders anyway, so no man on the ship knew what he ought to do.

Round about dinnertime there was so much water in the engine room that everyone had to get out, and no one was having any dinner. But I was going aft with another fellow when we found that the seas had been breaking over her so badly that the barman had abandoned the bar, and everything was left so that anyone could have what he wanted. So that other fellow and I hopped over the counter and started opening the bottles, because we thought if we had to go to the bottom of the sea it would be easier to go down tight than sober. So when we had drunk all we could hold, we stuffed some bottles in our pockets and went away back to the others and soon everyone round us was just about as drunk as we were.

The ship was still pitching like a buckjumper[10] and her list was getting worse and worse. The passengers had all started to put on their lifebelts, but no one had been ordered to boat stations, and the women were all crying and we were as drunk as lords.

I must have been pretty drunk because I went down to my cabin and started packing my suitcase, which is not a very sensible thing to do when you are going to the bottom of the sea. But while I was packing my suitcase a kid engineer came down to the cabin and grabbed hold of me. "You're wanted in the engine room alleyway," he said, "they're going to lower the Second into the engine room to shut off the main stop valves on the boilers."

Now perhaps you will not understand what a main-stop valve is for, but you know that a ship's boiler is filled with boiling-hot steam, and if the cold seawater gets on to a boiler filled like that there is going to be a big explosion. So the thing to do in a situation like this is to shut off the main-stop valves and then everything is all right. Well, there was about six feet of seawater in the engine room already, so it was about time someone had thought of shutting off the main-stop valves.

10 *buckjumper* a jump like that of a wild horse to throw off a rider on its back.

3

Well, when I got up to the engine-room alleyway they had the Second Engineer with a rope round him, and we all hung on to the rope while he was lowered through the trap. I have told you how the ship was pitching and rolling, and the seas were washing right through the engine-room alleyway, so it was like standing in a rushing river during an earthquake, but even though I try to describe it you could not tell what it was like, standing there balancing the engineer while he swung over the boilers, unless you had been there lending a hand yourself.

At first he swung like a trapeze artist limbering up for his act, but at last he got his bearings, and landed on the top of those boilers, while he reached out and shut off all the valves. Then he gave a tug to show that he was coming up.

We felt the rope go tight as he swung off the boilers into space, and at the same minute the ship gave a terrific lurch. The next minute there was a bit of a bump and that engineer gave a screech, and when we hauled him up he was as white as the paint in the first-class passengers quarters, and both his legs were dangling as if they were made of string—broken. He gave another screech when we hauled him up and landed him into the alleyway, because it was impossible to be gentle with a man when the ship was more drunk than we were, but all the same it must have hurt getting dumped down the way we dumped him, with a pair of broken legs.

It happened through him swinging against an iron girder when he stepped off those boilers, and now he had just about fainted, so we gave him some whisky and carried him up to the boat deck and put him down there. It was cold and wet up there and the angle of the deck was more like a roof than a deck, but we thought we would be ordered to the boats any time now, and if he was left down below he might never have got carried up at all in the excitement. So we left him there, thinking he would be all right, but it seems he was forgotten after all, for he was not amongst the ones who finally escaped from the ship.

4

Well, after that time with the Second Engineer, we thought we would like another drink.

So we went back to the after[11] bar, but we found that someone had got wise, because the carpenter had been there before us with orders

11 *after* situated in the rear.

to board it up. But we could not bear the thought of good drink going to the bottom, so we got axes and broke down the boarding, and put all the bottles we could manage in our pockets, though a lot were broken already with the ship lurching the way she was.

By this time the list of her was so bad that the fish plates[12] on one side were out of the water, and the passengers were rushing up and down, walking in the "V" between the fish plates and the side of her, because the decks had such a slant that you would need to have had suckers on your feet to keep your balance.

But we are now getting to a stage where my memory is somewhat hazy, and I do not remember very much more of what happened, except that by now passengers were jumping overboard and being lost, and the ones left were shrieking so loud that even the wind and waves couldn't drown it. So we looked up to the masts and saw the SOS messages crackling out at last, but we knew they would be too late to do us much good, because anyone could tell by now that a matter of minutes would see us all in the water.

Boats were starting to be lowered, and one of the first to get away had the bo'sun[13] in it with four South American millionaires.

But there were not enough boats to save all the passengers because the ones on the port side, which is the side she was listing from, were too far out of line with the water to be lowered, and on some of the others the ropes were so old and worn that they came away and the boats were lost.

The passengers were jumping overboard in swarms now, and I thought it was about time that I jumped too. I remember seeing the kid engineer that had got me out of my cabin hold his nose and jump ahead of me. Then I went, and when I came up first I could see nothing at all. But I had a life belt, and I paddled, though the seas were still enormous, but I felt to see the two bottles that I had were still safe, and then I struck out, hoping a boat would come along.

Well, I was luckier than some, because after a few minutes a boat did dive over the swell,[14] and I yelled but they didn't hear, so I grabbed over the side, and then they saw me and hauled me in. They all wanted my whisky when they saw what I had in my pockets, but I said, no,

12 *fish plate* also known as a "flounder plate": a steel, triangular plate with openings at each of its corners for towing bridles.

13 *bo'sun* a variation on "boatswain"; a petty or warrant officer with responsibility for the deck crew and the vessel's cables, anchors and rigging.

14 *swell* a long wave or series of waves, frequently crestless and very large.

we would keep it in case we needed it more later, because I didn't see why I should let a lot of black men (which were all that were in this boat) have my whisky, after I had worked so hard to obtain it.

5

Well, we cruised around in those seas till the old ship went down— stern first she went, just diving quietly under the water. There were some small explosions when she vanished, but nothing else.

The Captain, Sparks,[15] and Second Engineer and over 200 others went down on her, but you never would have known from watching her that all those people were being killed. It was mostly a matter of lights being there one minute, and the next minute no lights at all. But it seemed rather dark and cold after she had vanished, with nothing but wind and waves as far as we could tell all round us, and I kept having swigs at my whisky, because I knew if I let my head cool after having come through so much I would start and get depressed. And I did not want to get depressed when I was alone in an open boat with a whole lot of niggers, because after all a white man is supposed to set an example.

So after we had been afloat in this lifeboat for about an hour we saw rockets going up on the horizon and we knew that the ships which had heard our SOS were coming. It felt good to see ships all alight come steaming up. There were six of them altogether, and they found quite a lot of lifeboats cruising around in the dark. Our lifeboat was found by a little Norwegian tramp[16] and we were taken to New York where we landed amongst crowds of people wanting our autographs, and photographers, and reporters.

All the reporters wanted me to answer their questions. But I said I was too busy, though it was quite an experience being a hero for a change. Some of the people made a whole lot of money talking from the radio station, but just then I was not wanting too much publicity, because there were people who wanted to find where I was.

So my experiences in the wreck have never been told to any section of the public before.[17]

15 *Sparks* the ship's radio operator.
16 *tramp* a ship that that does not adhere to a fixed route, but rather transports cargo to any destination.
17 *So my experiences . . . the public before* The preceding is clearly an account of the last journey of the s.s. *Vestris*. While on a voyage to Barbados and South America, it sank off the Virginia Capes on November 12, 1928. Moore's estimate of the number dead is mistaken: there were 113 lost.

6

As I was not seeking publicity at that time I went away to stay at Heinz Billings' speakeasy in Hoboken because that is the kind of place where people do not ask you questions about where you have come from or anything like that. Heinz Billings was really a German, but he had changed his name to Billings so as to be patriotic in the War. He had a big Alsatian dog that used to sleep outside his room at night and stop with him in the daytime, so unless you had a gun it would have been very difficult to take advantage of Heinz Billings, but that did not worry me because I did not need to take advantage at this time. . . . You see I was just staying with Heinz, but I did not need a job just now as I had been promised another ship as soon as one was available owing to my sufferings in the wreck.

So soon I was made second engineer on a ship which I shall call the *Alpha* that was sailing to Santos and Rio and Buenos Aires. I was a little bit worried when I heard about Buenos Aires because I remembered the old lady that had been going to set me up in business, but I thought I would be careful and I probably would not meet her because after all we would not stay very long in Buenos Aires.

So I went on that ship and she was an old tub if ever a ship was.

But I did not seem to be able to keep out of trouble in any port that we called at all the time I was on that ship so I think there must be something that has a bad influence on a man about the climate of South America. But the funny thing about those parts is that though I was in trouble in every port I was only in gaol in one of them and that was when I had not done anything to deserve it, so I really think fate is very ironical the way it behaves to a man.

It is really a wonder that we were not all drowned on the *Alpha* because she was the most unseaworthy vessel that I have ever put to sea in. Her plates were so rotten that when a man was chipping at one of them he suddenly went right through her side and the water started rushing in. So we had to put a plug in the rivet hole till Chippy could come to fix it, and when he tried to block up the hole there was an awful flood in the engine room because the side of the ship was so rotten that the whole plate came away. We were very lucky we did not go to the bottom of the sea over that and it used to get on my mind to think our ship was so unseaworthy so perhaps that is partly what helped to make me get into trouble every time we were in port.

But I will not tell you about all the times that I got into trouble. I will just tell you about how I was unjustly put in gaol.

It was in a place called Rosario[18] where there is not very much that you can do, so I had gone ashore with the Second Mate who was a very religious quiet-living sort of man. Our ship was sailing at six in the morning so we did not mean to stay out late and when we had had some food in a café we were walking along the street. We came to a place in the street where there was a man playing an accordion and he was a real artist, that fellow, he could make that accordion speak.

So while we were listening to him making that accordion speak, some more men came out of another café and stood beside us listening, and the next thing we knew a big police van had driven up and we were all rounded into it and taken away to the gaol. When we got to gaol I kept telling them that we were respectable ship's officers, but they did not seem to think we were respectable at all, so it was no good me talking. We were all put in the gaol.

It is not very comfortable in a gaol in South America, because they are all built of stone and they are wet and there is nowhere at all where you can sit down. So we had to lean against each other to get some sleep while we were standing up, because you could not sit on the floor owing to there being water there. But there was a window with some bars across it through which I could see some officers playing cards. I called out to them how it was all a mistake us being in gaol but they would not listen to me.

So, as the night drew on the Second Mate that was with me started to be very depressed because this was the first time he had ever been in a gaol, and I must say it was not a very good introduction, and besides that he seemed to think that now he had been in gaol he would lose all his reputation.

I really felt more sorry for him than I did for my own predicament because I think it must be a worry to lose your reputation, but that is never a thing that I have had to bother about because I have never had any reputation to lose.

The night drew on and it got so cold that we were shivering, and it makes your legs ache to have to stand up so long on them, and we really could not get any sleep to help us to forget our sufferings. But I kept thinking how this would be a useful lesson to me because now,

18 *Rosario* a city in east-central Argentina on the Paraná river.

if I ever commit a crime, I will not do it in South America because I would not like to be put in gaol where it was all wet and there was no place to sit down.

Only it seemed like that night would never end, but at last we heard our ship's whistle blowing so we knew it must be nearly six and they were blowing for us because we had not come back on board. So the poor Second Mate was nearly weeping by this time because he kept thinking how now his reputation would be gone.

But I told him I would speak up for him and say how he had not done anything and it was not his fault, so after he had heard that he felt somewhat better.

But the ship's siren kept on blowing and we could not do anything about it, so we kept wondering if she would sail without us, but by nine o'clock someone came to the door of our cell and called, "Are two Americans in here?"

We were taken out and we found it was our ship's agent who had searched all the town for us. He asked us what we had done and we said we had not done anything. But the police who had brought us in said we had been making a disturbance in a café, and then it turned out he meant the café where the other men had come from, and we showed how he was wrong because we told him how we had not been in that café at all.

When he heard that he bowed like anything and made a lot of apologies in Spanish, but we said we would see our consul because we wanted something more than some apologies and in the end we got it. We got £5 each compensation from the authorities in Rosario, so it was not an unprofitable night after all.

7

But when we went back to the ship everyone lined up and cheered us because we had kept the whole ship waiting for over three hours and the Old Man was mad at us till we explained how we had been the victims of a miscarriage of justice.

But it was a good idea getting £5 compensation from the authorities because it made me think how there was an avenue for making money that had been right under my nose all my life and I had never thought to explore it.

Of course the trouble about compensation is that something has to happen to you before you can claim it, but if you know how to utilize your opportunities it need not be anything very big.

It was one day when I was thinking like this that I fell off the boilers and though I did not plan for anything of the kind to happen, and it really was very painful, I knew that at last my chance had come. Because this time I really had broken some ribs—not like in Alexandria, where the doctor was deceived. But this time I was quite a wreck so I was taken ashore and put in hospital but I came on by another ship belonging to the same company in a few weeks. All the way home I was thinking how much I could get out of the company in compensation because I was really very ill and would have to go to an Officers Convalescent Home in New York.

But when we got into New York I was really treated very badly because they all went ashore and left me for five hours. So I thought no one was coming at all and at last I made a man bring a taxi to take me to the nearest hospital because by now I was feeling very sick.

The last thing I remember is getting into that taxi and then everything became blank because later when I recovered I was lying in a Roman Catholic Hospital in Hoboken and there was an ice pack on my head and the nuns were telling beads over me.

Well, it gave me quite a fright to see the nuns telling beads over me, so I asked what was the matter and they said I must not talk because I had pleurisy and double pneumonia,[19] but I made up my mind that I would not die yet. Because where would be the use in dying when there was money coming to me from the company for compensation? But I thought that the company might now try to cheat me through me being weak and helpless, so I asked the nuns to send for Heinz Billings to visit me because I knew he would handle the situation for me if he thought there was going to be a profit.

So when I was well enough the nuns sent for Heinz Billings, but Heinz could not come himself because of the police, but he sent two of his henchmen, and they brought me a lot of fresh gear and a razor because all my gear had been stolen when I was ill in the taxi, and they also brought me some invalid food and a chicken. So though I will not deny that Heinz Billings is a mean man you could not say that he had no good in him even though he is a gangster.

Heinz Billings' two henchmen sat down beside me and talked, but it is a great pity that they found the bottle of rubbing alcohol. For rubbing alcohol is not really meant to be drunk—it is coloured to warn people—but they would not take any notice when I told them

---

19 *double pneumonia* impacting both lungs.

they might get a withered arm, because when a man finds something to drink when he is thirsty he always seems to think that he is going to be the exception.

So they took the rubbing alcohol out of my locker and drank it, and it really was a disgrace the way they behaved after that in a room full of sick people.

After that, Heinz Billings used to send a woman out of his speakeasy instead of his henchmen to see me. It is a funny thing about this woman because she was a waitress married to a man called Hauptmann, and the other day I read in the paper that the man who had been arrested for kidnapping Colonel Lindbergh's baby was a man called Hauptmann and his wife was a waitress too.[20] So I think it must have been the same woman, because you would not be likely to have such a coincidence for nothing in your life.

But at this time I did not know anything about Colonel Lindbergh's baby so I used to have Mrs. Hauptmann come and see me when I was sick.

8

But as soon as I could come out of hospital I went to stay with Heinz Billings while we saw how much compensation we could get from the company.

I had no money when I went to stay with Heinz Billings and he would not give me any so I had to work in his speakeasy, though I felt it was very degrading for a man of my skill and education to be working picking sailors' pockets and serving drinks behind the bar.

Heinz had girls in his speakeasy and the sailors used to stay all night and the girls would take most of their money to give to Heinz in the morning, but sometimes in case they missed some I had to watch too. Heinz used to throw me the keys through his door in the early morning and then I would go through all the rooms, and after that I had to open up the bar and start business for the day.

We used to break down our own drinks in a back room in that speakeasy and sometimes I would be sent to get the pure alcohol

20 *Colonel Lindbergh . . . waitress too.* Charles Augustus Lindbergh (1902-1974) became the first aviator to fly across the Atlantic Ocean alone after completing a celebrated flight from New York to Paris on May 20–21, 1927. His first child was abducted and murdered in 1932. A carpenter, Bruno Hauptmann, was found guilty of the kidnapping and was executed. As Moore indicates, Hauptmann's wife, Anna, was a waitress.

from the bootleggers on the ships. I used to go aboard with a rubber breastplate that was hollow like a hot-water bag strapped under my vest, and when that was filled up on board with alcohol you would look just the same only more prosperous because you were fatter than when you went on board. It used to be a ticklish moment coming through the customs but if you gave them some cigarettes they generally did not bother you. We used to get quite a lot of alcohol ashore in that way and then we would break it down into different flavoured drinks in the back room.

You used to put brown sugar in when you wanted to make whisky and for the other drinks we used different essences. We used to get 25 cents for every drink we sold and we could get 75 cents for specials. But specials were not any different really only a man thinks he is getting something different when he pays 75 cents for it.

But all the time I was working for Heinz Billings we were trying for my compensation. Heinz Billings had an Irish lawyer that he said I could have the use of and we were going to try for $25,000. The lawyer was to have a third and I wanted the rest but I could see that Heinz thought he would get half the remainder, but I did not see why he should have my compensation when I was the one who had had the broken ribs and the double pneumonia. But I did not tell Heinz that I thought he should not have some of my compensation because then he might not have let me go on using his lawyer.

So we started out our campaign by writing letters to the company, but right from the start the company showed what twisters they were, because they wrote back that since I had left the ship in a taxi before their ambulance arrived and had not waited for their ambulance they were no longer responsible for what had happened me. So they were going to get out of paying for my broken ribs over a little detail like that, only we were not as soft as they thought we were going to be.

Heinz Billings' Irish lawyer was a very clever man and he said what we ought to do was to go down and label the ship. That is a way they have in America by which you go down and pin a notice on the mast of a ship every time she comes into port, and when you have done that the captain cannot move anywhere until he has gone and reported himself to the court. But though we took a lot of trouble and did this every time the ship was in, the company still would not pay anything, so we decided all we could do was to take my case to the courts.

But the company were very clever and they had a lot of money so they kept getting the case put off, and I did not really have any money much while I was working for Heinz so I was driven to go and ask for advances from the Irish lawyer. But I did not tell Heinz that the lawyer was advancing me money because that might have prejudiced the case in court, because you never knew what Heinz might not get up and say before everyone if he happened to get wind that I did not see why he should have some of my compensation as well as the Irish lawyer. But though I did not tell Heinz he found out about the money and then he tried to play a very dirty trick on me. He said that if I did not sign a deed promising him most of my compensation he would squeal and then I would get none.

So when I heard how Heinz was double-crossing me I went to the Irish lawyer and we thought out what we would do.

So we wrote again to the company and said the case was so long coming on that if they would agree to settle out of court we would reduce to some extent the size of my compensation. So we asked for quite a small sum, but they would not give it to us but in the end we got £250 and a first-class ticket for me in the *Homeric*, only I did not use my first-class ticket. I sold it to a guy in Hoboken for £4 10s. 0d.[21] I then paid the Irish lawyer his third but I did not give Heinz Billings anything, because I did not think he deserved it after the way he had treated me.

I did not stay in his speakeasy after I had got my money because I thought he might find out, and besides I wanted a holiday. So I left one night and I took all the money in the till with me because I think he owed me something after the way he had treated me.

But Heinz Billings was very angry when he found I'd gone in the night and taken some money with me, and he swore, I was told afterwards, that he would wait all his life to get me. So after that I could never go back to Hoboken, but I went to Atlantic City with my money and had a very good time.

---

21 *£4 10s. 0d.* Prior to decimalization in 1971, the pound sterling's sub-unit was the shilling, denoted by an "s." Twenty shillings equated to £1. The shilling's subunit was the penny, symbolized by a "d." Twelve pence (pennies) equaled 1s.

PART THREE
Mitchell and China

CHAPTER X

1

THE part of my life that I am now coming to is what I think you would call the climax of my career. But first I must tell you about how I came to meet Mitchell, because though Mitchell has been a terrible trial in many ways and has led me into a great many difficulties, I would not like to ignore him in my reminiscences, because I think if a man has been through things with you it is only right that he should be remembered.

Well, it was through being broke that I came to meet Mitchell. I had spent all the money that I got for my compensation and I could not go back to Hoboken so I had to look for work elsewhere. But I did not like very much to go about in the daytime because I was still in New York and I did not know when one of Heinz's henchmen might not see me, so I was rather handicapped in trying to find work.

But one night I heard there was a man wanted to cook in a coffeepot, which is a coffee stall, so I went along to wait in the queue of people that were applying. It was midnight when I got to the place and we had to wait till five in the morning so that will show you how hard I was trying to find myself some honest work.

But when I saw how many people were waiting along with me I knew I would have to think up something if I was to secure the job, so I spent the night writing out some references that I thought would impress the man when it came to my turn.

But besides writing out my references I got talking to a limey who was standing next to me. Well, it seemed to be a long time since I had met anyone from the Old Country so I took a fancy to this limey, and he told me his name was Mitchell, and as we stood waiting for the dawn we talked all about ourselves. It seems he had been through things the same as I had, so I told him if I got this job he must hang round when I came off duty because I would swipe some grub and then we could have a feed.

Well, dawn came at last and the Greek that owned the coffeepot came along to interview us. He was a very fat Greek and he did not know who to choose there were so many of us, but he said he liked limeys so he thought he would have me, and he made up his mind for sure when he had seen my references. Because there is no sense in writing yourself a reference if you do not make it a good one, but in case he should notice that I did not seem familiar with the running of a coffeepot I told him that until now I had always worked at cooking in the big hotels in Chicago.

That made him think I was quite a swell guy and he told me that I could start right away. I winked at Mitchell and told him to hang around that evening and I went in and started to cook for the coffeepot.

You did not have to do a lot really—just make coffee and cook eggs and hamburger steaks and bacon, so I watched the Greek boy who was supposed to be my offsider[1] and pretty soon I had the hang of it like an old hand.

I did well all that day and after I had finished I came away with half a chicken and rolls and ham, so I went to where Mitchell was waiting and we had a great feed, but it was on the second day that disaster overtook me. Because though I did my best perhaps I was not so careful on the second day. I was lifting a huge can of fat and I slipped and it all spilt over, and the next thing I knew the whole place had caught fire. So I out of that coffeepot like a streak of greased lightning and bolted down the road before the Greek could come after me. I expect the coffeepot was all burnt up but I really did not wait to look, and as I had not collected any wages I was not any better off after my waiting and all my trouble.

2

I waited till it was daylight and I went down to the docks at New York and there was a ship called the *Golden Arrow*, and she was going to China. I thought how a change of scene might do me good and I went on board and asked if they were wanting any engineers.

Well, that was a piece of luck because they were wanting two engineers and I was signed on as third right away. As soon as I was signed on the Skipper asked me if I knew of another engineer who could be signed on as a junior, so I thought at once of Mitchell, who though he was not an engineer would be all right if I told him what to do, so I said I would go ashore and look and went to find Mitchell.

I found Mitchell in a speakeasy where he had got a man to buy him a drink and I said if he would come along I thought I had a job

1 *offsider* assistant.

for him. I took him back to the *Golden Arrow* and I said this was my great friend so we could be on the same watch together, as I thought if we were on the same watch no one would be likely to find out about Mitchell not being a qualified engineer.

Before this he had been a waiter, but it does not take a lot of intelligence just to be a junior engineer. So Mitchell was signed on the *Golden Arrow* and we were to leave for China in three days' time.

Looking back I think that all my life I have been too generous in helping people when they do not really deserve it, but I had taken a fancy to Mitchell, only I never would have got him the job if I known all the trouble that was in store.

He was a real crazy man, was Mitchell, and he did not seem to understand that not being what you could call secure in his position, it would be wise to be very polite to his senior officers on board. But instead of that we had not been two days out when nobody on the ship could stand him.

Our ship was making for Shanghai via Panama and Japan, so it was going to be a long voyage and though he did not mean any harm it would have been much better if Mitchell could have been tactful. But instead of that he would come down to the engine room and talk like this to the Chief:

"Hallo, Chief," he would say, "how's the old coffee grinder?"

That is the way he would talk of a huge 40-foot engine that the Chief loved like a daughter, so you will understand that when the Chief loved his engine like that it was not very easy for him to love Mitchell as well.

I tried to explain to Mitchell, but Mitchell is not the kind of person that you can give a hint to. The only thing that he would do was to laugh out so loud that half the ship could hear him, and then he would go right back and do the same thing again. I really used to wonder sometimes why I bothered with Mitchell, but I did not know at first what a trial he was to become.

3

It was not an exciting voyage going through the Panama Canal and I don't know what I would have done to pass the time away if Mitchell and I had not found a way to keep on winning at cards. I will not tell you what our system was because it is a very good system and someday it may be worth money to me, but you must not let anyone know you are using it, because they will put you out of your club, or just draw a gun on you if they find out you are using it. But it is all right so long as you are careful and it makes you win every time. We played for cigarettes with one of the kid electricians. He was a nice kid. I liked him. He never got tired of playing because he always seemed to think that if he went on long enough his luck would turn. We did not like to tell him that we had an infallible system, but we used to give him a cigarette sometimes, just so that he would not think that we were mean.

That was all that we did till we got to Yokohama, and then I had a very sad disillusionment about that fellow Mitchell because up till now I had thought he was my friend.

But at Yokohama I went ashore to buy some silk shirts only you cannot buy them straight out, you have to get them made there, so I came back to the ship and lay down in the cabin that Mitchell was sharing with me so that I could have some sleep.

I was still sleeping when a steward came to wake me to say that the Jap had brought my shirts and was asking for the money. So I sat up and put my hand in my pocket and the £7 10s. 0d. that had been there when I lay down was now all gone.

So you can imagine that I had rather a shock. Seventy yen[2] all gone. I jumped off my bunk and I ran along the deck to the Skipper calling out that I had been robbed. But the steward called after me, "It's your mate that took it. I see him ashore in a café with a whole roll of money."

When I heard that I halted in my stride and became very disillusioned to think that I had been shipmates with a man who was a thief.

I went straight back to our cabin and broke open his locker and took out his gold Waltham watch that was worth nearly £20, and after I had that I did not feel so disillusioned, but I thought I would go ashore and find Mitchell and I would not say I had his watch but would charge him with his crime.

So the Jap and I went downtown in a taxi. We went to a joint that is called the Kaio Café where they have music and women, and as soon as we were out of that taxi there came Mitchell through the door, as if he had been thrown out, and he really was very drunk indeed.

But I did not feel sorry for him when I thought how it was my money he had got drunk on, so I took him by the shoulder and I said. "What have you done with my money?"

2 *Seventy yen* Moore again confusingly mixes currencies. However, £7 10s. 0d. and ¥70 were about equal in the 1920s.

But it seems he had spent all my money because he had been with a woman, and Japanese women take all the money in your pockets just the same way that other women do. He emptied all his pockets right there on the pavement to show me and there was nothing in them but some crumbs and some dead matches.

So I took out his watch then, and I dangled it before him, and I said, "Now I will keep this watch till you pay me back my money." But he was too drunk to be impressed with what I said.

<h2 style="text-align:center">4</h2>

I did not forgive Mitchell all the time we stayed in Yokohama, because I was very disillusioned. It was not till he was accused of killing the Angora rabbits that I really forgave him, but I forgave him then because he had no friends left on the ship.

It was funny about the Angora rabbits. It happened when we were going to leave Yokohama. The Skipper and the Chief did not come back till it was nearly time to sail. We were all on the deck watching and there they were coming up the gangway each of them nursing a fluffy white Angora rabbit as if they had been carrying a baby. If you had seen them you would have been most amused. But they did not think it was funny because they had been having a few, and they told the carpenter to build a hutch[3] in the poop.[4] Even when they were sober they still took an interest in those rabbits. All the way to Kobe they would talk about Angora rabbits, and then all of a sudden the rabbits disappeared.

You have no idea what a fuss there was about losing those rabbits and everyone said it must be Mitchell, because who else would think of such a thing?

But I did not think it was Mitchell, only who was I against so many? And somebody must have done it. Mitchell said it was the Skipper's dog. But though this was a clever dog it could not open the catch of a hutch and then close it when it was finished, so this suggestion of Mitchell's did not vindicate him at all.

Mitchell was under suspicion all the time till we got to Kobe. If it had not been for a quarrel amongst our crew—who were all Chinamen—that is a mystery that would never have been solved.

But the morning we got to Kobe a sailor came and said that he would tell us about the rabbits, and then it came out that the Chinese crew had *eaten* them.

3 *hutch* a cage or a small, enclosed space.
4 *poop* an enclosed space above the main deck and at the ship's rear.

All the ship laughed like anything when the Skipper and the Chief were not looking, but we could not laugh when they were looking because they were not amused at all.

5

Mitchell had to pay me back my money when we reached Kobe. The Skipper made him give it to me out of his draw.[5] Then we went ashore together to see the sights of Kobe.

Kobe is the pick of all the places I have visited. It has little winding streets all hung with lanterns, so that at night it looks like a party, and in the daytime you look away up to high hills. There are pretty little Japanese houses and pretty little Japanese girls, and there are cool breezes and the air smells sweet. I think if I could retire from life I would go and live at Kobe.

When we had berthed a man came aboard our ship giving out cards for a place called the Rose Bar. So Mitchell and I thought we would go and look at it. But it was not really a very good place when we reached it because the girls were quite old and wizened so we did not go in at all. But we went along the street in the dark looking for another place, and all the time an old Jap was following us. We walked for about an hour, and I was starting to feel worried because there he was still behind us, and every time we crossed the road he did, and every corner we turned he came round, and if I turned to tell him to clear off and mind his own business he would not take any notice, but would be lighting a cigarette. It is horrible to have a man following you even in a country where you know the detectives do not want you, so by this time I was starting to be alarmed.

But fortunately we were now opposite a nice-looking café so we thought we would not lose our dignity by starting to run away but would turn in here, and we had just turned in there and found our way to a table, when lo and behold that Jap had followed us inside.

But he did not come up to our table, or cause any disturbance. In fact he did not look at us at all. Instead he went straight to the counter and said something to the girl who was there and we saw her look at us and then she gave him some money. So we guessed that he was telling her that he had brought us to this café, and now he was getting his rake-off. It seems that they do that just the same as in America, so that was why he had been following us. We need not have been alarmed at all.

5 *draw* an account or line of credit.

6

It was a nice place that we had come to this time. The girls were quite young and they made you laugh like anything, and it really was not very expensive at all. But I was never a man to save my money so I did not go back to the ship at all that night, but stayed ashore in one of the hotels.

The next night I was on duty on the ship and I was very surprised when a sailor came to me and said that there was a woman at the gangway asking to see me, because I did not know any women in Kobe at all. But I went to the gangway to see if there could be a mistake and it seems there was not a mistake, because there was a woman all right, but she did not look like a woman. She was more like a child of 18. She looked sweet standing there by the gangway. She was as pretty as a painting, and she was wearing a kimono with one of those sashes round her waist that take half an hour to unwind. She was looking up at the ship in a funny little lost sort of way so that I had to run down and say, "Hullo," and then she smiled.

I did know her. I had met her in that café. She couldn't speak a word of English, but in the hotel I'd written down my name and the ship's name on a piece of card.

So here she was come down to look for me. I didn't know what to do with her, but the others said, "Fetch her on board." So we took her down to the engineers mess room and we sat her on the table and made her a cup of tea. She wouldn't drink milk in her tea, I remember. She was looking round at everything, and touching things and laughing. But she couldn't talk to us and we couldn't talk to her.

One of the chaps said, "Go on, fry her a haddock."[6] And everybody laughed. But we didn't do that. We gave her a cup of tea.

I took her up on deck in the end and gave her a little push down the gangway, and she looked back at me and smiled. But she went all right. She was a pretty little kid. She must have taken a fancy to me.

7

Well, after that you can understand that I was not in a mood for Mitchell. I was feeling quite uplifted, which is a new and a strange feeling for me. So I went away to my bed and did not think unpleasant

---

6 *haddock* a fish related to the common cod.

thoughts, but thought about my mother and when I was very young instead. But round about morning Mitchell woke me up coming in, only coming in is not quite the word because his legs were not answering properly and his face was in an awful mess with two eyes already going purple, and his clothes looked as if they just come through five years of war.

So I sat up and said, "Christ, what have you been doing?"

"I've been scrapping, Bob," he said, "I feel crook."[7] And he wanted me to give him the beer I had under the mattress.

But I did not see why I should give him my good beer, so I said it would be better if he had some rum out of the suitcase. "There's a bottle full there," I said.

But he shook his head at me. "It's all gone," he said. "I drank it."

A whole bottle of rum!

I never can tell you why I bothered with Mitchell. He did not seem to be impressed with his behaviour, however, but just sat dabbing at his black eyes so in the end I had to get up and open the beer for him.

You would think that scrap would have cured him, but you cannot cure a man who is as far-gone as Mitchell. The last night we were in Kobe he disgraced himself even worse. He was left in charge of the engines that run the four big dynamos that supply light and power for the winches on that kind of a ship. But when the Second came aboard late at night he found the winches stopped and all the lights out, and when he went below there was Mitchell asleep on the floor of the engine room with an empty bottle beside him. So you can imagine that he was not very pleased.

He did not do anything that night, however, being somewhat oiled himself, but in the morning he told the Chief.

The Chief, who did not like Mitchell, was not very pleased either, so he thought he would come along to look for Mitchell in our cabin. Mitchell was sleeping himself sober on a settee and I was still in my bunk, so we did not hear when the Chief knocked on the door. That made the Chief think that the door must be locked so he ran against it with his shoulder—like a battering ram. But the door was not locked at all, so the Chief came shooting into our cabin like something out of a gun. As he could not stop himself he went right across our cabin and it was not till his head hit the corner of our wardrobe that he was really held up.

7 *crook* unwell (Australian and New Zealand).

It was awful to see his face when he turned round after that, though it was not our fault that the door was not locked. Mitchell did not even know that the Chief had come to see him because he was still asleep, so it was quite a shock for him when the Chief picked him up in both hands and threw him across the cabin just as if he was a sack of oats.

But he looked up and blinked to show he was still living, and he still did not seem to know what all the fuss was about. You would have laughed if you could have seen the Chief trying to tell him, because he was so angry that he could not talk in words at all. I think he would have liked to kill Mitchell because his hands kept opening and closing and his neck was quite swelled up. But at last he seemed to remember the dignity of his position, for he swung round and went away, and the next thing we heard was that Mitchell had been put off watch.

He had to work on the deck then, but he did not suffer any chagrin. He just used to wait till the Skipper or the Chief was passing and then he would give them the raspberry.

By now I was the only man who would even speak to Mitchell. I think I must be too kind-hearted because I did not feel that I could desert him in his trouble so the best thing I could think of to do was to leave this ship and take him ashore at Shanghai.

But before we arrived in Shanghai he did a thing which nearly set me against him. It was over one of the Chinese greasers. He was a greaser on my watch and one night when I went down to the engine room there he was lying on the floor rolling and writhing as if he had been taken with a fit. So I ran to the engine-room telephone and called up to the bridge.

The Skipper and the Chief both came in answer to my call and by the time they arrived this greaser had passed right out. He was lying quite stiff with his eyes shut and the first thing the Chief said was that it was opium. But I said no I did not think it was opium because this boy was on my watch and I would know if he took opium, so we worked away and presently he came round.

Then they began to ask him what was really the matter. And it seemed he had taken a fit because he had no pay. He did not have any pay because when he was leaving New York he had a bottle of medicine under his pillow, and when the customs officers found it they said it must be analysed. So the analysis was sent across to meet the ship at 'Frisco and it said that there was opium in the medicine so he would have to be fined. But the amount of the fine was more than his pay for the voyage and no one had told him this until now when we were just due in Shanghai. He was having a fit because his wife that he had just married had been living on credit till he came home with his wages, and now that he had no wages he would have to go to gaol for the debts.

So you see there was really some reason for him to be worried and I felt very sorry because he just lay on the floor and kept moaning, "No money, no money," so I said, "Don't you worry, you have plenty money." And I went all round the ship and took a collection for him. But I was very unwise to put the collection in my cabin because it vanished out of there and it seems that Mitchell must have taken it. So I do not think you can say a good word for Mitchell over that because it really was a very mean thing to do.

8

The next morning we got to Shanghai and I told the Chief how I was planning that here I would leave the ship. So he said, "For God's sake take that Mitchell with you. They will kill him if you leave him here."

So I thought I had better take him. I never could be hard on Mitchell; though looking back I do not think that he has been a good influence on my life.

I was quite excited over my first look at China. I had a feeling I was going to do well there.

You go right up the river to Shanghai and tie up right in the town, but already before we had landed I had an experience which showed me the kind of land that I had come to. I was leaning on the rail beside the Chief watching them throw out the rope to fix our big hawser to. It had a lump of lead on the end and the man that threw it swung it crooked so that it caught a man in a junk on the head and he crumpled up and passed right out. All the crowd on the wharf started to laugh like anything when they saw the man pass right out. But though I have seen much violence in my life it did not strike me as being at all funny. I was very surprised to find that people could be so callous, but the Chief just said that that was what they were like in China. So I thought if that was China I would have to look out for myself.

9

When we were tied up, Mitchell and I were given £10 each advance because no one but the Chief knew we were going to desert the ship. But next day when we were properly oiled Mitchell said why not go back and see what everyone was doing, and like a mutt I said well why not, because I did not see how he had an ulterior motive.

And we would not be arrested because they did not know that we were deserters yet. So we went back to the ship. Everyone was on shore so I went down to the engine room to talk to the man that was on watch and for nearly an hour I did not see Mitchell at all. Then he came down to the engine room and he was laughing like anything and he seemed to want me to hurry up and come ashore. I still did not know what had happened but I ought to have had my suspicions now that I was so disillusioned with Mitchell, but I did not think a thing until we were right off the ship.

Then he brought out a camera and said, "Now let me take your photo!"

But I did not let him take my photo because I was too shocked. "Where did you get that camera?" I said to Mitchell, though I knew where he had got it because I recognized it as belonging to the kid electrician that we used to cheat at cards.

Mitchell did not mind me knowing. "I swiped it," he said, and he started to turn out his pockets and they were full of things that he had taken from everybody's kit.[8]

I am not what you would call a pernickety[9] man, but I must say I was ashamed of Mitchell over that. I was very sorry that we had gone back to the ship because now if I did not do anything, I would be an accessory after the fact. Yet I knew I could not influence Mitchell, so I just had to be worried over it being a very wrong thing to do, especially to shipmates.

I took the film out of the kid's camera though, and posted it back to him. I did not feel so bad after I had done that.

But Mitchell did not feel any remorse at all. He thought that he had been clever. So you see I am not really the same kind of man as Mitchell whatever people may say.

8 *kit* collection of personal items.
9 *pernickety* persnickety; fastidious.

10

I will now tell you about the time we had in Shanghai. You must remember we had never been in a Chinese city before. Because when I know all about the etiquette of a city I do not get thrown out of the best hotels very often, but in Shanghai we were thrown out the first night we were there. You see it seems that in a Chinese city you must not take your women into a hotel. It does not matter so long as no one sees you because then you can all pretend.

But we did not want to pretend, so we took our two Chinese girls up to our room in our hotel, but you should have seen all those old majors and colonels who were drinking highballs[10] in the lounge when we walked through on our way to the elevator. You would think they had never set eyes on a Chinese woman in their lives. So when we got up to our room the telephone was ringing already and we had to pack up our bags and go away from that hotel.

They gave us back our deposits and we took the girls with us so we were not greatly inconvenienced after all.

We found Shanghai a very nice city until we had spent all our money, but after that we did not like it as well.

I do not remember how long we were in Shanghai before we finished our money because while I have some money I am never in a condition to remember very much. But the time that I can now remember is after our money was spent and we seemed to have lost all our luggage and we were not feeling very well, but I think perhaps that was the strange food and the climate.

We had nothing left except the clothes we had been living in and the kid electrician's camera and Mitchell's gold watch. So we went and sold Mitchell's gold watch. But they are sharks in China and they would not give us much for it so by nighttime all our money was gone.

There we were in the Chinese part of the city,[11] with nothing to trade but a camera, and we had to have somewhere to sleep. We could

10 *highballs* a cocktail consisting of a liquor—particularly whisky—and water or soda, served in a tall glass and with ice.

11 *Chinese part of the city* While the notion of a Chinese neighborhood in a Chinese city may seem odd to today's reader, parts of Shanghai, named "concessions," were once under foreign control. After its defeat by the British at the end of the First Opium War in 1842, China signed the Treaty of Nanking, which allowed for unrestricted foreign commercial access to Shanghai and also ceded Hong Kong to Britain. Soon China signed similar agreements with other imperial powers. The British, French, Americans, and Japanese all held portions of Shanghai.

see the Chinese spreading their mats and lying on the pavement, but that does not tempt a man who has been used to a mattress, besides being rather public, so we thought we would ask at an eating house if they had a place where we could sleep.

The place that we chose in the end was the sort of place that a policeman would not like to go in by himself, but we had to go in places like that because now that we had lost our luggage and had been sleeping in our clothes we did not look respectable anymore.

It took us a long time to make the old chap who was in charge understand what we meant, but then he nodded very hard and took the camera and looked at it. Then he nodded some more and put it out of our reach.

After that we supposed that we could stay for the night. We were taken to a back room where there was a ladder going up through a hole in the ceiling. We did not like having our backs to him as we climbed up the ladder to the ceiling because you never can tell what a man is going to do you when you have your back to him, so we did not waste any time getting to the top of this ladder, and then we came into a loft that was as dark as pitch and that smelt so that you found yourself wishing you had been born without a sense of smell. The old Chinaman came up after us and put some sheets down on the floor. Then he asked us if we "wantem girl," but we said, "No, we wantem sleep," so he went away and left us in the dark, and we lay there thinking how easy it would be to make away with a man if he was fool enough to come in a place like this.

As soon as we began to warm the boards the bugs came out and crawled on us, and later, when they thought we were asleep, coolies came and crawled on us too, looking for our valuables and money. But they did not get anything because everything was gone. But we let them crawl and did not move when they felt in our pockets because you never know if a man will stick a knife in you if he is disturbed at such a moment.

I think if we had had any money we might not have been alive in the morning. It was dangerous to go in that place for no one in Shanghai would have missed us if we had disappeared.

We did not say anything about the people that had crawled on us when we climbed down the ladder in the morning but the old man who owned the house kept looking at us when we were not looking so I think he was wondering if we had found him out. He did not do anything to stop us leaving, however, nor did he offer us any breakfast though we were now very hungry.

We went out into the hot morning and we felt very limp indeed. All the Europeans we passed were dressed in white duck[12] or silk, whereas there was I in blue serge[13] and Mitchell in Harris[14] tweeds. What with lack of food and the heat we seemed to be disintegrating and running down on the pavement.

We felt also that our clothes made us conspicuous and a man does not like to be conspicuous in the state that we were then in.

It seemed that this day was some sort of flag day[15] in Shanghai, for all the smart women were out in the streets with little boxes seeing if they could wheedle some money out of the men. But of course we did not have any money.

When one of them came up to us we went to walk by as if we had not seen it, but I expect you know that if you try not to see a thing it always turns out to be the very thing that you see. However, in this case, the thing that we saw was so lucky that looking back I am inclined to think that it must have been an act of God.

For it said on the box that the flag day was in aid of "Distressed Foreign Seamen" and Mitchell and I did not see who that could be except us. So we grabbed each other by the arm and ran down the street past the lady so that we nearly knocked her down. I am afraid she was very surprised. But we were in such a hurry to get to this place where they had all the money to aid the distressed foreign seamen.

When we got to the place we were shown into a room where there was a sympathetic lady, not young, but nice. So we told her our sad story and she said we were two silly boys, but all the same the trouble we were in seemed to go right to her heart. So she took us to a room where there were silk shirts and socks and white trousers, and we were allowed to choose ones that would fit us. I also picked myself a topee[16] and Mitchell had a panama hat. When we were all dressed everyone came and looked at us, and then they gave us some money, and told us go to our consul.

So first we had some breakfast and then we went to look for the consul. But it was another official that we saw. His wife was a

12 *duck* a strong cloth, typically of cotton.
13 *serge* a strong, twilled fabric of wool and worsted, or solely worsted.
14 *Harris* a type of tweed produced on the Scottish island of Lewis and Harris.
15 *flag day* a day when donations to charity are sought in exchange for small flags.
16 *topee* pith helmet.

Eurasian and he started to tell us that he had two nice daughters. He seemed to think we would be welcome in his home, but we said it was work we were looking for so he sent us round to a few shipping firms.

In the end we came to a petroleum company who have their own boats taking stuff up to depots all along the Yangtse Kiang as well as coastal boats going north to Manchuria and south to Hong Kong.

It was a very aristocratic man that we saw when we went to this office. He was the kind of man that wears a monocle all the time. He was very nice to us though, so we thought perhaps it was just the way he had been brought up. He was an R.N.R.[17]

He said we had been very foolish and then he looked at our credentials and at last he said he thought he could find me a job. He was not so sure about Mitchell, though, because you see Mitchell is not a qualified engineer. But I did not see how I could take a job and leave my friend stranded in Shanghai so I said I would let him know in 24 hours.

Then Mitchell and I went along to the bar at the Swan where they have "Red" Watson, the pugilist who was bouncer, and after we had had a drink and talked we said that we would stick together, so I got a man to ring the commander at the company's office and say that I was sorry but I could not take a job there after all.

So after that Mitchell and I spent our time playing at billiards. Later in the day there was a 'phone call for Mitchell and when he came back his whole face was wreathed in smiles.

So I asked him if he had been left a fortune, but it seems that all that had happened was that he had been given a job.

"I have a job as an engineer," he said.

"Who have you got it with?" I asked, and you will admit that I had grounds for being upset when he told me the job was with the same company who had hired me.

I lifted off the hand that he had put on my shoulder because I would not deign to have him touch me, and I said with icy precision, "So you are going to take it, after me turning one down for you?"

"Aw, look!" said Mitchell, "I will give you half me wages."

But I did not want half his wages. I was once more greatly disillusioned with Mitchell. I did not have a word to say to him but went back to the bar and had another whisky.

17 *R.N.R.* Royal Naval Reserve. A corps of civilians and retired Royal Navy sailors that aid the regular force whenever necessary.

Next day, however, I thought it would not do any harm to go down the river with him to have a look at his ship. I do not think that there is any sense in a man cutting off his nose to spite his face, and though I was still disillusioned with Mitchell I was quite curious to have a look at his ship.

What happened on that visit proves that I am right in my contention, for I never would have met the Chief, who helped me, if I had borne a grudge against Mitchell and refused to look at his ship.

This ship was called the *Ma-a-Haing* and the man that was the Chief Engineer was a very nice fellow. When he heard my name he said that he knew all about me, because it seems how people had been talking about me turning down a good job in order to stand by my pal.

"Why do you carry that fellow on your back?" he said to me, so seeing how Mitchell could not hear, I explained what we had agreed and how I had now been disillusioned about Mitchell. So he asked me would I take a job if I was offered one now.

When I said I would he promised he would 'phone the commander, and it was because I met that Chief on the *Ma-a-Haing* that I came to be made a supernumerary[18] chief engineer. It was on her sister ship the *Ho-a-Haing* which was a river boat carrying paraffin[19] between Ichang[20] and Chungking[21] on the Yangtse Kiang, but at present she was down in Shanghai, anchored off the Woosoo Forts.[22]

The day after I got that job I had to go and see the commander. He had to tell me about my duties which I found would not be anything unless the Chief was taken sick. And for staying on that ship and not doing any duties I was to be given double pay. Double pay started when we got beyond Ichang and it was to be £62 10s. 0d. a month. It seemed to me like the kind of job you have dreams about after many whiskies but I never made such a big mistake in my life.

After all a business firm does not give a man double pay for nothing. This was first brought to my knowledge when I saw the *Ho-a-Haing*

18 *supernumerary* above the typical or designated number.
19 *paraffin* kerosene.
20 *Ichang* also known as Yichang, a city in the east-central province of Hubei.
21 *Chungking* also known as Chongqing or Ch'ung-ch'ing. A city located the Yangtze in the southwestern province of Sichuan. China's capital from 1937–1946.
22 *Woosoo Forts* Moore misspells "Wusong"; most sources refer to a single "Fort." The British captured it in June 1842 during the First Opium War.

in the river. She had armour plating six feet high all round her decks, and when I asked what it was for, I was told that if they did not have that they would never keep enough men alive to get the ship to her destination.

So then I saw I was not being paid just for nothing after all. It seemed that the trouble was Chinese bandits.

But at first when I got the job I did not think about bandits at all. I got an advance on my pay and I went and bought another topee and several white suits. I thought that now as I was a supernumerary chief engineer I would have to dress in keeping with my position.

I did not have to join the ship until midnight so I went to have a few last drinks before saying good-bye to Shanghai. I had to be at the Bund[23] at midnight for the launch that was to take me to the ship and when I got there I was not fully oiled, but I had a couple of bottles of whisky in my pocket as I thought I would need them to see me through till morning. But if I had known more about the ships on the Chinese rivers I would not have wasted my money on that extra whisky because I could get everything I wanted and only had to pay 4s. 6d. a bottle.

But at this time I did not know anything of the facilities of Chinese travel.

11

It was a big launch that was waiting for me. There was a yellow flag flying from it and when we started down the river I went and sat in the wheelhouse with the Chinese captain. I did not know at this time that the way you must treat a Chinaman is to give him a kick in the pants, so I thought they were just like other human beings. But it seems you could not have any prestige in China if you treated a Chinaman like a human being, so when I started to give the captain in the wheelhouse drinks out of my whisky bottle I was really breaking a very serious rule.

But at the time I did not know this and the Chinaman did not think to tell me so it was not till later that I learned what a mistake I had made.

It was nine miles down the river to the Forts and all the way the captain and I were drinking out of my whisky bottle. When we finished one we started on the other and after that I was giving him

23 *Bund* an embankment and boulevard along the west shore of the Huangpu River in Shanghai.

dollar bills. He was laughing like anything so I think he was quite happy and the launch seemed to be trying to write her name on the river. But we did not mind about that as so far we had not hit anything, though when we came to the *Ho-a-Haing* we experienced some little difficulty in getting alongside.

It is a good thing it was a river boat, because I would not like to have had to climb a ladder, but this boat had a lower deck so close to the water that you could step right on it so I was all right.

The Chief Steward, who was a Chinaman, came up when he heard me arriving and he picked up my bags and took me down to my cabin. But it was not a cabin at all, it was really a stateroom. There was a carpet on the floor and a bed instead of a bunk, and armchairs, and a settee, and a desk, and a wardrobe. In fact there was just one thing that we needed and that was some shelves with holes in to hold all my bottles. So the Chief Steward said he would see to it, and when he had gone away and left me to myself I felt there was not really any more to ask of life.

But I did not have much time for thinking because soon he was back again and this time he said that the Chief would like to see me, but when I went up on deck to see the Chief there he was stretched out like a dead man. But he was not really dead—only drunk.

It worried me, however, to think about what this would do to his prestige before all the Chinamen, so I thought we should carry him below and hide him in his cabin. He was a big red-faced fellow and he weighed so much that I could not lift him alone, but one of the Chinamen helped me and we got him down to his bed. Then I sent the Chinaman away so that the prestige of the Chief should not suffer anymore, and when we were alone he opened one eye and looked at me and then he said, "There will be a grand crowd at the Central Station tonight." At first I did not know what he meant, but after all I am also a Scotsman, so presently it came to me that this was the month of July and that it was about the time of the Glasgow Fair[24] holiday, so I guessed that must be what he meant, for I could tell by his voice that he belonged to Glasgow. His name was Martin.

---

24 *Glasgow Fair* Falling on the second Monday in July, the Fair has been an important part of Glasgow life since the late 12th century. Originally a market for the sale of cattle and horses and the hiring of staff, in the 19th century it began to attract entertainment such as circuses, rides, and shows. Later it marked the start of Fair Fortnight, when those with the means would go "doon the watter" to resort towns on the Firth of Clyde. (See *http://www .scotland-quide.co.uk* and *http://www.theglasgowstory.com*)

"You're frae Glasga'?" he asked. And then he started to cry. He was one of those fellows who always start to cry when they are oiled.

"Oh, I wish I was in Glasga'," he said. "Tell me, what is it like in Glasga' now?"

But I said I had just come from the States, so then he began to cry more because he said he was like that too and that he had not seen his old home for 20 years.

So I sat beside him and tried to stop him crying, and thought how this was a funny beginning for a job as supernumerary chief engineer.

After a while he cheered up and said we would have a little drink for old times' sake, so he sat up and clapped his hands, and a lot of Chinamen came running. That was the first time I saw the way they wait on you in China. He ordered them to bring drinks and then he lay down again. I asked him would they do that for me and he said I must boot them if they didn't. So I saw that I was going to enjoy myself while I was aboard the *Ho-a-Haing*.

When Martin went to sleep I returned to my cabin, but I did not go to sleep because Martin had now roused memories of Glasgow, so I thought I would write a letter home, and I went to ring the bell for the Steward. Then I thought I would clap my hands like Martin. But I had never done that before so in the end I decided that after all I would ring the bell. It was between two and three in the morning but Chinamen seem to stay on duty all the time, so when I had asked him about the mails I wrote a letter to my mother and then I went to sleep.

But I had only just gone to sleep when someone was shaking my shoulder, and I sat up and there was Martin. He had a bottle in one hand and he was crying like anything. So he sat down beside me and made me stay awake and talk.

By five or six it was light and he wanted me to dress and come ashore. He said we wouldn't sail till next day as the Captain had not come aboard, so in the end he persuaded me to get out of bed.

We had to go ashore in a sampan[25] because there were no motorboats, and then Martin said he would take me to his bowling club. It was only seven o'clock, but places open early in the East, only I kept being worried in case the Captain came back and found us missing, so I did not enjoy the bowling club and as soon as I could I slipped away and left Martin, but the Captain had still not returned when I arrived at the ship.

25 *sampan* a small, flat-bottomed Chinese boat typically propelled with two short oars.

CHAPTER XI

1

WHEN I was on the *Ho-a-Haing* I had two Chinese servants. They would do everything I told them, even put my clothes on—down to my shoes and socks. One of them would curl up like a dog and sleep on the mat across my door. It is no wonder that a man back in England starts to feel the call of the East.

There was a barber to shave and do your hair. He did not get any wages but all you had to pay him was one Chinese dollar (about 1/2)[1] a month. He was supposed to make a lot of extra money out of smuggling opium. We had a Chinese crew of 40. Most of them used to make money out of smuggling. When it was not opium it was salt. Salt is the only thing the poorest peasants up the river can buy. They live on the rice they grow and have practically no money. But if they do not have some salt with the rice they catch some disease and die. It is very hard to get money out of poor Chinese peasants, but the government is always wanting money, and since the peasants must have rice, they thought the best way to get some would be to put a tax on the salt. But the peasants get out of it every way they can, and that is why the sailors smuggle salt up the river to them.

All of our crew was Chinese. They slept on mats on the fo'c'sle.[2] Then there were the Chinese engineers and stewards. They slept aft. There were four white men, counting me. The other three were Martin, the Chief; old Taffy, the Mate, who was a Welshman with a little organ that he used to play hymns on; and the Captain, who was an Englishman that I did not get on with very well. Martin did not like the Captain either. He had been much longer on the river and he

---

1 *one Chinese dollar (about 1/2)* From its establishment in 1910 until 1935, the value of the Chinese dollar, known as the Yuan Shin Kai, was equivalent to the fluctuating value of little under an ounce of silver. For amounts of less than a pound sterling, sometimes a slash was used to separate shilling and pence values: "1/2" signifies one shilling, two pence.

2 *fo'c'sle* a variation of "forecastle"; the forward part of a merchant ship where the crew's quarters are located.

would not take much notice of anything the Captain said. But Martin was a good engineer so the Captain did not quarrel with him.

The *Ho-a-Haing* was a ship on which the company had spared no effort. We had a refrigerator and electric fans and hot baths. Our job was to take over paraffin that the big ships (like the one Mitchell had been put on) brought up as far as Ichang, and deliver it to depots along the Middle River. The Middle River is between Ichang and Chungking, so we did not come down to Hankow[3] and Shanghai very often.

It was morning when we started off. There were three Chinese pilots to get us away. These men have spent all their lives learning the river, but it seems that you can never be sure of the Yangtse Kiang because there is a current which keeps moving the bed somewhere different all the time. There are bell buoys, but they are not always right because sometimes the bed has shifted before anyone has found out and moved them, so you will see that the Chinese pilots have to be pretty sharp.

They work one at a time, standing by a coolie on a platform that is slung out over the water. The coolie poles the depth all the time and the pilot keeps signalling the steersman with a finger. You hear him calling in a sing-song voice all the time.

It is a funny thing about Chinamen, but they do not seem to be able to work without singing. In the towns the coolies call "Yo-he-ho" all the time they pass backwards and forwards with cargo. Even if they work all through the night they make it. You hear it from your hotel or from your ship, if you are tied up close.

"Yo-he-ho," they call, "Yo-he-ho." It is like the voice of China, only you do not like the voice of China when it comes through the window and keeps you awake at night.

In the daytime it is better. The coolies pulling junks up the river on a towrope call, and the ones floating on the junks have a kind of song too. You find that you do not forget it. I dream I still hear it sometimes.

2

When you first leave Shanghai for Ichang the country that you go through is flat. When you walk around the decks and look through holes in the armour plating, you do not see anything but maize and rice fields and yellow water. There are villages set in the rice fields made of huts built of mud and bamboo.

3 *Hankow* formerly a city in east-central China. It was merged with Hanyang and Wuchang to form Wuhan, the capital of Hubei province.

When the kids see you coming they run down to the water and jump up and down and shout to make you look at them. If you throw them your empty bottles they will dive for them.

When you get farther up where all the land is not cultivated you come to the tiger grass.[4] You can hide a whole army in tiger grass. It grows up to eight feet high.

There are not many bandits on the lower reaches of the river so you do not risk your life every time you take a breath of air. Some people think that this is due to the Chinese gunboats, but as matter of fact, when you get to know about things you find that the Chinese gunboats are only there for show. They steam up and down showing all their guns of course, but they never shoot at the bandits because they have no shells to shoot with. The government will not let them have any because they might sell them to the bandits. So you see what I mean when I say that the guns are only there for show.

It is the Japanese, American, and British gunboats that really keep down the bandits. But even they are not much good after you pass Hankow.

Our ship had machine guns and steam hoses, so we did not really need any gunboats to do our fighting for us.

There is quite a lot of traffic low down on the Yangtse Kiang. You pass junks that are being hauled on a rope by coolies. Each junk has a big eye painted on either side of the prow. The coolies think that this will keep away evil spirits.

A few passenger boats go up as far as Hankow. Then there are the gunboats and a few oil ships.

Nearly all the time at the beginning you are passing some kind of ship. When you pass a ship you do not semaphore as you do when you are out at sea, but you write up on a blackboard that they can see from your deck any message that you want them to know. Some times you will read on a blackboard that there is shooting up the river. It is useful to have this warning because then you know when you must look out.

We did not strike any shooting on the lower side of Hankow.

3

When we got to Hankow I put on a white suit and a topee and went ashore. It is really quite a big place. There is a Roman Catholic hospital and quite a lot of Europeans. When you walk through the

4 *tiger grass* a relatively short fan palm.

streets it is almost like a modern city. It is the only place you pass like this after you have left Shanghai.

But when you have been ashore a while you realize that it is not really like a modern city at all because underneath the veneer of civilization you keep coming on signs of the immemorial and unchanging East. Here is something that happened when I was passing a vacant allotment.

It was just like a big allotment that you might see in a city in the States. There was a high hoarding across the front and scaffolding behind. You would not have thought anything about it except that here were some building sites for auction, if it had not been for a very funny smell. And then if you looked you found the smell was coming from behind the hoarding, and there were a lot of coffins stacked there and there were dead men in them, only they had been dead a long time, and the rain had soaked on the wood, and some of the bottoms had fallen out, and everything was coming through. So I thought, "Well, they cannot be very efficient in China." But when I asked someone about it they said they were put there on purpose because it is part of their religion not to bury a person till one year after he is dead.

So it seemed to me after that that China is a very funny country. But I did not know what a funny country it really was till after I had seen a Chinese funeral. It seemed to be all the dead people that I was meeting the first time that I was ashore in Hankow. I suppose it is true how they say it never rains but it pours, but perhaps afterwards I got so used to seeing dead people that I did not notice them anymore.

However, with regard to the funeral, it came to me with a shock to realize what it really was. For they made such a noise and they got so excited that they did not seem to be showing respect for the dead at all.

I could hear this funeral coming before I could see it, and there was noise of people calling out, and a lot of Chinese whistles going, and a band was playing "Tipperary"[5] and "John Brown's Body,"[6] and then some squealing Chinese music. You never would have thought they were escorting a body to the grave.

---

5 *"Tipperary"* "It's a Long Way to Tipperary," a vaudeville song that gained enormous popularity among troops on both sides during World War I.
6 *"John Brown's Body"* also known as "The Battle Hymn of the Republic." A popular song among Union soldiers and their supporters during the U.S. Civil War.

I came round a corner and there they were marching along, with some of them calling out and some of them shedding tears and throwing themselves about as they walked. In the middle there was the band and then there was a bamboo cart. There was a big box in the cart cut out of a whole tree trunk and this box was covered with leaves. More people walked behind the cart and they were calling out too. I had to ask a European who was passing before I found out that this was a funeral.

When I went back to the ship I told them about the funeral and how I had seen the dead bodies, and the Chief said, "Oh, that is nothing. When you get farther up the river you will see how life is cheap in China. You will see hundreds of bodies floating every day on the river. The river police fish them out and every station is full of them, but no one comes to claim them so they have to be buried as unknown." I thought that he was telling me a story but after we had left Hankow I saw with my own eyes. You can tell a dead woman in the water because she floats face upwards. The men float face down.

The day we left Hankow the Chief called out to me, "Come over here and I will show you something," so I went to the side of the ship and he pointed to a place where the end of a cobbled street ran down into the water. There was a dog standing there dragging at a sort of bundle that had floated against the side. He would get it partway out and then the wash of the river would send it back again. Then he would catch it again and tug, and give a low growl as he tugged at it. People were passing on the bank but no one seemed to take any notice.

"Have a good look," said Martin, "and see what that bundle is."

It was a dead girl!

I did not feel very well after seeing that sight with the dog, so I think we will pass on to pleasanter things.

It is a long way from Hankow to Ichang and the biggest place you pass on the way is a town that is called Shasi.[7] This is a rebel town where you will often meet trouble, but the first time we passed there everything was quite quiet. It is built mostly of bamboo huts and they fly a red flag all the time, so you see they mean to let you know that they are very defiant. One day when we were near Shasi we met the rebel army on the march and I think I will tell you what they looked like because I am sure that it will make you laugh.

At this time that we saw them they were marching on the bank of the river and they were in single file so that they stood out against

---

7 *Shasi* also known as Sha-shih; city in south Hubei.

the sky. They had on khaki uniforms and full army equipment, but as it was a hot day every one of them had a parasol up to keep the sun off!

It seemed to me very funny to see soldiers using parasols but they do not appear to think anything of it in China.

Every night when we were on the Yangtse Kiang we used to tie up to a boulder. Our name is painted in white on the ones where we used to tie up so that you can tell them each time. All up the Yangtse River for fifteen hundred miles you will see boulders with "Ho-a-Haing" painted on them.

You have to tie up at night because the river is unsafe to navigate when you cannot see. We used to haul in to the bank and put a steel hawser round a boulder. Then we would all go to bed, but the Chinese crew would keep watch, because it is when you are tied up to the bank at night that the bandits come and try to board you.

But we were not attacked that first time till after we passed Ichang. It took us 24 days altogether to get up the river to Ichang because we had the current against us all the time.

After Hankow we did not pass nearly so much traffic. There were no passenger ships and not so many junks.

There were fewer villages and you could see they were not used to white men because one night when we tied up outside a village all the people came down to the bank to stare at us, but I was the one they stared at most, and I could not think what was the matter, because though I am not unattractive to look at I had not thought before that I was conspicuous at all. But as I kept leaning on the rail there was no doubt that this time I was the centre of attraction. Some of them were giggling and some were pointing and some of the kids looked quite frightened.

"What is wrong with me?" I said to Taffy.

So he laughed and said, "The sun is on your hair," and as I could not see whatever he meant by that he explained that it seemed to be the very first time the people from this village had ever set eyes on a blond!

So naturally I was very surprised, but I was glad it was no worse.

4

When we arrived in Ichang we had started on our real job, because from here we had to carry paraffin to the unknown interior of China. No one is allowed on the river beyond Ichang unless they have important business, because it really is not safe.

It was from here that our pay doubled and the insurance on our boat stopped. We had to leave all our clothes except one change of things at Ichang, so you really began to feel as if you were going into war.

I will not say I was nervous, but as we had to be there for some days loading paraffin, Taffy and Martin and I thought that we would go to church.

Besides the oil installation manager and his clerk there were no white people in Ichang except the missionary and his wife who had the church.

Now it may make you laugh to think of me being friends with missionaries, but as a matter of fact Dr. Scott[8] and his wife were very nice people. I do not expect they could help being missionaries and I always think it is very narrow for a man to be prejudiced about his friends.

I do not remember very much about the service that we went to because I do not think we can have been quite sober, but when we were coming out the missionary was standing at the door and he shook us all by the hand and asked us to come to his house so that we could have a cup of tea.

He was really very nice for a missionary because he had a bottle of whisky and he did not seem to want to drink very much of it himself. He had a big Alsatian too, but he told us how he was afraid that now he would have to shoot it because only that morning he had found it tasting human flesh.

I could not imagine where a dog would get human flesh because I did not think that they were cannibals even in China, so I asked Dr. Scott where it was that his dog had got it and he said it was because when

8 *Dr. Scott* Rev. Dr. Forbes Scott Tocher (1885–1973). An ordained Missionary of the Church of Scotland, he served in Ichang from 1909 until 1915. Tocher fought with the Royal Field Artillery from 1916 to 1919 during World War I, and received the Military Cross. He returned to Ichang to continue his missionary work in 1920. In 1927 he successfully negotiated with Yangtze pirates for the release of a captain who had been abducted from his ship near Ichang. For this effort, in 1928 he was made a Commander of the Order of the British Empire and an Honorary Doctor of Divinity by Aberdeen University six years later. Tocher was interned by the Japanese in Shanghai beginning in 1940. After the war he continued his work in Ichang for three more years. In 1948 he returned to Great Britain to serve as the minister of the parish of Botriphnie, Banffshire in northeastern Scotland. Tocher retired in 1955. His first wife, Johanna, the first woman to serve as a lecturer at a Scottish university, passed away in 1957. Dr. Tocher married Helen Dickie Wilson, with whom he had been interned in Shanghai, in 1965. (See *http://www.botriphnie.org.uk/ministers.htm* and *http://www.mundus.ac.uk/cats/4/1082.htm*)

the Chinese are poor they did not bury their dead very deep.

"Sometimes," he said, "stillborn children are just left lying on the ground, other times they scrape a little hole and just cover a body over. But the dogs find where they are and dig them out."

He said he had got up that morning and found his dog with something on the mat and when he looked he saw it was the thighbone of a child.

So now he would have to shoot his dog in case it should become dangerous through having tasted human flesh.

"The Chinese do not like being so poor that they cannot bury their children," Dr. Scott said to us. "Have you noticed how the children nearly all have silver bangles on their arms? Well, their parents start to put those on as soon as the children are born. They must never take them off and rich children will have dozens. Poor coolies will go hungry so that their children can have a few bangles. You would wonder why they think decoration is so important, but it is not really decoration—it is the price of their funeral!"

Dr. Scott was a very interesting man and he told us a lot of things until it was time for supper. Then his wife called us and we went into the other room, and on the table there was a real fresh salad.

"Don't be afraid of the salad," Mrs. Scott said to us, "it is quite all right because it has been grown in our own garden."

Now being new to China I did not know what she meant, but Martin leaned over and explained how you must not eat a salad in China because the Chinese who do the gardening do not have our ideas about the kind of things that you cannot use for manure.

You see it seems that they are so poor in the interior of China that they do not have any animals to make manure for them, and they cannot afford to buy artificial fertilizer, so they use the only kind they can get, but even that is expensive because there are people in the interior who have made a "corner" in it. They have a monopoly of all the public conveniences. It is just like the stock market, only here it is not wheat or cotton or pepper, but the result is the same because the people who own the monopoly have all the supplies and you cannot get any for your garden except through them. A man who has a monopoly like that in China is set up for life because there is nothing to stop him making people pay through the nose.

After I had heard about this I knew what it was that the peasants store in ditches by their fields in China, and I used to be very careful when I was out walking, because when it has been there some time a mould grows on it and hides it, and if you do not look where you are going you will have a catastrophe.

When Martin had finished explaining to me about the salad Mrs. Scott gave us all a helping and then she told a story that made us laugh very much. I will tell you this story because as Mrs. Scott was a missionary's wife I am sure she would not tell one that was not sufficiently refined.

Well, it seems that when Dr. and Mrs. Scott first came to live in Ichang they started a vegetable garden and they were very careful to tell their Chinese gardener that he must not use any of the local manure on the plants. So he said he would be very careful and they gave him some superphosphates. He started to grow them most beautiful tomato and lettuce but the superphosphate seemed to last for a long time. So one day Dr. Scott went down to see what was happening and he nearly fainted when he found the Chinese gardener had been using the wrong kind of manure all the time.

So he shouted, "What for you do this, when I tell you not to use the town manure?"

And the old gardener shouted back, "That all right. You no worry. *Quite* all right. It not town manure—it your own!"

So Mrs. Scott said that after that they got a different gardener.

5

After we had loaded up our paraffin we pulled out from Ichang and the next place that we made for was Chungking. Chungking is situated in a very wild part of China and to get there you have to go through the Yangtse Kiang Gorges.[9] These gorges are very dangerous but also very beautiful to see. They are made by a mountain range blocking the way of the river, and after a lot of trouble the river has cut through. In between each gorge there are a lot of dangerous rapids so you have to keep your wits about you when you are going up.

You will be interested for me to tell you what these gorges look like because if you are an ordinary traveller you are not allowed to go up them. Only one oil boat besides ours was allowed up, so I am really one of the very few white men who have seen this wonderful sight.

9 *Yangtse Kiang Gorges* the site of the Three Gorges Dam, a $30 billion project. It is the world's largest hydroelectric dam, and has displaced over 1.5 million people. By raising the Yangtze's water level, the project submerged adjacent cities and towns, including significant archeological sites, changing the landscape forever.

It is not very far from Ichang to Chungking but the current is so strong that it used to take us four days to get there, but when we were coming back and the current was with us we could do it in 24 hours.

I was very much afraid the first time we went through the Gorges, not that I am a nervous man, but really if you did not know you never would expect to come out the other side alive. I do not like the dark much either, and when you come into the Gorges the shadow is so dark and the walls are so high and cold that you find yourself starting to shiver though you do not know quite what for.

You look away up where the bright sky is like a strip of blue ribbon stretched across the top of the gorge. You would not feel so bad if there was more noise. But the water runs like oil in here, though it makes enough noise in the rapids. When you first look at the water it seems to be quite still and you do not realize how the current has caught hold of you till you look at the gauge and see you are on "Full Steam Ahead"—yet the boat is scarcely moving! Sometimes it is not moving at all. You just hear the current sucking a bit, that is all.

You cannot walk about and take in the scenery when you are in one of these Gorges because if you do someone may drop a rock on you. There are people who live in caves up on the rim of the Gorges and they do not like to have visitors so they roll down rocks on them. Sometimes if a rock is big enough it will wreck your ship like a bomb. But we did not actually get wrecked in the Yangtse Kiang Gorges. I used to ride on the bridge which was covered with armour plating specially to keep off the rocks, and all the crew had orders not to show themselves but to keep below.

We would go slowly through a gorge with the water boiling at our bow, and then we would come to a part where the gorge widened and you could see paths like crooked ribbons, away up. These are tracks the coolies make who pull junks through these gorges.

You can train the glasses[10] on them when there is enough light. They are not much bigger than flies and they crawl along in single file. They are harnessed together with a bamboo hawser. They do not wear any clothes except just a loincloth. Sometimes while you are watching one will lose his footing and fall. You will see his yellow body turning over and over as it falls down the face of the rock and you hope it will not hit the ship because that would make

10 *train the glasses* aim the binoculars.

such a mess, but it generally falls in the water and after that you do not see it anymore. It does not rise because of the current, but is carried down to where the river widens and there it floats and the scavenger hawks get it. You are not supposed to shoot at scavenger hawks because they save the police a lot of trouble. They take out the heavy part of the intestines in a body, so that it sinks to the bottom and then there is no bother about having to fish it out and bury it. You will always see a lot of scavenger hawks flying above the Yangtse Kiang.

The coolies up the gorge do not even notice when one of them falls in the water. It does not occur to them to stop, or even look round.

6

After your first gorge you are glad to run out into daylight though you plunge right into the rapids and they do not give you much peace.

You cannot hear yourself speak when you are right in the rapids and the boat has hard work to keep going because really it is travelling uphill. The water comes boiling down on top of you and sometimes the decks are all covered and the way she is rolling and pitching you think that each minute she will tear out her bottom on a boulder. These boulders keep sticking out of the water and you cannot steer her clear of them because of the way she is pitching, so it seems to be mostly luck. Really going through those rapids is a very trying time.

Sometimes the current is so strong that she stands there pitching and tossing and will not go forward at all. Once we were stuck in a rapid till the Captain got 300 coolies to dig in stakes to rig a wind-lass[11] for a steel hawser off the bank. That gave us the extra pull that beat the current. Otherwise we would never have got through.

It was worse that time because there had been floods upstream. Generally we would be shaken all to pieces but we did not actually get stuck.

After the roar of a rapid you would plunge into another silent gorge. Those gorges always made me shiver, they were so dark and cold.

We used to battle like that for four days, making for Chungking. Every night we would tie up in slack water and get our breath for the next day.

11 *windlass* a hoisting machine.

The open hills between the gorges are full of wild orange groves. We tied up in a place like that after coming through the worst gorge.

7

This gorge is so high and steep that the walls lean in and nearly meet. The only light you can see up above is a tiny wavy line like a piece of cotton thread. It's more like a cave than a gorge. The Captain rings a bell as soon as you are in this gorge, and that means "Look out for rocks" so all the crew drop on their faces, because here you are a helpless target if the hill men fancy to attack you. Generally the bell is rung when you must be warned of shooting, but in this gorge rocks would be worse than guns.

It only lasts 20 minutes, but that is quite long enough. The boat strains as if it was hurrying to get out too, but of course it is really the current that gives you that impression.

There is a village just past this gorge, and when you come out into the light and draw your breath again because no one has dropped a rock on you, you are glad to tie up beside it for a while.

This village has some bamboo huts and a pagoda on a rise.[12] The first time we tied up there Johnny, our cook, was just getting ready to go ashore and buy some eggs and chickens when a funny old man came down from the village and asked to come aboard.

He was a very old man because his hair was quite grey, and he had a pigtail coiled round his head. He had on a blue jacket and trousers just like all Chinese peasants, but it seems he was really more than a peasant because he had come to ask for "cumshaw"[13] which is money, and he said if he had some cumshaw he would make all the "bad men" keep away from our ship.

But Martin was up on deck when this old man was asking for cumshaw and it seems that he recognized him for when he had given me a wink he said something in Chinese, and the old man stopped what he was saying and did not know what to do next. When Martin saw that he started laughing, and at that the old man left off[14] looking upset and started laughing too. And when he laughed he went on laughing till you would not think he had ever heard a joke before.

12 *rise* hilltop.
13 *cumshaw* According to *Webster's Ninth New Collegiate Dictionary*, its etymon is "ka sia," Amoy Chinese for "*grateful thanks* (a phrase used by beggars)." The *Ninth* defines cumshaw as "present, gratuity."
14 *left off* ceased.

So I said to Martin, "What is all the fun about?" And Martin said, "It is this old chap, the way he keeps on asking for cumshaw. Do you know the first time a British gunboat anchored in this village he came down, asked for cumshaw to keep the bad men away from them! So the skipper said to take him along and show him the six-inch gun. But he had not seen a six-inch gun so he did not know what it was, and he took out his knife and started scraping it to see what it was made of, so they thought they would fire it for him.

"They took aim at a big piece of rock and blew it right out of the hill. They meant to impress the old chap, but he did not wait to be impressed. As soon as he heard the bang he dived overboard with all his clothes on."

But now he was laughing like anything, so it seems they can see a joke even in the middle of China. So we thought we could give him some cumshaw as a mark of appreciation.

Now that we had so much protection we thought it would be safe to go ashore, so Taffy and Martin and I went with Chinese No. 1.

When I went ashore this time was the first time I tasted samshui, which is a spirit that the Chinese make out of rice, and the only explanation I can give of the events that then happened is that Chinese samshui is really extremely strong.

I had had several drinks of samshui by the time we came to the pagoda, but I did not really feel as if anything was the matter. In case you do not know, a pagoda is a Chinese temple, but it is narrow with a lot of storeys, so it is also used for a lookout tower.

The ground floor is where they keep the gods, and as there are not any windows and only a small door you cannot see very much when first you go inside. The floor space in this pagoda was the size of a small house and it was covered with poppy seeds that were being dried for opium. An old priest like a mummy was sitting looking at the seeds.

He did not move when we came in but we could feel his eyes upon us.

When our eyes got so that they could see we noticed four porcelain idols sitting around the walls. One was very large, more than life-size, but the others were smaller. One was so small that you could put him under your coat.

When you come into a pagoda you throw coppers[15] at the gods' feet and then the priest comes to life and shuffles forward and lights bunches of incense sticks in jars. When Martin threw down a couple of silver dollars instead of just coppers the priest was so impressed

15 *coppers* coins.

that he could hardly light the sticks in the midst of his excitement, so that will show you how poor they are, because two silver dollars is only half a crown.[16] But Martin said that was enough to feed two of them for a month, so I suppose it would seem a lot of money if you looked at it in that way.

It made me feel like a millionaire to think of them being so poor and I thought, "Well, probably I could buy up this whole pagoda for under a week's pay." So I went to where there were some coffins cut from logs stacked against the wall and I thought that just for a start I would make him a bid for one, but I thought he was rather a shark when he said it would cost a hundred dollars, because what would I do with a heavy log coffin that I was only buying for charity? So I decided I would not have it after all.

I began to feel annoyed at this, however, because it had been pleasant to feel that I could buy the place up if I liked. I took out the cigarette I was smoking and stuck it on the end of my stick and went to put it in the god's mouth . . . just to show that I was not impressed. But I will not do that when I am in a pagoda again because it nearly cost me my life.

This priest did not seem to be able to see a joke for he pulled out a knife and jumped at me, and if Martin had not stopped him he would have cut my throat.

It was not a pleasant incident and there would have been more trouble, only Martin explained that I had been drinking samshui, so after that he put down the knife and said he would not cut my throat, but he did not look at me anymore.

So I thought if he was like that I would show him who he was dealing with, and I swiped the little god and put it under my coat.

Nobody saw me take it and as we were walking down the hill I kept thinking how some day I would sell it at Christie's for a lot of money, for anybody could see it was hundreds of years old.

The people in the village did not notice anything strange though if you had looked closely you could see the bulge of my coat.

But they might have thought that was my figure, only once when a dog nipped my ankle, and I reached out to hit it with my stick there was nearly an awkward moment, because I forgot about the god, and when I took my arm away I had just time to clutch myself again before it fell to the ground. So after that narrow squeak I began to think I would like to go straight back to the ship.

16 *crown* a coin, typically of silver, worth five shillings.

But it seems this was not to be, for as we turned down the hill to where the ship was tied up a commotion started back by the pagoda, and all the others were puzzled, but I could have told them what it was. You could see the priest running down the hill waving his arms above his head, and there was yelling and wailing and dogs barking and the noise spread and spread.

I began to be rather upset, because I saw there was going to be trouble. I had not thought they would make such a fuss about the god.

"What can all that commotion be?" asked Martin, and as by now they were pouring down the hill in a horde, I began to see how I had been foolish, and I thought I had better confess so that one of them could tell me what to do. So I took the god from under my coat and I said, "I suppose that this is the trouble."

Well, when Chinese No. 1 saw that god he nearly passed right away.

He said, "We will all die for this." And I must own I was rather upset, because I did not want to die miserably in the interior of China when I had not done any thing to warrant death either.

"This is what comes of going to uncivilized parts," I said, and the best thing I could think of to do was to say, "Let them have their silly god." Because really I did not want it if there was going to be all this fuss. I never would have taken it if I had known how the Chinese do not seem to be able to see when a thing is done for a joke. They have not any sense of humour like us.

So Chinese No. 1 took the god and started running with it to the priest. The priest was heading the mob that were pouring down the hill, and you could see from their faces that they were bent on murder. But when they saw the god murder died out of their faces and they began to look very reverent instead. But they did not look reverent when they turned their heads in my direction, so I was glad Chinese No. 1 could say how it was samshui that I was not used to that had made me do it, because I really think they would have attacked me otherwise. But as it was they turned and marched back to the pagoda with the god at the head of the procession and Martin took me by the arm and came with me back to the ship.

8

After that I did not leave the ship until we came to Chungking.

Though Chungking is buried right in the middle of China there is not as much trouble there as at Ichang and Shasi. This is because all the people in the town pay the bandits an indemnity not to bother them through the year. I really think this is much better than waiting to be raided, because then nobody is killed and everyone pays something so that you know where you are.

There is only one white man living at Chungking. He is the installation manager for the paraffin tanks. You cannot go past Chungking because the river is too narrow, and even if your boat would go you would get into trouble with the bandits, so nobody ever goes farther inland than this.

They are so poor in Chungking that their money is split up into very tiny fractions, but the coins they have to represent these fractions are really quite large, so when you go ashore to do some shopping you have to take a boy with you to carry your money in a sack. I used to like having a boy to carry my money in a sack because you feel as if you are very rich when you cannot lift your money by yourself.

Chungking has not any of the amenities of civilization. It is very smelly and dirty with tiny winding streets and most of the houses are only one storey, made of bamboo. There are beggars on all the street corners. Women cripple their children so that they can make money as beggars.

There is one who can always tell when a white man is coming by his walk. She is an old woman and she has no arms or legs and she is blind, but she has a piece of hide tied on her forehead so that she can beat her head on the ground to attract attention. I expect her family would not lose her for anything. She must make them a lot of money because you cannot refuse a person who has no arms or legs and is blind.

When I was in Chungking I went into a tea shop where they were smoking opium. There was so much smoke and incense that you could not see anything at first, but afterwards you could see figures lying about like logs. These were public tea shops where the men bring women and children. No one seems to think any thing of smoking opium.

They had a gramophone playing, but it was Chinese music, so it did not seem out of place. When a white man goes in a tea shop like that he is stared at at first, and if he cannot use his chopsticks everyone starts to laugh. But I could use my chopsticks quite well so presently they got bored and did not take any more notice of me.

There was no light in the tea shop except what came through the door, the floor was only earth, and there were bamboo stools to sit on. The women had bound feet so that they could hardly walk and they carried their babies slung on their backs.

You can order a meal of nine or ten courses in these places and it will only cost about sixpence.[17] You can have some samshui with it. The Chinese do not drink it like white men, they use it to flavour their food.

While I was eating my meal a pig came and rooted[18] round my legs. They have pigs everywhere as we would have dogs, but in China the dogs are outcasts. I expect that is because you can eat a pig and not a dog.

Though you do not strike bandits in Chungking there is still a lot of death about because there are more ways of killing a man in China than shooting him with a gun.

People are not much worried when they pass a dead body, and they do not do anything about it. Only the relatives will come and see what the person has died of, because they can go to the government and collect a sum of money if there has been foul play. So I expect that makes for quite a lot of foul play in China, because some relatives cannot be worth much alive.

When I got back to the ship after going ashore at Chungking I saw one of these bodies myself, but I do not know if there had been foul play. I saw it as I was walking on the pontoons[19] before stepping on board and there it was down in the water wedged between the ship and the fenders.[20] It was rising and falling with the lap of the water, and when at last the ship crushed it it came to pieces and spread out so that when you looked at it you did not feel very well.

But nobody seemed to think they ought to do anything about it so I averted my eyes and went aboard the ship.

9

As soon as I came aboard the ship when we tied up in Chungking I could smell a very funny smell. And when I said, "What is that smell?" they would look at one another but would not tell me, only they told me not to worry. So I still did not know what it was when we pulled out from Chungking and began the return trip.

As I told you the return trip is only 24 hours because the current is with you, so when I woke up in the morning we were nearly there.

17 *sixpence* a pre-decimalization British coin that equaled six pennies.
18 *rooted* dug up with its snout.
19 *pontoons* floats strung together to form a temporary bridge.
20 *fender* timber or rope hung over the side of a dock or boat to cushion against impact or friction.

The first thing I saw when I opened my eyes that morning was an envelope on my table. There was no writing on the envelope, and when I tore open the flap I did not find a letter inside, but instead 300 Chinese dollars. So I could not make out what this was but I thought I had better put them away at once, before anyone came back and found out their mistake.

But after I was dressed it seems it was not a mistake, because the Chief said to me when no one was about, "Did you get yours?"

So at first I did not know what he meant but then I thought of the envelope and said did he mean that.

So he said yes he meant that and I asked what it was.

"Nobody knows," he said. "It is something to do with the opium. We all get one but we do not know where it comes from. You will get one every trip."

"Where is the opium?" I said, because I had not seen any, so he sniffed and then I remembered about the funny smell.

"I can't tell you where it is," he said, "because it is smuggled, but that is it."

So each trip I took my money and did not ask any questions.

But it was the Chinese crew who used to smuggle the opium. It is not that smoking opium is illegal in China; it is not, but the Chinese do not like to pay the government duty. Every time you come into a port the customs officers come and search the ship. They have a stick with a spiked point and they go around stabbing things. You would get a surprise at the places the Chinese hide opium in. One trip they took all the cork out of the life belts and put tins of opium instead! That is all very well in a ship that does not go to the bottom but it would not be very nice if you were in danger of being drowned. That is the worst of the way they do not value human life in China. We think a man is useful in Europe, but in China they always think, "Oh, well, you can get plenty more."

But they do not always put opium in the life belts.

One time they hid packets of it under my mattress, and that was not very nice because if the officers had found it it would have looked as if I had been getting myself mixed up in crime.

The Chinese engineers were the worst because they had the most brains. They made a false bulkhead in the engine room, working when we were not below, and stuffed it full of opium without us finding out.

You could always smell it on the ship but they did not smoke it except when they were in port and not on duty. At those times they would have a party for their friends. They would wait till it was dusk and then they would set out little tables on the pontoons and their friends would come and eat and after they had had their meal they would chatter and sing and go down to the crew's quarters, where they would lie about and smoke opium till nothing mattered any more.

If we had to start early in the morning Taffy and I would take our torches and go down about five in the morning and sort them out. If we could not wake the visitors up we just had to throw them ashore. I often wondered what Taffy, who, I told you, was very religious and liked to sing hymns, thought about all this sin taking place on our ship. He used to look sad sometimes but he never said anything.

There is one thing about opium in China—it does not seem to hurt a Chinaman.

If you are a white man and you smoke opium it is sure to ruin your career. But a Chinaman can take it and it will not affect his work.

We had 12 Chinese engineers on the *Ho-a-Haing*, three for each watch. They all used to smoke opium, yet next to a Scotsman, I would rather trust a Chinese engineer. You could depend on them. Sometimes Martin and I would not go to the engine room for days. Even though they were smoking opium they never came late on watch, and when they were on duty they would not even leave the engine room for a blow of fresh air.

I used to wonder how they could do it, because when a white man smokes opium you cannot depend on him to be anywhere except at his own funeral. But it seems that the Chinese have more self-control.

C H A P T E R X I I

1

I HAVE now given you an outline of the routine of life on the river so I will pass at once to the high spots that happened to me there.

The first high spot was one night when we tied up before reaching Ichang coming down from Chungking. It was a very hot night so we thought that we could have a party, and by the time we had finished you could only tell Martin was alive by the noise he made with his breath. He made plenty of noise with that though, so there was no need to worry.

We carried him down below so as not to affect his prestige, and then I thought, since it was such a hot night, I would not go down to my cabin but would sleep up on deck. I had a camp bed that you could put up on deck and there was a net fixed over it because the mosquitoes were bad.

The air was still and hot but you could hear shouting in the distance, though we did not think much of that because it was always happening.

When I got under my net and lay down to go to sleep I thought I saw four men on the skyline, but Taffy said it was imagination, and I thought that if it was not imagination it might at least be gin, so I did not worry very much but settled myself for sleep. But just as I was dozing off Chinese No. 1 came and shook me, and he said, "You look out, master. Bad men. Plenty trouble coming."

But I had to think of my prestige and could not show him I was nervous, or that I had been drinking gin, so I pushed him away and told him not to be a fool. So he did not warn me anymore, but went away below, and though I was very nervous the gin made me go to sleep.

Then suddenly there was a shot and I who had been asleep jumped up before I was awake and became caught in the mosquito net that was over my bed. I thought that I was attacked from behind and was being strangled, so I fought with all my strength and I had the mosquito net torn into shreds and was out of breath and gasping before I realized that I was not attacked at all.

Then I felt somewhat foolish so I went below to where I had some gin, and after having a drink I came back on deck feeling calm and able to face what had happened.

It was pitch-dark on the deck but I found the Captain and Taffy, and they were talking about how no one could wake the Chief who was still in a drunken condition, and wondering what was happening on the bank, which you could not see for the darkness, though you could hear bullets pinging against our armour plating and dropping off into the water.

The Captain said, "They will not attack while it is dark." But we said, "How can you be sure?" So I decided I would get the steam hoses out just to be be on the safe side.

"I will get out the searchlight, and we can see how many attackers there are," said Taffy.

The searchlight was over the bridge, higher than the armour plating. You could work it from down below, but first there was a water proof cover that had to be taken off. Taffy offered to go up and do it, but he had on a white suit that would have marked him out for a target. I thought I had better do it as my clothes did not show up so much. But when I got up with the guns shooting from the bank and no armour plating to protect me I felt just as if I was naked, and I whipped off the cover and jumped down as fast as I could. I do not think they even saw me, but I felt most conspicuous even though it was quite dark.

We turned on the searchlight from the deck and swung it along the bank and you could see hundreds of bandits massed along the edge of the water. They shrank down when we turned the light on them and while we kept it on them they did not try any more shooting. But while we were watching the bank they were creeping on us from the water, unawares.[1]

We would not have known till they were on us but for the Chinese on our boat who suddenly gave a yell, and when we swung round the searchlight there was a big junk drifting down with the current, and it was crammed to the gunwales[2] with bandits waiting to spring aboard.

They were all armed with rifles and they crouched down watching us.

The junk swung broadside[3] on in the current, and we waited with the steam hoses ready. Nobody made any noise. The firing on the bank had ceased. It was the feeling you have in the calm before a storm bursts.

Suddenly the junk bumped us—quite gently. They rose in a wave and broke over our decks. The steam hoses met them. Boiling steam. It swept them into the water. They squealed like pigs. They were

1 *unawares* without warning.
2 *gunwales* the top edges of a ship's sides.
3 *broadside* sideways.

scalded. They were drowned. They were crushed to death in the panic. For 10 minutes there was bedlam. Then they went down and vanished. The empty junk bumped free and drifted on down the current. The ones on the bank simply melted away in the panic.

In no time there was dead quiet. Even the shooting in the distance had stopped now. You could not hear anything except our own breaths panting with excitement. But the danger was over. There was no cause for more excitement. It made you feel rather flat for it all to be over so quickly. We did not know what to do. We stood about and looked at one another. Then we thought we had better have a drink. So someone fetched a bottle and glasses and we sat on the deck and talked about how they squealed when they fell off into the water.

We did not go to sleep again because soon the sun came up and it was daylight.

But the part that will make you laugh is how Martin came up on deck in the morning when it was all over, and saw the dead bodies on the bank where we had shot them, with the heads of some of them hanging over into the water.

And when he saw them he blinked and said, "Has there been an accident?" Because he had slept right through and did not know a thing that had been happening!

2

We were quite heroes when we came into Ichang next day, and two ships from down the river that were already tied to the pontoons sent officers to welcome us and hear all about our story.

And what was my surprise when I found that one of these ships was the *Ma-a-Haing* on which I had left Mitchell after he disillusioned me about taking the job with the oil company. But by now I was so glad to think I would see Mitchell that I forgot all about how he had disillusioned me and all I could do was ask where I would find him, and everyone I asked told me I would find him ashore.

So I jumped into a rickshaw and started up from the river watching out for all the places where I thought Mitchell might be.

But at last it was in another rickshaw that I saw him, and when we recognized each other we each felt so excited that we called out across the street and jumped out of our rickshaws and caught hold of each other, and talked and laughed so much that a crowd began to collect, and we had to move into a tea shop or we would have held up all the traffic.

This was the first time Mitchell had been up the river. His ship had been trading up the coast to Manchuria, so we thought we would go inland and have a look at the country, though we had been told that inland was very dangerous, but we are not the kind of people who believe all the things they are told.

Mitchell wanted to find a cemetery where he said there were crabs that ate people. He said there were a lot of them in China.

"They are like tarantulas," he said. "You go into a cemetery at dusk and suddenly the ground is crawling, where they have come from their meals in the graves, and they chase you. . . ."

But I said I did not think that would happen unless you had too much samshui. But Mitchell said I was wrong, and though I have never seen this kind of a cemetery, from what people tell me it seems that he must be right.

However, we did not find one this day when we went inland, but though our quest was fruitless you could not say that we were bored.

First we went to a pagoda, but this time I was very careful because I remembered how the Chinese have no sense of humour where their pagodas are concerned.

So we did not swipe a god, but climbed the stone spiral staircase up to the top instead, and as it was 80 feet high you could see out all over the country.

You could see where the hill fell away to the river, and the narrow sweep[4] by the pontoons where our boats were tied up. Besides Mitchell's and mine there was an American and a Japanese gunboat. The town was just a jumble of mud and bamboo houses, but the company's paraffin tanks stood out and made a big landmark. Behind us open country rose to the top of a hill.

Mitchell and I thought we would climb down the tower and go to see what we could find on the other side of this hill.

At first there seemed to be nothing to walk through but rice fields, and this was not very exciting as once we were over the crest you could not even look back and see Ichang and think how how high up we were. But after we had gone about two miles we came to a village and then the excitement began.

Because it seems that the poor peasants who live in these villages never come into the town and do not see any white men, so they think everybody is their enemy and they do not know anything about civilization at all.

4 *sweep* curve.

Mitchell said, "Do you think they will attack us?"

But I said, "You must be nonchalant. They will take advantage of weakness." So we thought we would walk abreast and keep in the middle of the street and then probably we would be all right.

So we entered this village alone with an air of great sangfroid, and you never would have thought we were two against about a hundred.

As soon as the peasants saw us coming they all came out of their houses and the way they looked at us was more like animals do than men. They did not seem to know how to lift their heads. It is as if they have been cowed, like scavenger dogs.

So we did not need our sangfroid as much as we had thought we would.

The older peasants were too cowed to come very near us, though they followed us along the street and gaped. But the children had more courage and some of them came quite close. We did not mind them coming close so long as they did not do anything, but when two big boys who were nearly men tried spitting on our necks to see what we would do, we began to feel it was a difficult situation.

"Do not take any notice," I said to Mitchell, because I thought if we enraged them they might attack us, and who would know we had been killed right out here in a lonely village, so I thought, we must not enrage them at all costs.

But we must also preserve our sangfroid.

So we kept on walking through the village just as if nothing was happening. But when the other peasants saw that we did not do anything when the boys spat on us they crowded up and joined in too.

So soon there were about a hundred peasants following us and spitting on our backs. They kicked up dust with their bare feet and threw that on us too. Before they were finished our necks and our bodies were in a state from this treatment that it would make you sick to hear described.

But we did not lose our sangfroid. We kept walking as if nothing was happening, and all the time we were bearing round so that we came at last to the crest of the hill from where the slope ran down to Ichang and the river.

When we saw that we knew that we were safe, because the peasants began to fall back and show that they were afraid to come over the crest of the hill. All except one boy, who it seemed that nothing would shake off. He followed us for 300 yards after the others had dropped back and as he was still spitting at us we thought we were never going to be rid of him at all.

"Plug him one!" said Mitchell.

And I pulled out my gun and shot him. Until that moment Mitchell says he did not know I had a gun. He says he meant for me to hit him, but I thought he meant shoot. I had to turn round to shoot the boy, and it was at such close quarters that half of his face was blown away. But we did not stay to look at that. As soon as we saw him fall both of us started to run.

We had a start on the peasants who forgot all about their nervousness when they saw the boy drop, so that they began running after us, and hooting. But we beat them down the slope and gave them the slip at last in the twisty streets of Ichang, so that when we emerged and came back to our ships we thought we had got clean away.

There was no one aboard to notice our clothes at close quarters and we walked across the pontoons as if we had just been for a stroll. I left Mitchell at the *Ma-a-Haing* and went on to my own boat. As soon as I was aboard I went down to my cabin and put on a clean shirt. Then I took my gun out of my pocket and extracted the empty case. I threw this through the port hole and reloaded the chamber. Then I pulled a vaseline rag through the barrel and wiped her over with some oil, and after all that you would never know she had been fired. I threw her in the drawer and went up on deck just as if nothing had happened.

I hoped there would not be a commotion, but I had forgotten how the Chinese can claim compensation for a relative when he has been killed by foul play. For this is what was worrying these people. When they could not catch Mitchell and me they went back and picked up the corpse and carried it downhill to the police. But the police did not want to pay the indemnity if they could collect it from someone, so they brought the whole procession down to the pontoon in order to find out who had done it.

It is a good thing there were four ships in Ichang at this time, because when there were so many sailors ashore all at once there was no reason why we should be the guilty parties. So when the police came and asked us questions I had to seem very surprised.

I had not even had my gun out of my drawer, I said, and I had only been for a walk as far as the pagoda. I waited with the Chinese official while the Chief and Captain went below to test my evidence and they said any fool could see my gun had not been out of my drawer, so then I was acquitted of suspicion and the police apologized for causing trouble. The ragged lot of villagers who had been crowding round the ship were ordered to pick up their corpse and go away. So they did, and when last I heard they were still looking for someone to pay the indemnity. I was sorry I could not pay it because I really only killed the boy from an impulse on the spur of the moment due to what Mitchell said. But all the same when people spit all over you they must take what is coming, and they really should not expect a payment of money as well.

3

I was only in Ichang for two days after that shooting because then I began to swell up and get awfully sick. Soon I could not walk and they put me in the mission hospital, but when I did not get better I was given sick leave to go down to Hankow.

By this time Mitchell had gone and I was quite alone with my trouble, so I really thought I would prefer to go down to Hankow for a rest.

I went down on a gunboat and they put me in the Roman Catholic hospital. The doctor who saw me there took a serious view of my case and said I would have to have an operation. But the trip down the river away from the scene of my worries had made me feel much better so I was not very apprehensive at all.

But even if you are not apprehensive, it does not do you any good to lie brooding about how you are going to have an operation, so I was glad when they put me on a balcony with two other Europeans, one of whom had a club that he said that he could 'phone to send over three bottles of whisky.

He was as good as his word, and when that whisky came I did not have to brood and get apprehensive any longer because he let me have one bottle to keep under my bed. We kept the bottles under the bed so that the sisters[5] would not find them, because they were very religious and did not believe in whisky, as well as it being bad for us. But they were pleased when we said we would like a nice drink of soda water, so they got that for us and then they went away and left us in peace.

When the time came for me to go the operating theatre I was not in a state of mind to be apprehensive at all.

I believe it is very dangerous to be drunk when you take an anaesthetic so I suppose I was lucky to come through alive. The last thing I remember is lying on the operating table and then I seemed to be in a dream where Chinese No. 1 was chasing after me, and as I

5 *sisters* nurses.

was running he was throwing dollar bills at me, and I was catching them and putting them in my pocket.

When I recovered consciousness the stitches had been put in and I was back in bed on the balcony and as soon as the sister had gone I could feel for my bottle again. It kept me from feeling depressed after the anaesthetic.

It did not kill me, however, for in two days I could sit up, and that was the day that we heard there was going to be a Chinese execution. As I had not yet seen a Chinese execution I thought that I would like to witness this spectacle. So when the sisters were not looking I put on my clothes and walked out of the hospital just as if I had been paying someone a visit. No one stopped me on the way out, and though I was feeling somewhat weak I kept on down the street in the direction that the crowd were going till I came to site of the execution. This was an open space right in front of the gaol and when I arrived there I found the execution had already started. They had a man standing up on boxes with a policeman on each side of him and an open space had been cleared between him and the crowd.

It was a big crowd and there were men, women and children in it. They were all very excited, so that they were laughing and shouting and throwing their hats in the air.

The man who was on the boxes had two ropes round his neck. The policeman on the right held one and the policeman on the left held the other. As I came up they each began to pull on their ropes, pushing their feet on the boxes to get some extra leverage. It takes a long time to kill a man in this way, and it was watching this execution that made me realize that I am really more kindhearted than a Chinaman, because after a while I could not take any more pleasure in it but began to feel as if I would vomit, whereas the Chinese who were looking on kept laughing and cheering till the end.

But at last I could not wait any longer because the sight became more than I could bear, as it is not very quick or efficient to strangle a man in this manner. So I turned and pushed through the people. But instead of going back to the hospital I thought I would have to take a walk down the street just to have a breath of fresh air.

I did not have any real idea of running away from the hospital, but you never can tell what will happen when you start to walk down a street and the rock that I perished on was when I stopped to look in a window where a Chinaman was sitting making shoes.

It is interesting the way they make shoes in China because they do not have any machinery, but they have a narrow paper tape and you put your bare foot down and they tear off bits of tape the size of your different measurements. Then they cut out the leather from your measurements, and they sit in the open window and sew that into a shoe by hand.

So this is what I was watching when a European lady walked past with whom there was a little girl. As she was not very a young lady and she had a little girl with her I did not take much notice of her. And what was my surprise therefore when she stopped and spoke to me.

"Hullo, Bob!" she said. And you could have knocked me over with a feather to find a lady in the middle of China addressing me by name. But I did not forget my manners though it did not seem to me that I knew her, so I held out my hand and she shook it and then she said I must come to her home. So I began to hope that there would not be any complications. But as we walked along she said that I must meet her husband, so it was evidently nothing like that.

I still did not know who she was, but I did not show anything, and at last she began to talk about being in Glasgow, and then I took another look at her, and I saw how she had changed what with marriage and with the climate, but that she was a girl that I used to be friends with in Glasgow when I was only a boy.

So I felt relieved at this discovery as I did not want to be mixed up with strange women at present, when my health was rather delicate, and I went willingly to her home.

When we were in her home she told me how that night she was helping to organize a ball in one of the big hotels. The next thing she said was would I come. And I was now in an awkward predicament for the time had passed for confessing that I was a hospital case who was walking round with an open wound under his clothes. So I thought I would not disappoint her, but would have some drinks to combat my weakness and would go back to the hospital and have a rest in bed the next day. I was sorry to think how the sisters would be searching everywhere for me, but it was not possible to reassure them as if I did that I could not go to the ball. So I thought how when I had some money I would buy them a present instead.

4

It was really quite a big ball. Nearly all Hankow was there. I do not remember much about it after the first few dances as my weakness increased very much under the strain of the excitement, and I had to keep having drinks to enable me to carry on. I remember a big Russian Jew though, and a woman that was his daughter, and I seemed to be always with this daughter, though I cannot quite think why, because from what I can remember I did not really like her much at all.

But it seems she was one of those women that you do not get away from at dances, unless you abandon your manners, because there is not any competition for her company, and if you are a gentleman you cannot just go away and leave her sitting against a wall. So the last thing I remember is still being with this woman and starting to feel alarmed in case she should be tempted to take advantage of my weakness, so that I would come round and find that I was now her husband. And that thought alarmed me so much that I took her to find some more whisky so that my strength should not desert me. And I cannot think what happened then because when I came round in the morning I had somehow escaped from this woman, but I was with another woman and I was asking her to come up the river to have a house in Ichang, so it seems that my strength must have deserted me after all.

I said that I would pay for her to have a house in Ichang, so you can see how she had taken advantage of me in my weak state. I was very surprised when I came round and heard what I was saying, for I could not remember having ever seen this woman before. She was not Chinese, she was Russian, and she was not really the kind of woman a man would want to put in a house in Ichang at all.

She was lying on her side when I came round, and she was not looking at me but instead she was playing with something that she had on her finger.

Then suddenly she reached over and put her face close to mine. And she put both her arms round my neck, and she whispered, "Tell me please, how much you pay for it?"

So I was very much puzzled, though I was flattered by her affection, and I asked her, "Pay for *what*?"

"This that you give me, silly boy!" and she brought her hand round where I could see it. But I could not answer at first when I saw what she had on her finger, for it was not the kind of thing that you give to a woman who is a perfect stranger, for it was a solitaire diamond, and the setting it was in was platinum, so it must have cost hundreds of pounds.

"Where did you get that?" I said when the first wave of sickness left me. For I was hoping I might be mistaken. But there was no mistake about it.

"You give it me . . . of course . . . silly!"

So the sickness came back again, only it was worse this time for all doubt was now swept away. I could not ask her where I had got it, for that would not have been diplomatic, but the one thing I had to think of was how I could get it back from her, because wherever I had got it I could not have come by it honestly, and you can not get away with a thing like that in China—the way you can in the States. But of course she did not want to give it to me.

I said, "Here, let me look at that ring," but she must have had her suspicions for she would not take it off her finger, but showed me with it still on her hand. So I took hold of her hand as if I was going to stroke it, because by now I was desperate thinking how the police would be after me. And when I had her hand between mine I started to pull off the ring, but she tried to clench her fingers and she fought as if she was a savage, but she was not really a match for me, for I twisted her arm and knelt on it so that she could not use it and then I put a pillow on her face to keep her from calling out, and I leant against the pillow with my back to keep it in position, while I reached forward with my arms and pulled off the ring.

Then I jumped up off the bed and picked up my shoes with one hand and putting the ring in my pocket I fled out of the house in my bare feet, so that I would escape before she could raise the alarm.

I was sorry to have to do it for I do not like to be unchivalrous, but there are times when a man must save himself at all costs.

As soon as I was in the street I called out for a rickshaw, and when it came I scrambled in and told the boy to go as fast as he could because I thought perhaps she would chase me. But she did not have the nerve to do that, and I arrived at the hospital without further mishap.

I put on my shoes in the rickshaw and I tied the ring up in my handkerchief and then I spent the time while we drove trying to think back over the events of the night before in case I could discover how I had come by this ring.

But I could not remember anything except being with the other woman whom I thought might take advantage of my weakness and going once to the washroom because I did not feel very well.

5

So when I got to the hospital my troubles were still unsolved. I got down out of the rickshaw and walked straight inside, and when I got inside there you would have thought I had come back from the dead. For there were the sisters kneeling down saying prayers for me and I really was very perturbed to think I had upset them so much. When they saw me they all fell on me and hustled me up the stairs and took me out of my clothes, so that I would be back into bed looking as if nothing had happened before the doctor came. For they thought the doctor would be angry that they had not guarded me better, but I said I would take all the blame for I really was sorry to see how upset they were.

I did not mean the doctor to find out, but it seems that rumours had reached him for he said when he had examined me that I had incurred a great risk. I might have caught anything he said, and I nearly smiled when he said that, for how could he know that what I had really nearly caught was two strange women and a spell in gaol for stealing a platinum and diamond ring. I had got away from the women, but the ring was still under my pillow, and I lay there all that day wondering where I could have got it and how I could return it to its owner before the police came.

But I did not manage to return it before someone came to claim it, for that very evening the big fat Russian Jew who had introduced me to his daughter at the ball came shouting into the hospital saying I had robbed his daughter. So I guessed from the tone in his voice that she was the one who owned the ring.

"You steal it in the washroom where my daughter leave it. My boy see you do it." So I started to think that perhaps it was a frame-up so that I would enter the family rather than be sent to prison, but perhaps I was doing them an injustice and it was just my habit of not being able to let slip an opportunity. I do not know which it was, but I saw that I must act quickly, so I pulled out my handkerchief and untied it and took out the ring.

"If this is what you want," I said, "I have been holding it for safe keeping." And when I said that in a very convincing tone it took the wind out of his sails. So then I said I was tired with the effects of my operation, so I closed my eyes and leaned back on my pillow. But I watched him through my lashes and I saw him look carefully at the ring, and when he had made sure it was the real one he put it in his pocket and stopped saying I had robbed his daughter and the sisters came one on each side of him and tiptoed him away.

So that was a very difficult corner rounded safely, and after the sisters had given me some brandy to revive me I went off to sleep soundly for I really was very tired.

CHAPTER XIII

1

FTER my operation I recovered quite rapidly and soon I was well enough to go back up the river. I will never forget the last sight I saw before I left Hankow.

I did not see the Russian Jew, or his daughter, or the woman I gave the ring to anymore, but as I was going down from the hospital to join the ship that was to take me back to Ichang I saw something that was much worse. It was a procession—a procession of Chinamen in cages. The cages were not big enough to let a man kneel up straight, the only way he could manage was to crouch down with his head sticking forward; but even if there had been room he could not have moved from that position for each one had his hands tied to his heels. They were trussed worse than turkeys for market. The cages were mounted on poles and four men were carrying each cage. They must have suffered very severely for they had been days in these cages, and now when they were approaching their journey's end they did not receive any sympathy, but instead all the people in the streets crowded round and jeered. So I asked what these men had done since everyone was so unsympathetic, and I was told that they were guilty of being Communists. So evidently that is a very bad crime in China, but I think they are more to be pitied than blamed, for what can you think of a man who goes in for politics when all he will get out of it is being put in a cage?

2

The *Ho-a-Haing* was tied up at Ichang when I got back from Hankow and she would not be ready to sail till next day, so when we saw we would not be needed Martin and I went ashore. We did not mean to get into mischief, but you never know what is round the corner, and what was round the corner this time was one of the strangest experiences that ever came into my life. It was through meeting some American sailors off a gunboat that it happened, for they began to boast that the only two white men who had ever walked through the tunnels under the mountains outside Ichang were two American sailors, and it seemed to us that this was a challenge to our national prestige. For these sailors were saying that no one else would ever do it, and Martin and I thought that two Scots from Glasgow could not let that pass. So we decided we would go out and walk through these tunnels without delay.

We took two electric torches[1] and some gin and a haversack,[2] but we did not tell people we were going for we thought that would spoil the effect. We thought it would be much better to just walk back into Ichang after it was all over and say in the course of conversation that we had just come back through the tunnels, say it very casually, as if we were in the habit of coming through the tunnels every day.

So no one knew where we had gone to and there was a lot of speculation after we had disappeared.

The tunnels about which I am talking are a very ancient feature of this country. They are supposed to have been cut out by hand by Chinese soldiers thousands of years ago. They run right under the mountains. No one ever goes near them for they do not lead anywhere special and also the Chinese have superstitions about them. So we did not have much information except that it was supposed to take 36 hours to go through.

To get to the mouth of the tunnels you walk out of Ichang along the bank of the Yangtse Kiang River for a little over a mile. Then you come to the mountains, and right at the foot of the mountains you see what you have been looking for—a big gaping hole about six feet high and twenty feet wide.

You walk into this and you find yourself in a pitch-black passage that goes straight into the mountain. There is not any noise at all, only your own footsteps and your voices when you talk. But you do not talk much because it sounds so strange. We had to be careful where we walked because the surface was wet and slippery and we did not want to sit down without warning because there was always a risk that something would happen to the gin. There was nothing alive in the tunnel—not even bats, so soon we began to feel lonely, and we would require to have a drink to keep out the damp when this happened for we could not risk losing heart now that our hands were to the plough.

When we switched on our torches to see if there was anything to look at we found there was nothing but stalactites that were growing down from the roof. It is supposed to take hundreds of years to make

1 *electric torches* flashlights.
2 *haversack* satchel.

an inch of stalactite and some of these were a couple of feet long. So this made us feel we were in touch with something very ancient and we felt a great respect for the Chinamen who had hollowed out this tunnel without any machinery so many thousand years ago.

When we walked we kept one torch going because Martin thought there might be a hole in the floor where we would fall into deep water or an underground river, but I said he must have been reading penny dreadfuls,[3] but we kept sharp watch on the floor just the same.

At first it was very exciting walking in the bowels of the earth, but after we got used to that sensation there was not much variety and soon it seemed just monotonous so we became bored. If there had not been some gin to drink I think I should have lost interest. But Martin kept saying, "We must show those American sailors," and then we would be spurred on by the thought of our national prestige.

It was so much the same in the tunnel that we would have lost our sense of time if we had not both had watches. You could not have told if you had been in there two hours or 10. I am glad that we had our watches to tell us how time was passing, because otherwise we might have thought that we had been in there for days and that the tunnel was unending and that might have shaken our nerve so that we would have started to run. It would not have done to start to run because then we might have fallen exhausted and never come out to greet the day.

So we took great care of our watches and did not start to worry until we had been walking in the tunnel for 18 hours. By this time we were expecting to reach the other end. We were going on what we had been told about the trip taking 36 hours. But still we kept walking and still there was no sign of daylight so at last it began to be clear that someone had made a mistake.

It was an awful feeling to think that now that we were down in this tunnel perhaps it went on forever and you never came out at all!

We sat down and had another drink before we could face that idea, and then Martin said No, he did not believe that was it. He thought it was more likely that it took you 36 hours to get through the tunnel *each way*.

Well, it turned out that Martin was right. But before we had proved his theory it seemed to be almost as bad as the tunnel having no end at all. For 36 hours each way is a long time to travel with

3 *penny dreadfuls* cheaply printed novels with violent, fantastic stories, popular in the 19th century.

nothing but gin to sustain you, and we did not have very much rest as when you tried to sit on the stones and have a little sleep the cold damp would come through and wake you, so you had to struggle on again.

At last we were nearly exhausted and still the tunnel did not seem to end. Our heads now felt as if they were floating off our bodies and swimming along the roof, but our legs were still rooted to the ground like great lumps of lead and you could not escape from them. Thus we were not in an altogether happy state.

I think perhaps we would have died in that tunnel if the end had not come soon after this. The 36 hours were long past and we were approaching despair when suddenly Martin called out and caught hold of my arm. My heart, that was a moment! For at last after all this time the darkness was getting thinner.

We started to run with all the strength that we had left and soon there was no doubt that this was not an illusion, but we were really at the end of the tunnel and were coming out into the air.

But it was very strange when we first came out into the air. For though there was light in our eyes we could not see anything—everything was a blur. It must have been through being such a long time in that tunnel, and perhaps also because of our weakened condition. But after a while we could distinguish the kind of country we were in and it was all deserted hillsides that seemed to be swimming in a haze.

We did not go far from the mouth of the tunnel for besides feeling very weak we did not want to meet any people, as the people in these parts will often kill a stranger before he has time to explain who he really is.

So we just stayed by the tunnel and had some of the remains of the gin. We felt that the best thing to do was to start back while we had the strength, for we now saw that what lay before us was a very dangerous time.

As well as this, Martin was worried about what they would be thinking on the ship, for the time was now past when she had been due to sail, but she could not possibly have sailed without any engineers. But I thought that this was no time for trivial worries when what was really the matter was that our lives were at stake.

It did not seem to me that Martin had any sense of proportion, for really they could not quibble over time when they were going to be lucky if they got us back at all.

3

I do not remember very much of the return trip through the tunnel. We were so weak with hunger and exhaustion and so drunk with what we had been drinking that I do not think we had any clear ideas. Afterwards, when the gin was finished, we seemed to become delirious and it really would not have surprised me if we had lain down and died.

But it must be true what they say about the sense of self-preservation because at the end of two days we were still walking in the tunnel, though you could not rightly call it walking, but at least we were moving along.

Then suddenly we thought we heard voices and we did not know at first whether this was the end or real people. But at last when they came right up to us and took hold of our arms we knew that we could not be just dreaming so we realized we were saved.

We were blind so we could not see them, but one of the voices we knew. It was the missionary doctor and he was leading a search party; after combing the country they had come to the tunnel as a last resort. When we knew that at last we were safe the remains of our strength seemed to vanish and we could not walk anymore. In fact we could hardly stand. We could not call out either. We could only beat our hands in the air.

But they got us back to the ship and put us to bed to recover, but for two hours I could not go to sleep because my sight had not come back. I kept wondering if I was struck blind and I did not think I could bear it, so that at last when my eyes began to see again I found I was starting to cry. But I did not cry much because I was too tired for the effort, but instead I dropped off to sleep and lay like one dead for many hours.

It was really a great adventure after it was all over for we were now quite famous. There was almost a column about us in the *Shanghai Daily News*.

4

I had been so busy when I first came back from Hankow that I did not notice the climate, but now that I was convalescent I observed that we were in midsummer and that the temperature was rising to 127 in the shade. You could not call this comfortable even in the best conditions, and conditions were not best on the Yangtse Kiang River, for besides the great heat there was a lot of humidity as well. It is all very well to say people will pay money to have a Turkish bath at home, and here were we given one for nothing, but at home you do not have to stay in your bath all the time.

It may have been very cleansing but it seemed to take away all your strength. As I was supernumerary and did not really have to work I used to stay in bed all day and get up when it was dark. Then I would go along the deck and look for a cold shower. But unless it was very late at night your cold shower would only scald you because the water was stored in a tank that the sun shone on all day and in the end it would be heated nearly to boiling point.

This is where I envied the crew, because they had river water that was pumped into big clay tubs that stood on the deck. But though this water was cool it was very dirty water having come straight from the river and if you got any in your mouth you would risk having typhoid fever. But the crew would put alum in it to clear away the sediment, so sometimes I thought they were lucky in spite of the risk.

The only time we could get cool was when we swam in the pools between the Gorges where the water was not so bad.

I used to go swimming with Martin because now we had become great friends after going through that ordeal in the tunnel together. Martin knew more about China than anyone I met on the river and while we were swimming together he used to tell me stories about the things they will do to white people in China, so that even in that climate he made you feel quite cold.

He said they do things that drive you mad even if they do not kill you. He said he knew a man who is mad from what bandits did to him. He was rescued at last by a missionary who went unarmed to the bandits camp to give them the ransom, and whatever you think of missionaries you cannot help admitting that that was a very brave thing to do.

But what they do to women is worse than what they do to men because you can rape a woman and this is said to be worse than death. Martin said he knew a missionary's daughter that was raped by a whole regiment and you must admit that that was carrying things rather too far.

So after hearing what Martin said I used to keep my eyes open.

The very next time I was ashore in Chungking I saw my second public execution. But this one was not as bad as the one I had seen in Hankow.

This time the man who was being killed was a bandit. We saw a crowd making down the street so we followed, and when we pushed into the front we found the man that was going to be killed kneeling with his hands tied behind him and standing over him was another man with a four-foot sword. But the man who had the sword did not look like a public executioner so Martin thought he must be granted a special privilege, and when we asked we found this was so, for it seemed he was a rich merchant whose small son had been kidnapped for ransom but instead of waiting for the ransom they had killed the little boy. Now this bandit had been caught for the crime and the father was to be allowed to kill him.

He lifted the sword with both hands and made one swipe through the neck of the bandit just where the back of it was poking up through his clothes. And I must say that this was a much neater execution than the one that I witnessed in Hankow, for there they did not get it over quickly and the result was very untidy, but here, in the time that it would take you to click the shutter of a camera the man's head was lying on the stones and his body was toppling over, so that his dead eyes were looking across a stone space to his dead carcass before he can even have had time to think what it was that had hit him. And that is the way that I think an execution should be done.

The man that had made this execution stood leaning on his sword, looking down at his work for a minute, but as soon as he saw that another cut would not be needed he handed it to the bearer to be wiped, and then he turned and marched away.

Everyone now started to disperse and Martin and I went too. We lighted cigarettes as we went and really did not feel at all sick or excited, which just goes to show how soon you can take things for granted, for a public execution is quite a serious matter, yet here we were feeling as if we had just been out fishing.

5

In the middle of summer in China you have a lot of storms. These storms do not cool the air much and they make the humidity worse; but besides that they flood the river, so that sometimes it rises one foot an hour and when that happens the current gets too strong for you to go up to Chungking. I remember one storm that floated a ship from her moorings and when she came down past us we all ran up from our dinner because we thought she might have rammed into us but instead she just shaved past. There was a Chinaman and his wife on board her and they were jumping up and down and yelling because they could not get off and she was out of control. But we could not do anything and at last they were carried away right over a rice field where she grounded. And when the water went down they had to set up house in their boat because it was months before there was another flood to float her away.

I remember that flood on the river because it was the night after that that old Martin was so much upset. It came through us having a singsong when we were tied up to the bank. The Chinese started us singing, because after it was dark they had a sort of guitar down aft and they were chanting away to it and you could smell the opium.

It was a hot, still night and we were in a lonely part of the river. There were no other ships and no villages. You could only see the yellow river, and hear it sucking a little, and see the sky that was so big that our boat seemed very small. It made you feel you were almost the only people in the world. You started to feel sorry, but you did not know what you were sorry for, only it was not unpleasant, although there was a lump in your throat.

I expect you have had that kind of feeling so you will know what I mean. When it got very bad you started to sing songs. I expect it is a feeling like that that makes animals sing to the moon. But of course I do not mean to imply it was an animal feeling in us.

Well, it was the Chinese and the loneliness that started us. Then Taffy pulled out the little organ that he kept under his bed (for hymns) and Martin said, "Well, what about a wee cocktail?" and after we had all had that Taffy started "Land of our Fathers,"[4] which was his favourite, and I accompanied him on a mandolin.

It would have sounded funny to anyone walking on the bank to hear such sounds coming from a little boat in the middle of China, for after "Land of our Fathers" we passed to anthems and hymns and bits of Harry Lauder,[5] as well as other songs.

When we stopped for a rest you could hear the Chinese singing but most of the time we were louder than they were. At last we started to

4   *"Land of our Fathers"* "Land of My Fathers" ("Hen Wlad fy Nhadau"), the Welsh national anthem.

5   *Harry Lauder* Sir Harry MacLennan Lauder (1870–1950), a very popular Scottish vaudeville singer and comedian.

sing a song called "I Belang tae Glasga'"[6] and when we started this one Martin did not join in. He had been drinking a good deal in between the songs we were singing and now when he heard this tune something seemed to stir inside him, for he got up and wrenched my mandolin out of my hand, and broke it across his knee, and walked away leaving the pieces lying on the deck. So you can imagine I was surprised and somewhat vexed.

But I did not follow Martin to tax him with his behaviour because he is a big man and when he has been drinking you never know what he will do. But we did not sing very much after that for it seemed to have dampened our ardour, so we left the coast clear for the Chinese who were still at it and went to our cabins to sleep. But presently old Martin came bursting into my cabin.

He did not say anything at first but just sat down on the bed, and then he started:

"Have you ever seen Bert Fleming's grave outside Shasi?" And I did not know what he was talking about because this was the first time I had ever heard of Bert Fleming, but it seemed that I was now going to learn if I would only be patient.

"A Chinese Christian pulled him out and buried him. He was a good chap," said Martin. "His ship was tied up at Ichang when it was boarded by bandits. All the Chinese crew joined the raiders so Bert and the Captain and the Mate had to lock themselves in the bridge to keep from being killed. They were there for three days, but the bandits did not break in. They just camped round on the decks. At the end of three days a French gunboat and a British passenger ship came up the river. The passenger ship had wind of the trouble and she was carrying armed bluejackets.[7] When they drew level with the ship that was in the hands of the bandits they signalled for Bert and his friends to jump overboard. And they did, before the bandits could stop them. When they came up the Mate started to swim for the French ship and the Captain to the British one. But what happened to Bert, Bobby? He did not swim anywhere, because Chinese No. 1 saw him come up and aimed a rifle at him. He was shot and he sank in the water. His body went

6 *"I Belang tae Glasga'"* "I Belong to Glasgow" was a vaudeville song written by Will Fyffe (1885–1947), a contemporary of Lauder and a fellow Scot. Fyffe offered the composition to Lauder, who declined it for its positive take on hard liquor.

7 *bluejackets* sailors.

down in the current and the Chinese Christian at Shasi saw it and pulled it ashore. You can see his grave there. He was my great friend, Bobby, and that song you were playing when I took away your mandolin was one that he was always singing."

He gave a big sigh then and went on sitting on my bed, staring in front of him.

So after that I could not be angry at him breaking my mandolin but I wished he would move off my bed so I could get into it, but he did not seem to be concerned with a little thing like that.

6

But next morning he was better and we came down to Ichang and tied up beside the pontoons for a couple of days. I did not have Mitchell to go exploring in the country this time, so I took Martin instead, and we were not looking for trouble because I remembered what had happened to Mitchell and me the time we went looking for the cemetery where there are crabs that eat people. But this time we saw something that was even worse than that.

We were walking back up the river not expecting to meet anything when we came to a little village, and you could tell from the way the crowd had all come out of their houses that something important was happening, but we did not dream what. For you never could dream the kind of things they think of in China. Not even when you are having a nightmare you could not dream them.

For in the middle of this group there was a woman tied to a stake. Her hands were behind her round the stake and her clothes were stripped off her body and Martin said when we got near, "I do not think you will want to look at what they are doing. They are punishing a woman for being unfaithful to her husband." And when I looked I knew that he was right, but I could not take my eyes away for it was one of those sights that burn themselves into your mind and come back when you cannot sleep at night. It was too horrible to describe but I will tell you part of it. They had taken out their knives and they were cutting her breasts off.

Martin pulled me back because after I had seen this sight I did not know what I was doing and I would have plunged in and tried to attack these villagers, but as Martin said I would only get myself killed and not do the woman any good. But I could not get her out of my mind all the time we walked on past this village. "Will they kill her when they have finished?" I said to Martin.

"They will throw her outside," he said. "She will die in the end. The man who seduced her will not have anything done to him." So it seems they have never heard of sex equality in China.

But that night when we were back on the ship Martin called me over and pointed to something that was floating down on the current.

It was this mutilated woman who had been thrown, stake and all, into the river to drift until the scavenger hawks got her. And even now after all these hours she was not dead. So I took out my gun and shot her. And I think looking back on China that that was my best action all the time I was there.

7

Coming down to Ichang the next time after that we broke our propeller shaft, and as we could not mend it up the river we had to start down to Hankow on one screw to get fixed. But it seemed our luck was out that trip, because when we were near Shasi a boat passed us coming up and on her blackboard there was the notice that there was firing a little way down.

So we were warned, and just in time.

We were now approaching a part of the river where you have to go right in by the bank to get the deep channel and just by the bank where we swung in there was a boy with a rifle. He picked it up and took aim at us so I did not waste any time. As he pressed the trigger I fired. I did not aim badly because he at once dropped his gun and caught his stomach with both hands. Then he toppled over on his face and stayed there. The next minute hell was let loose.

They turned a bombardment on us. Not rifles—field guns.[8] We were plated against bullets but no one had reckoned on shells.

The first shot to tear through the plating exploded in an engine-room steam pipe, so that not only was an engine put out of commission but the engine room was filled with scalding steam and the Chinese engineers lost their heads and bolted.

Out of control, the ship began to heel round, while I chased the engineers along the deck with a gun. You could not make them pull themselves together unless you threatened to shoot them, but when they saw that I had them covered they forgot to be frightened of the shells and I drove them back to their posts at the point of my gun. Every time there was a shot from the bank they tried to lie flat on the floor, and I

8 *field guns* movable artillery.

had to get them up again by saying I was going to shoot. We had to keep the remaining engine at full steam ahead. It was our only chance.

But at first we were not successful in managing to run through the bombardment. The shells kept falling all round us and with each new one you kept thinking, "This one has got us!" But for some time there was no serious loss of life. Then there was a huge explosion somewhere right amidships, and from the shrieking and groaning you could tell that perhaps it would be better not to go and have a look at the damage. You did not need your eyes to confirm that a number of people had been killed.

I do not know what I should have done at this juncture if fate had not decided for me, for at this moment a piece of hot fire tore through my face and clapping a hand to each cheek I felt the blood running through my fingers where a bullet had gone in one side and come out the other.

When I felt the blood running down my face I seemed to lose interest in the fighting for I dropped on my hands and knees and started to crawl out of sight. It is funny the things that come to your mind in a state of crisis, for in my case it was a memory of how someone had once said that the best place to be in when there was shooting around was the bath. So I found myself crawling towards the bathroom leaving a trail of blood on the floor, but after I got into the bath I felt more secure for I realized the bullets would not come through it.

I lay there all through the barrage, and as my face kept on bleeding it was not long before the bath was not a pretty sight to look at. But of course this was not the time to worry about things like that.

A bath is not at all comfortable when there is no water in it, and presently when the shooting slackened I found I had time to notice this. It seemed to be finding all the corners of my bones. The wound in my face had stiffened so that my mouth was no longer full of blood, but my cheeks were now set like leather and were aching very severely. I was glad when the shooting stopped enough for me to crawl out.

I crept along the passage[9] to the companionway and climbed up on deck. The first thing I saw when I got up on deck was Martin stretched out—dead. That shook me badly. I had liked old Martin. But there was nothing to be done for him now.

---

9 *passage* corridor.

I turned my eyes away because I did not like to see him dead and the next thing I saw was 18 dead Chinamen. The deck was running blood. They had been blown to pieces. That must have been the big shot I heard just before I was hit.

At first I thought I was the only one left on board, but after a while I found the Captain and Taffy, locked up in the bridge. They were quite shocked when they saw me for my face was something of a mess, and when I told them about Martin they did not know what to say. There was nothing to say really except that we must see how many of the crew were still alive, and try to carry on with them till we met help on the river.

For we did not intend to fall into the hands of the bandits.

We found that three of the 12 Chinese engineers were dead so that made us one whole watch short, and now for the first time I was not supernumerary but was really Chief Engineer. I could not enjoy this when I thought of Martin lying dead, however, and I thought of the irony of life which had brought me promotion in this way.

I told you we had only one engine, so it was hard work to keep the ship going, but we had the international distress signal flying from our mast so we hoped help would come before long.

And now it seemed our luck had turned, for in a very short time we saw two British gunboats on the river and when we came close we could see they were the H.M.S. *Bee* and the H.M.S. *Tern*.[10] When we had signalled our story they sent boats across to take off our dead and poor old Martin went along with all the Chinamen.

As soon as they had done this the gunboats steamed on up the river and I read in the papers when I was in hospital in Hankow what they did to those bandits who had bombarded us. They steamed up to Shasi and found 7,000 men entrenched, but they did not open fire first because it is a law on the river that foreigners must not fire unless they are attacked. But the bandits could not resist the chance to shoot a British gunboat so they began to shoot and then the gunboats replied.

10 *H.M.S. Bee and the H.M.S Tern* Both ships were Royal Navy river gunboats serving on the Yangtze. All but one of the Royal Navy river gunboats patrolling in China had the names of either birds or insects, according to *www.hmsfalcon.com*, a site devoted to the subject. The *Bee* served as the Royal Navy's flagship on the Yangtze beginning in 1920. On December 12, 1937, the *Bee*, the H.M.S. *Ladybird* and the U.S.S. *Oahu* took aboard survivors of the U.S.S. *Panay* after it was sunk by Japanese aircraft.

They really have strong guns on those gunboats for the barrage they got back blew half the hillside away. You could not find any bandits afterwards for it was the part of the hillside where the 7,000 men were.

We read all about it in the papers, for we went on down to Hankow and I was put in hospital to have my wound treated while the ship was being repaired. It was not a serious wound, though painful. It left a scar on my face but you could not call it a disfigurement, and I really would not mind at all if it were not for the fact that you cannot hide a scar from the police.

But I have not been in trouble with the police since I came back from China and I think that perhaps I am leading a reformed life.

But after all that fighting I began to lose my taste for China, for I thought how I was still young and why should I waste my life by being a target for bandits just to please an oil company? So it seemed to me I was a mug to go courting what had happened to Martin. For where was the sense in risking your life for nothing? And besides the climate was not good.

I decided I would leave the *Ho-a-Haing*. It was a wise decision. I have no time for those people who imagine I was losing my nerve.

I signed off the *Ho-a-Haing* and booked on a ship back to Shanghai but I did not want to give the Captain my rifle and two revolvers. They are issued to you to use while you are with the company. But I did not feel it would be safe to travel all that way down the river without any kind of protection, so after I had given them to the Captain I sneaked back into his cabin and swiped a revolver for myself.

I think it was very necessary for me to have a revolver.

But by this time my health was not good, due to the effect of the climate, and I had to drink quite a lot in order to keep up my spirits. So while I was staying with the installation manager waiting for the ship to take me down the river I ran up quite a whisky bill.

But my mind was not altogether clear and when the time came for me to go I did not remember to pay it, so the boy to whom I owed the money came with me on the launch that was going to take me to the ship. But I did not remember he was the one to whom I owed this money, so when he came over and started to make demands from me I did not understand what he wanted, for I was not quite myself, and I drew out my gun and shot at him, but fortunately I missed.

I was the only white man in the launch and everyone else crouched away from me in a heap, when they saw that I was excited and was shooting with a loaded gun. But now I came to myself and saw that I might have done a murder, so I was very remorseful to think what whisky can do to you, so I called the boy across, and at first he was afraid to come.

But at last he did come and then I asked what was the matter, so he told me about the bill for whisky and I said, "Well, why didn't you *say* so?" But he was shaking like a leaf and did not seem to understand me, so I put my gun away in order to reassure him, and when I took out my money to pay him he nearly jumped into the water because he seemed to think I might be drawing out another gun.

Some of the Chinese are really very cowardly, but of course you cannot blame them seeing they are not white men.

8

It was a passenger boat on which I went back to Shanghai and there were a hundred passengers.

Most of the passengers were being evacuated from a place up the river that had been attacked by bandits and two of them were American women missionaries. These two missionaries had lost control of their reason through being in the hands of the bandits and now they had to be locked in their cabin all the time. But even then you could not forget about them for most of the day and night you could hear the way they were screaming. It quite gets on your nerves to be cooped up on a ship where two mad women are screaming.

The day we got into Shanghai I was down in my cabin packing when suddenly the ship heeled over as if she was going to turn turtle. So that I should not be trapped if this was what was going to happen I bolted up quickly on deck, but it was only a false alarm for nothing had gone wrong. There was only a Chinaman standing up on the deck rail making ready to jump over and everyone had run to the side to watch him and that had made the ship heel over. But I did not even bother to watch because I knew what he really was—he was an opium smuggler. The life belt that he was wearing was lined with tins of opium and after he jumped over everyone thought he was drowning but he was really swimming quite easily. And soon a junk that had been waiting sheered across and picked him up. The passengers were very excited, but I did not think anything of it because it is a thing that you can see any day in China.

9

There were two men waiting to meet me when I arrived in Shanghai. They were Chinese messengers and they had the oil company's badge on their caps. They had a message for me which said that they would take my bags to the Astor House Hotel and that I was to go right along and report myself to headquarters.

So I went around to headquarters and the commander was waiting for me. He was angry at me for having left the ship when she was up the river, but I said I was played out. Anymore would have meant my death.

So when he heard that he said I must be seen by the company's doctors and if they ordered me to hospital I would be put there on half pay. So I went to the company's doctors but they wanted to put me in the International Hospital, so I did not say anything to them but I did not go to any hospital, for what I wanted was not hospital but a holiday.

I was given the company's car and two Chinese boys to drive with me to the hospital, but after we had started I said first I would like to stop for a drink in the Cathay Hotel. So I went inside the Cathay Hotel and after an hour I was still there. The boys in the car were feeling worried but at first they did not like to say anything, only after two hours they came in to look for me. But by now I was feeling how a man is not going to put up with being ordered about by Chinamen, so I told them they could go away. I said if they did not go away I would knock them down and dance on their faces. So after that they decided they would not bother me anymore.

I told them I would go to the hospital later on in a rickshaw, but of course I did not intend to go to the hospital at all. I think it must have been all the privations that I had endured up the river, for now I began to have what I will call a reaction. I did not seem to want to remember anything at all. I just wanted to stay in the bar having drinks all day long and I do not remember where I slept at night. I think I must have slept in a different place every night. It was not till six months later that I went to the Astor House Hotel to collect my gear that had been taken there the very first night.

But my reaction did not last six months. If it had I think it would have killed me because at the end of three months I was so weak that I could not lift a glass from the table. When I had my first pick-me-up at six o'clock in the morning the barman had to hold it to my mouth or I would have spilt it all before any of it got to my mouth.

When I landed in Shanghai I had an account for £800 in the Hongkong and Shanghai Bank. I sent £200 to London, but all the rest I spent.

By the end of three months I was known in all the bars in Shanghai. I was spending £200 a month and I was going into the bank 10 and 20 times a day to put money in or draw it out.

The Hongkong and Shanghai Bank[11] is the coolest place in Shanghai. They have specially conditioned air and there are stone seats and tables where you can have a rest. It is wonderful to come in there out of all the heat, so I thought it would be a good idea to take my bottle and go and sit there. But they did not like me having a bottle and they used to put me outside. But I said they could not put me outside when I was one of their clients, so they said in that case I could not be a client anymore. So I took my account away.

Well, there I was with nowhere to leave my money, and I had to put it all in my pockets. But so that unscrupulous people would not take advantage of me when I could not protect myself I used to give it to hotel managers to mind. But whenever I did that I would be sure to want some more about two or three in the morning, and the hotel managers did not like being got out of bed so I had to be always taking it to a different hotel.

It was an awful reaction that I had for these three months. All Shanghai knew about me. All the rickshaw boys knew me. All the men in the bars knew me.

I had one rickshaw boy that I used to pay by the week to wait outside bars for me. When I did not come out all night he would just lie down and go to sleep in the road. But after a while I got tired of seeing the same face always so I told him to go away.

I do not think I can have told him politely for after that the rickshaw boys joined together and tried to murder me. Perhaps he told them I was carrying money and they could all have a share. It happened one night when I was not in a state to notice that the boy who was pulling me had turned into a blind alley and I only came to my senses when he suddenly put down the shafts and I turned and saw the alley full of men. They were all massed barring my escape and I saw that I was in a trap.

11 *Hongkong and Shanghai Bank* The Hongkong and Shanghai Banking Corporation Limited, founded in 1865, was the founding member of the HSBC Group, which today is one of the world's largest banking and financial services organizations. The building Moore describes, located at No. 12 the Bund, was completed in 1923. No expense was spared in its construction, and its air conditioning system was one of the most advanced in Shanghai. The building is in use today and is owned by the Pudong Development Bank.

This was a shock that made me feel rather more sober and when they began to close in my brain had come quite alive. I remembered I had the gun I had swiped from the oil company, and if it was not for that gun I would not be writing this tale.

I put my hand in my pocket and felt the stock of the gun and at the same time I brought my foot down on the "tram." The tram is the plate at the side which rings a bell on the footboard and this was to distract them as well as to give the alarm. At the same moment I pulled out my gun and started shooting. That broke them. They never thought that I would have a gun. At the first shot they scattered like rabbits. Two, and they were clearing for their lives.

But I was not taking any chances. I went on banging the tram and shooting the gun at intervals till two Sikh policemen came running. Then I knew that I was safe.

I told the Sikhs what had happened and they could see from the deserted rickshaws that my story was not a fabrication though by now there were no coolies in sight. So they took the cushions out of the rickshaws, for these cushions are numbered and the police know who the numbers belong to, so that is all you ever have to do to punish a rickshaw coolie. But when they had collected the cushions they wanted to take me to headquarters, but I could not allow that as these policemen were Sikhs. They are only meant for keeping coolies in order, so I said they must get a white policeman and one went away to fetch one while the other stayed to watch. It was a white sergeant that they brought back and I said that of course I would go to headquarters with him.

But when I got to headquarters he asked what was I doing with a gun. So I told him how I had been up the river on the *Ho-a-Haing*.

He told me that my firm had been combing Shanghai for me, so I said for him to stand by me and not breathe a word that he had found me. For I did not want to go back with the company yet. So he was a sport, that sergeant, but he said he would have to take my gun. He said he would have to send it back to the company, but so that I should not get in trouble for having swiped it, he said he would put it in an envelope and say I had 'phoned from my hotel for a policeman to come and collect it. It is only sometimes in life that you meet with a sportsman like that.

CHAPTER XIV

1

WELL, after that I went back to my drinking. It was an awful burst[1] I had. It was partly the time up the river, partly the money, and partly the heat, that made me do it. The heat was awful, even in Shanghai. When they wouldn't let me go and sit in the bank anymore to keep cool I found there was a swimming pool at the American Y.M.C.A. Now all you can buy in a Y.M.C.A. is Coca-Cola, but I used to sit in the shallow end and send a Chinese boy out to buy gin. I used to squat in the water then with a bottle of gin, drinking it. Oh, I was awful all right, that time in Shanghai.

I told you how I got so shaky in the end I couldn't lift a glass up to drink it. I was a hospital case all right. But instead of going into hospital I went away again up the river. My money was getting low and a man found a job for me.

It was in a pub owned by a Chinaman but there was an American bartender and the licence was in his name because a Chinaman isn't allowed to hold a licence in the British Concession in Shanghai. Well, I was in this pub when a swell-looking Chinaman came in. You could see he was rich and while he was having his drink he started talking to the barman. He was talking about a ship that had been in dock getting her engines repaired and I got listening and chipped in with a question.

"You know all about engines, eh?" He was a bit sarcastic at first, because I wasn't looking my best after the time I'd been having.

"Christ, Johnny!"[2] I said. "I've got a chief's ticket." So he started to take an interest in me then.

"You want a job, eh?" he said. "Maybe I find you one."

So I said that would do me and when we finished our drinks we went out together.

He took me down to some docks on the river, to some dingy-looking little offices. Then he left me for a while, but in a minute he came back with about the worst looking Chinaman that ever I saw. He was

1 *burst* drinking binge.
2 *Johnny* chap, dude

cross-eyed, his mouth was like a wooden slit, and he had a quiet voice that make you feel there was a cold hand on your spine. A real bad fellow he struck me as, and I was right.

But at first he was awfully nice to me. He said he had a small ship taking cargo up the river and there'd been trouble with her engines so he thought it would be a good business to get an English engineer. He offered me £100 a month! So I forgot how ugly he looked and I said I would take it. I was still half-oiled or I'd have known there was bound to be trouble.

He seemed pleased when I said I would come, and he didn't give me time to sober up and change my mind. He said we were sailing that night and I had to go on board right away.

I must have been pretty drunk or I never would have gone with him. I hadn't any kit. Not a soul knew where I was going. It was dark when we got on board and I couldn't see much except coolies peeping at me everywhere round corners. The boat was anchored out in the river. From what I could see in the dark she weighed about 40 tons.

She was lighted with old paraffin lamps and she looked rather a comedown after the *Ho-a-Haing*. The captain called out to a Chinaman to come and show me my cabin, and he came up and pushed past me into the passage just as if I was not a white man at all. I remembered how I booted a boy overboard on the *Ho-a-Haing* because he so much as cast a look at me, and I thought, "This will have to be altered," and at that minute an other one pushed past me, and I saw another staring at me, insolent, and it came to me all of a sudden that I was alone on this boat with a mob of Chinamen all round me, and that no one would know where I was if they took it in their heads to do for me. An awful sort of feeling rolled up inside me and if I could I would have turned and run. But everywhere I looked they were watching me, so I just walked on till the one ahead showed me my cabin.

It was all right as cabins go, but no fan or anything. Rough after the *Ho-a-Haing*.

There was a dirty smell about it too, and the lamps made the place look grimy.

I sat down on my bunk and started to get frightened. I'd have got out now, if I could. I regretted more than anything that I didn't have any gun. I got up to go on the deck and there were two of them in the passageway. Wherever I went one would pop up watching me.

The Captain came down soon and took me to see the engines. I didn't like that Captain. There was something in his face I didn't like, but all the time he was awfully nice to me. He said could I start up now and I thought I would make out I was sick because then may be he would let me go ashore. I felt pretty sick too, what with worry and all that drinking. But he didn't let me go ashore. He didn't let me out of his sight. He sent a boy for some samshui and when I had a good drink of that I felt I didn't care very much what happened.

So I got the engines going and we started off up the river. I must have gone to sleep then because when I came round the samshui had worked off and I could feel we were moving up the river and I thought of being alone with all those Chinamen looking at me and I got up and made for the deck, thinking I might jump overboard. But when I got there the water was so dark and I remembered how a man would get caught in the treacherous currents, so I hung on the rail and I didn't jump, and when I turned round and looked there was one of them watching me.

He just smiled and did not speak. I pushed past him and went to my cabin. They had to watch the engines that night. I didn't.

2

Morning came and we were well away up the river. A coolie brought breakfast to my cabin. They hadn't any dining saloon. The Captain and the crew all ate together sitting on the deck. They used to sleep on the deck too. They slept on grass mats, spread out wherever they fancied. In the morning they rolled up the mats and put them out of the way. Mostly in the daytime they covered the decks with oranges. We were supposed to be carrying oranges. Also salt, and general cargo. But there was something funny.

I went up on the bridge and tried to get talking to the Captain. But you couldn't pump him, not in a month of Sundays.[3] He just stood there smoking a pipe a couple of feet long, looking at you with one cross-eye while he watched the river with the other.

Another funny thing was that when we passed ships I used to be sent below. We used to sneak into side creeks and lie out of sight too. Sometimes we would lie hidden in a side creek all day. When I asked the captain why he would just say, "You no savee."[4]

I knew there was something funny but I couldn't tell what.

3 *not in a month of Sundays* unlikely to happen.

4 *savee* know (Pidgin English). From *The Economic Journal*, Volume 11, No. 44 (December 1901): "You are invariably met with the too familiar expression, 'Me no savee', which conveys a world of meaning."

Though the river is so dangerous we used to travel mostly at night. They seemed to know the place as if it was their backyard. I tell you I didn't like it.

I'd given up ideas of jumping overboard but they went on watching me like cats. They must have known that I was worried. I kept feeling I would never get out of this alive, but at the same time I knew now I was safe for the moment because if they did for me there would be no one to manage their engine.

Knowing that let me get some sleep, but I still felt that unless I bolted I would never be free of them. And they took good care I had no chance to bolt.

We never stopped at a decent-sized place. Often we would just pull in to the side where there was nothing and they would put out a plank running into the tiger grass. Some of them would go ashore and we would wait hours for them. When that happened I would walk up on deck and stroll about and whistle, and look for a chance to slip off, but every time I would see their faces round corners watching me.

We would wait hours for the ones who went ashore to come back and when they did they would be carrying stuff in cases. I was dead curious to know what was in those cases but when I asked the Captain he always said, "You no savee." Only one day, when he was feeling extra-pleased he made out he was cocking his finger round a trigger and pulled it at me. I knew then what was in those cases. Rifles!

So we were smuggling arms. I watched after that and I used to see signals flashing from the bank to us at night.

That made me want to get free of them more than ever. I kept worrying that if I went out to it[5] no one would know what had happened me, so I thought I would try to smuggle out a letter. I wrote[6] it to my mother in Glasgow because I thought the Captain might read English and one time when we were pulled up beside the tiger grass and he was going ashore I gave it to him. Inside there was a note to my parents to cable the authorities in Shanghai where I was and what had happened, but all I said to the captain was, "England. You savee? Mother."

He said he saveed all right, but he must have thought it was a trap because home in Glasgow they never got the letter.

That time he went ashore with my letter he was gone six hours.

5 *went out to it* died (World War I slang).
6 *wrote* addressed.

3

When he came back it was nighttime and I was down in my cabin. I didn't hear him come back and when he pushed open the door to come in and speak to me I jumped up in my bunk thinking at last my time had come. But the Captain wasn't thinking of murder. He had brought me a cup of tea.

So he lit his long pipe and squatted on the floor of my cabin while one of the coolies brought in a low table with the little bowls of tea. He seemed to have got very sociable all of a sudden so I thought it would be a good chance to pump him some more about the ship.

I said what did he bring back this time, so he gave me a look with those cross-eyes of his and said as solemn as you like that this time it had been chickens.

So I said Oh, yes, I saveed about the chickens, because already I could smell the opium all over the place. It was opium as well as arms I had found out by this time.

There were some chickens as well though, because next day I saw them killing some for dinner. They cut their throats and shoved a tube in to drain the blood out. They save the blood to sprinkle their food with. But at first I thought he was just kidding about the chickens.

So I said what else had he got. So he grinned and said eggs as well as chickens.

"Go on," I said, "I savee eggs all right. Eggs go bang, eh?"

And he nodded and laughed like anything. I meant ammunition and I thought he meant that too, but he clapped his hands and the boy came, and he sent him away for something and when he came back there were two black things like pullets'[7] eggs lying on a dish and he told the boy to bring them over to me.

"Twenty years old," he said, and I had a good look at them.

After I had had a good look I guessed what they were. He was quite right. They were eggs—of a kind the coolies bury in their fields and leave for years with sticks up to mark where they are and how long they have been there. I'd seen them for sale in Ichang—the older the more expensive—but I'd never handled one before. Chinese would rather have them than oysters.

I reached out my hand to pick up one of these two, and it broke. The gas it let out in that cabin was overpowering, and it managed to

---

7 *pullets* female domestic fowls under a year old; pullet eggs are small and yokeless.

penetrate all over the ship. But they didn't mind it. They came over to have a look and there was a little shrunken yolk inside—quite hard. That is what they eat. I could see by his look that the Captain had his eye on this one so I gave it back to the coolie. He needn't have been afraid. The coolie took them away and the Captain sat down and went on drinking his tea and looking at me as if I ought now to be convinced that all he had gone ashore for was eggs and a couple of chickens.

So I let that pass. There wasn't any sense in arguing, and I asked instead could I go ashore next time, but he shook his head hard at that and said, "Bad men. You no savee."

So I asked him when the trip was going to finish. I reckoned by now that I would never get free unless I broke away myself but I asked him just to see what he would tell me. He just shrugged his shoulders and wouldn't say anything.

He smoked for a while, then looked at his feet, then smoked some more. Then he said, "Bymbye,[8] you savee, you have plenty money."

But that was what he always said when he saw I was getting restless. Yet so far I hadn't had a cent and now I did not expect any.

To all intents and purposes I was as good as kidnapped, and I used to spend all day scheming for a chance to get away.

I didn't like the work we were on, for I never knew when a 'plane or a gunboat would be after us and not knowing I was aboard I would be shelled or bombed with the rest. Oh, I tell you, what with thinking like that and having the crew watching me I had a lot of worry.

For the life of me I couldn't see how things were ever going to get better. We kept plying up and down the river between Hankow and Ichang, pulling into these little creeks and answering strange signals, and taking on cases at night, and giving them off on to junks—there was a regular network of arrangements and it seemed to me we might go on forever without my getting free.

After three months I was beginning to feel desperate. I seemed to see them getting uglier and more dangerous-looking every day. It got me down, having no sort of weapon and never being free of them. Every day they seemed to look bolder and push past me more cheekily. I hardly dared go to sleep. The way they looked at me now I reckoned they were just waiting for someone to give the word "go."

8 *Bymbye* by-and-by; soon.

Then one morning down in the engine room a greaser off with his sweat rag and hit me across the face with it. I think that was the crucial moment. If I had taken that quietly it would have been the end. But instead I brought my shovel right across his head and cut his skull like a cheese. He sagged from the knees and dropped. I pulled the shovel free and swung it up and stood over him. I thought the game was up and I might as well do for as many as I could before they got me.

But they were cowards. Instead of rushing me they fetched the Skipper. It seemed to me that would only put off the reckoning, but he was a funny chap that Skipper. He came down with his pipe and his cross-eyes and saw me there with the shovel dripping blood, and told me to come up on deck because he wanted to talk to me. So I took the shovel and came and all the others followed me. When we got up there he snapped at them all in Chinese and they cowered away, so I was puzzled. But suddenly he turned to me and said, with that funny grin of his, "You verry smart fellow. Maybe big chief down in Shanghai have good job for you!" And he threw me a loaded revolver.

So you never can tell how things will take people, can you?

4

After that they treated me better, and I felt safer, having the revolver, but they still watched me all the time, though once or twice they let me go ashore.

They picked their times though and took care it was never near a village. They used to send two men with me and they'd walk behind with knives in their belts, and guns, so that if I'd tried to bolt they'd have dropped me in half a second. I was just allowed to walk up and down the bank and then I had to turn round and come back on board.

It was a life. But I kept my spirits up thinking that if I only waited my chance would come. I waited four months altogether and then I was lucky. It was one time when we were up near Ichang and we had pulled in beside the bank and the Skipper had gone ashore. It was nighttime but it was moonlight and they were squatting on the deck playing mahjongg for bullets and drinking samshui by the light of the moon. They had a whole lot of samshui and they kept on drinking it so that for once in their lives they forgot all about me.

I started thinking what I could do and suddenly I decided.

I knew where there was some petrol in two tins,[9] and I crept quietly to the engine room with it. I was scared all the time the tins would make a noise—whatever you do tins always clank a bit, but the crew were so full of samshui that they didn't notice anything, and I crept around down there in the dark engine room pouring petrol everywhere. I flooded the whole place. A match now and the result would not have concerned any of us. But I did not strike a light until I was safe outside. Then I rolled some cotton waste in a ball. It lights well and you can throw it quite a long way without it going out. I threw it into the engine room!

The minute I threw it I ran to the side and jumped. As I was still on the rail there was a shattering explosion. A sheet of flame shot up behind me and the whole boat reeled. Pirates and samshui and mahjongg pieces flew into the air. I plunged and landed in the shallow water. I scrambled out and made for the bank. It was lit with the glare of the explosion but no one had time to notice me. The tiger grass was growing close and I slipped in amongst it. I don't know how many were killed, or if the boat sank, or when they came to miss me. I didn't wait for details. I kept hidden in that grass and ran.

I had on a shirt, a pair of trousers, and a pair of Chinese slippers. In my pocket there was my gun. I didn't know a thing except that it would take me weeks to get down to Hankow, but I knew that if I didn't get there I would never live to leave China, so I decided I had best keep moving as hard as I could go.

It was rough going in the dark, but I couldn't very well get lost while I had the river to guide me, so I ran through the grass and ploughed through the little creeks and stumbled over the roughs[10] till I was pretty certain no one from the ship would chase me and I could see it was near dawn.

I crept farther into the grass and had a wee sleep then.

When I woke it was broad daylight and I was consumed with thirst. I knew it was dangerous to drink the river water so I looked round for a village where I thought they might let me have a taste from a well. There was nothing but tiger grass in sight but I kept on down the river and presently came in sight of one of those little groups of bamboo huts.

My tongue was swollen by now so I made straight for it meaning to ask quietly for a drink and go on my way. But when I got near the

---

9 *petrol in two tins* gasoline in two metal containers.
10 *roughs* land overrun with high grass, rocks, and scrubs.

place a great mongrel dog rushed savagely at me so I drew my gun and shot it, and that brought the whole place out on me like a hive of bees.

They'd have killed me if I hadn't run. I turned and made down the bank but I was tired and they were gaining so I saw I must take to the water. I was lucky that day because I am no great swimmer and in most places the current will suck you down, but just here it was steadier so I took a chance and plunged.

There was a current, but no undertow. I felt the current grip me and begin to sweep me downstream but that didn't worry me so long as I could make my way against it.

The crowd of peasants that were chasing me strung along the bank and called and spat after me, but that did not hurt and none of them had guns.

Pretty soon the current carried me out of their reach and then I began to swim for the farther bank. It took some reaching but I managed it and I scrambled out on the other side, muddy and soaked, and still so thirsty that I bent down and drank the poisonous Yangtse water. If I died, well I would have to die. Thirst as well as germs can kill you.

I'd lost my slippers in the water so now I had to go barefoot and that ground is rough when you are used to having shoes.

After I had had a drink I sat back out of sight in the grass and felt in my pocket for some fags.[11] Then I remembered I had left the ship without any. That was the worst thing of all on my trip down the river—not having anything to smoke for days and days.

I started to feel depressed when I found I had not any fags, and what with being wet and hungry too, and having no hat and no shoes, and knowing there was going to be weeks of it, with everyone you met on the way trying to do you in, I didn't feel the immediate future had anything special to commend it.

But it seemed the only thing to do was to hop in and get it over, so I climbed to my feet and started sneaking down the river through the grass.

Every time I came near a village I made a wide detour, and I grew quite smart at sneaking past coolies standing on the bank scooping fish. I was never spotted at all.

At first my feet got awfully sore and when there was no one in sight I used to creep down to the edge of the water and put them in to cool. I was sitting like that one day when a Chinese gunboat hove in sight. I thought I was saved that time. I jumped up and waved to

11 *fags* cigarettes.

attract her attention. I thought when she saw me she would take me off but she kept right on and didn't seem to be taking any notice. I thought maybe she hadn't seen me, and I pulled out my gun and fired a couple of shots.

I only meant to show them I was there but they must have thought I was trying to attack, for the next minute they opened fire on me with rifles and if I hadn't turned and bolted into the tiger grass I would have been riddled with bullets. That cured me of hailing gunboats. I kept right on for Hankow and didn't let anyone get sight of me at all.

5

I was days making down the river. I lost count of time but altogether I think it took about three weeks. What with water and mud and sweat my clothes went to rags early. I soon had a beard. My mother would not have known me. I'd been pinching maize out of the fields and crouching in the grass to eat it. That was about my only food, except wild oranges now and then. I was getting weak and my head was getting funny, but the only thing I seemed to think about was how much I would like a smoke.

Well, one evening when I was thinking like that I came out of the tiger grass and there was a joss house standing by itself in a clearing. I hung round watching for a while before I made up my mind it was deserted, then I sneaked up to the door and had a look inside. It was a rather poor sort of joss house, but there was an idol sitting up the way they always have them and incense sticks in vases standing round his feet. Well, I was wanting a smoke so much that I thought maybe I would try what good the incense sticks were, so I sneaked in and took a handful of them and lit them.

But they were fools of things really, you couldn't smoke them at all. I tried for quite a long time and then suddenly I was seized with a rage. I flung down the sticks, grabbed a big sword that was hanging up on the wall, and I went up and began to slash at the idol. Slashing seemed to make me madder. I knocked it down off his stand and stood over him slashing and hacking. Then I turned and started tearing down every thing I could see. I smashed the whole place up. Then I turned and ran for my life. I ran into the tiger grass. I ran and ran, and as I ran I kept falling and getting up and going on running till at last I fell over and couldn't run any more. You'd have thought half China was after me, and all the time it was no one. I knew that really, but it was my head. My throat was all dry and I was gasping. Once I lay down I didn't dare move. I stayed there for hours and then I went to sleep and when I woke I felt better. I started off again.

About this time I began to see a change in the country. There was more cultivation and the villages were bigger so I knew that at last I must be getting near Hankow. I was glad about that because I was nearly done.

It was one evening that I came in sight of Hankow. Seeing what a sight I was I thought I had better wait till morning before going in there. I meant to hide in the fields outside, but then I thought I would just go close and have a look at the place first.

I tell you it was good to see a real town again and I was creeping along not thinking anything but how good a time I would have tomorrow, and how I would march in and make a big sensation with my story, when up there came behind me one of those Chinese policemen, and before I knew what had happened I was being marched to the nearest police station.

The way I looked you couldn't really blame him for running me in. You would think I'd been dug up out of a grave. And he couldn't understand when I tried to tell him what had happened so I just kept on saying, "Get policeman him savee English," and he just kept prodding me in the back and making me keep on marching, so that was the way we went on till we got to the station yard.

He took me into a room then and went out and left me, and I sat wondering if after all this I was going to end up in the cells. But when he came back there was a fellow with him who was a Russian, and he came over to me (you could hardly see me for beard) and said in the first real English I'd heard for four months, "Now what's all this about?"

I could have cried, but all I did was to ask did he have a fag he could spare.

He didn't want to give me one at first, but when I told him I was English and that I'd been captured by bandits and walked hundreds of miles down the banks of the Yangtse Kiang he got more sympathetic and gave me a light.

So I sat there in the police station smoking his cigarettes and talking till I got tired of talking and he had no more cigarettes. Then I thought I would like some food. But he said I would have to go to hospital after the time I'd had, so he 'phoned up the sisters where I had my operation and when they said there was room there I was sent right along.

Those poor sisters threw up their hands when they saw me, but after I was bathed and shaved and had borrowed some pyjamas they all crowded round and seemed to admire my appearance. But they would not give me a square meal, only invalid food.

After a while they went away to pray because they thought it was because of God that I came through that time on the river, but I think if it had been because of God He would not have let me forget my cigarettes.

6

Next day I was given a suit of clothes.

The doctor said I could go out then, so I went to look up some old friends, and there was the manager of a tobacco company who had been in hospital with me when I had my operation.

I told him all that had happened and how I wanted to get down to Shanghai, so he said he would pay for me to go on a passenger steamer and he gave me a few dollars as well.

So I said good-bye to him and I went on the steamer and sailed down the Yangtse Kiang for the last time.

I decided by now that I had had enough of China and when I got down to Shanghai I meant to go on home.

But I had no money when I landed so I told the rickshaw boy to drive me straight to the Astor House Hotel. That was where my gear had been left ever since I came down the river after being on the *Ho-a-Haing*.

But they wouldn't lend me any money at the Astor House Hotel and I had to get some of my gear out of where they had it stored, and pawn it. After that I went to another hotel where I used to spend a lot of my wages, but they wouldn't lend me any money either. So I thought I would go along to my old company. I knew they were not pleased at me not going into hospital that time when they sent me six months back, but you can never tell what will happen until you have seen a person, so I thought I would go along.

I was lucky that time too, because the commander with the monocle was away on his vacation and there was a deputy there who didn't know everything about me. So I told him my story and he said I had been very foolish but he was sorry because I had paid for it, he could see. I did look sick too. So he brought out a lot of dishonoured cheques that he said had come down the river after I had to take my money out of the Hongkong and Shanghai Bank, and he said what was I going to do about these because the people were wanting their money. So that was not what I had expected—to have debts when I thought that cash would greet me.

I said I was awful sorry but I hadn't a cent in the world so he said perhaps they could find me a job, though not the kind I'd been used to. The job was to look after the engines of the motorboats that the company had running on the river at Shanghai. Such a job would have been a great comedown for me. But I did not say I would not take it for I wanted an advance on wages, so he gave me fifty dollars and after that I did not go near him or the job anymore.

7

I was several days drinking in different hotels in Shanghai and one time I was talking to Red Watson in the Swan.

Red Watson is an ex-pug who is the bouncer in the Swan and while I was talking to Red another man came in. Well, this fellow was half-oiled and he was sprawling all over the counter.

"I work for the best company in the whole of China," he was shouting and he shook his fist in my face as if I wanted to contradict him.

So I said, "Here, steady on,[12] mate. Which company are you talking about?"

"The greatest oil concern in China," he said, and when I heard that I kicked Red under the bar for him not to say I was with that company too. But Red is not at his strongest from the neck up, so he blurted out just the same, "This guy is with the company you talk of."

So the chap had a good look at me and then he said I was lying because he reckoned he knew every man in the company.

"I *am* all the same," I said. "Will you take a bet on it?"

"I'll bet all the money you've got," he said.

So I took out my money and I had about £10. So I gave that to Red and the guy gave his to Red and then I took out my papers and showed him.

When he saw those he knew he was stonkered.[13] "Oh," he says, "you're Bob." And he turned out he knew all about me though he had never set eyes on me before.

So I collected the cash and asked him not to let on about me, and I bought him a drink, and soon we were good pals.

12 *steady on* hold on, take it easy.
13 *stonkered* defeated.

When he had had a few more drinks he said he knew how I could get back with the company . . . on a good job too. So I said, How?

"Well," he said, "there's a ship due in two days' time and the engineer on her is going to be sacked because he's no engineer."

"Which ship would that be?" I asked.

And when he said the *Ma-a-Haing*, I knew. "Would that be the Second Engineer?" I asked. And of course it was. And the Second Engineer on the *Ma-a-Haing* was Mitchell.

So I thanked him for that information but I didn't go after Mitchell's job. I got a rickshaw and went down the river to see him.

When the *Ma-a-Haing* came in she anchored opposite the gasoline buoys and it was a good long drive out there in a rickshaw. The river is wide just there and when I got to the place I could see the *Ma-a-Haing* anchored about half a mile out. I saw I would have to get a sampan and it being low tide, there was a 100 yards of mud between me and the edge of the water. So I yelled to a group of coolies who were fishing at the edge of the water and one turned round and came running across the mud to me. It was soft mucky mud and he sank past his knees at every step so it was a good job he didn't have any clothes on. I had on a white silk suit so I didn't let him come too near me but I yelled out that I wanted to go in a sampan and then it turned out that he didn't know a word of English.

I chinked[14] a dollar at him though and that got him interested, so he waved his arm to show that I was to walk along the top of a big sewer pipe that was running out over the mud to the edge of the water right near where his sampan was floating. So he ploughed along through the mud and I got up on the sewer pipe. But he was a fool if he thought I could balance on a sewer pipe after the life I'd been leading, so I had to straddle the thing and lever myself with my hands. I was a mess, I can tell you, in a white silk suit, straddling a dirty old sewer pipe.

Well, when we got to the end of the pipe there was about a 30-foot drop down into his sampan, and I wasn't having any, so I shook my head and yelled at him and turned round and straddled the pipe all the way back.

That made him scared because he thought he would lose the dollar, so he came up close and hunched his shoulders and pointed to his back, to show that he would carry me.

14 *chinked* made a little, metallic sound.

So I got down off the sewer pipe and climbed on to his back and he started off across the mud carrying me. For halfway it was all right. *Then he started to sink.* He started to sink deeper and deeper and soon he was up to his neck. He began to try and throw me off, but he couldn't get the leverage, being so far in, and I felt him going down under me and there was nothing but soft slimy mud all round us.

He was struggling, and my weight was pushing him deeper, and soon his face was in it and I could hear him choking. I started to yell then, but the other coolies that had been with him just went on fishing and never took an atom of notice. They heard me too because a Russian who was farther away heard, and began to run towards us. He started swearing at the coolies and his swearing moved them.

They started to come over, and the Russian made a detour round where the mud was firmer and they followed him. They got to the water's edge, and caught the rope that was holding the sampan and started to haul her (being flat-bottomed) over the mud towards us. But all the time the coolie under me was going down deeper and not struggling so hard now, and before they reached me I lost him and was lying on the mud, waiting for it to suck me down too. I had the sense, though, to lie out flat and not move, so as to offer more resistance. But I was shaking all the time and I still seemed to feel the coolie under me though he was quite lost now, and the mud all round was as quiet as if he had never been.

So I kept watching them pulling at the sampan and feeling myself sinking a little bit every minute and wondering if they could ever get it to me in time. It seemed to take years but it was coming all right. It seemed such a long time that I started to pull myself towards it, only that made my face and arms go down into the mud, and I thought I would be lost like that coolie. So I just lay while they kept ploughing and heaving, and in the end its nose came sliding where I could reach.

I heaved myself up then and grabbed hold of the side of her, and I never felt anything so good as the feel of that solid wood. I dragged my legs out of the mud and swung over into her. Once I knew I was safe and wasn't going down into the mud after all I came over all sick and couldn't do anything but crouch down in the bottom and shiver. Sometimes I can still feel that coolie sinking under me, but it's no manner of use brooding on things, is it? I think a man wants to have a drink when he finds himself starting to brood.

So I got into the sampan all right, and they pulled her back into the water and poled her out to the *Ma-a-Haing*. But you never saw such a sight as I was. Mud and muck all over my white silk suit, no hat, and my face caked with dirt. When I got out to the *Ma-a-Haing* I gave the coolies all the money that I had left in my pocket and scrambled up on board.

8

There was no one in sight. They all seemed to be sleeping or to have gone ashore, so I took off my wet clothes, rolled them under my arm and made for where I reckoned Mitchell's cabin would be. Sure enough there he was stretched out on his bunk, snoring.

"Hey!" I called to him.

He opened his eyes and sat up. Then he seemed to think he was having D.T.'s, but I explained it was only Bob come to see him; for you could not expect him to know me when I was not wearing any clothes and had mud thick on my face.

Then he let me wash and I borrowed a suit from him.

9

When we got ashore Mitchell asked what was I going to do now, so I said I was through with China and he said he was too, so we planned we would go home on a boat together.

Mitchell wasn't broke like I was, he had over £200, so we got drinking that night and the next day we went to the company to see about getting home. We were going home D.B.S. (Distressed British Seamen) and the cost of that was due from the *Golden Arrow* because we had landed from her, but somebody else had to make the immediate arrangements. So we went to the company. The deputy was hard on me this time, because some more dishonoured cheques had come in from up the river—they take an awful long time to work their way right down—and I had spent his 50 dollars and never gone to work on the motor-boats; but I explained how it was that I had had a tough time and got drinking, so he said the best thing was for me to get out of the country, and I said that was the very thing I had come there wanting to do.

So he rang up the British consul and said the company would pay half our expenses if they would advance the other half, so the British consul said they would, and Mitchell and I had to go round to the shipping master[15] to get everything fixed.

15 *shipping master* an official in charge of the hiring and dismissal of sailors below the rank of officer.

They booked for us to go on the s.s. *Dardanus*.[16] She was a cargo boat sailing that night, and the shipping master was awfully good getting us all fixed up, so Mitchell thought we ought to buy him something and he went out and got a pound of the best tobacco.

We gave this to the shipping master and he said it was too good of us, but he never should have said that because it impressed Mitchell so that he began to get sorry, and when I was talking to the shipping master out in the passage he swiped the tobacco back again, but the shipping master never let on if he guessed where it had gone to.

10

Well, after that we got in a motorboat and went out to our ship. When we got all our gear on board we asked where we would be sleeping and the purser took us down to the fo'c'sle where there was nothing but a stone floor and bunks—worse than steerage.[17] But we thought we would do better than that when the ship got out to sea, so we just dumped our gear there and went back on the deck.

The wireless operator was on deck and we asked where could we get a drink, and he said he didn't think we could have one, being D.B.S.

Well, by now we were getting tired of being D.B.S., but there didn't seem to be anything we could do about it, so we started to feel pretty glum. But the wireless operator said that since the ship had missed the tide we wouldn't be sailing till midnight, so why not go ashore again and say good-bye to Shanghai and bring back a supply of stuff for the voyage? So that cheered us up a bit and we decided we would go ashore.

Mitchell went ashore in shorts, a pair of sand shoes,[18] and an old blue blazer. I had a good suit on, but Mitchell had got awful careless since he came to China. I said he ought to have more respect for me, but you never could make any impression on Mitchell.

So we went ashore to say good-bye to Shanghai. Now Mitchell always starts to give away his money when he gets properly oiled, so

16 *s.s. Dardanus* The career of the s.s. *Dardanus* came to a close on April 6, 1942. After departing from Calcutta a few days earlier, it was bombed by a Japanese aircraft. Disabled, it was taken in tow by *Gandara*, a British steamship. The next day both ships were sunk by three Japanese cruisers.

17 *steerage* the substandard accommodations for passengers paying the cheapest fares (derivation from the initial location near the rudder).

18 *sand shoes* tennis shoes.

this time he gave me half his money to mind for him, and half of his money was about £100. Then we got in two rickshaws and went for a drive.

We drove right down the Bund and suddenly we heard a shout and there was a Chinaman chasing us, and Mitchell looked back and I looked back, and there he was running and waving with one hand, and in the other hand he had a pair of shoes.

"You buy my shoes," he was shouting, "you buy my shoes." And when he got up close he went to shove the shoes in the rickshaw, only Mitchell told him to clear out, we didn't want any shoes.

But he kept saying they were our shoes and we didn't know what to make of him so we asked the rickshaw boy to find out what was all the fuss.

Well, it turned out then that when we came in on the *Golden Arrow* he was one of the people who came down to the boat that we had ordered a lot of things from and never seen again. We never thought another thing about it, but this one had made our shoes and all these months he had been trying to deliver them to us. He never forgot what we looked like, and when we drove past in the rickshaw he saw us and chased after us.

So we said we didn't want the shoes now, but Mitchell threw him a dollar, and he caught it and rang[19] it to make sure it was a good one, because some of the dollars in China have had the silver scooped out of the middle by coolies and lead put in its place, so that you can't tell any difference from the outside. But this dollar was a good one, and the Chinaman seemed quite pleased with it. He grinned and trotted off still carrying the shoes.

That is nearly the last thing I remember about China, though I didn't get so oiled as Mitchell did that evening. I kept count of the time all right and when it was getting near midnight I got him into a rickshaw and started down to the river. But my rickshaw was ahead of Mitchell's and when I got down to the river I looked back and Mitchell had disappeared!

Well, I guessed pretty right where he would have gone, because there was a Polish woman that he used to go with, and sure enough there was his rickshaw sitting outside her house.

So I told my boy to wait and I went over and knocked. The Polish woman came to the door and she was in a proper temper.

19 *rang* produced a sound by striking.

"What for you make my boy always drunk?" she started, but I said her "boy" didn't need encouraging, and I pushed past her to where Mitchell was lying on the bed.

I went over and started shaking him.

"Come on," I said, "you'll miss the boat if you stop here."

But Mitchell opened one eye and looked at me and said he wasn't going.

"I've only got me mother," he said, "and she's in Canada. Why should I go to England?"

"Your gear's on board, Mitch," I said.

"Let it stop there," he said. "Go 'way and leave me."

So I tried shaking him again and he wanted to hit me. "Get away," he said.

So I went outside and got two Sikh policemen.

But when they came in Mitchell pulled their beards and laughed at them. "Get away," he said, "I'm not coming." And they couldn't make him come if he didn't want to. They said he was a free agent.

"That's it," said Mitchell. "I'm a free agent. I've only got me mother in the world. You can't make me do anything if I don't want to," and he winked at me with the one eye he had open.

"Well, what about your money?" I said.

"Keep it," he said, "keep it. You need it more than me."

So you see he was not in a normal condition.

At last I gave up and went back to the ship. I thought he would come round and follow later, but I stretched out and went to sleep in the smoke room, and when I woke it was daylight and we were away to sea.

So I did not see Mitchell again till he followed me to Glasgow, but I bought a lot of presents for my folks with his money so that when he asked me for it I could not give it to him back. It was really very funny to think how it was his money that had bought all the presents for my people, but he could not see it that way, even when I explained. I always think it is a pity for a man not to have a sense of humour, for then when these things happen he can have a good laugh and he does not get so upset. I am sure I do not know how I should have got on in my life but for my sense of humour, but a man cannot help it if he has not got one, and Mitchell was a good fellow in many other ways.

THE END

AFTERWORD
James Kelman

It is a pity there are getting to be so many places that I can never go back to, but all the same, I do not think it is much fun a man being respectable all his life.

I would like to go back to Hoboken, but if I did Heinz Billings might get me, because he said he would wait forever; though I think myself it is terribly mean of a man to say he will wait forever, when all you have done is to take some money out of the till in a speakeasy . . .

So, you see, I cannot go back . . . while [he] is alive, and I cannot go back to the rest of New York either, because there was the time the man was killed that held me up outside Kelly's Clam Broth House, and the police came with the gun and asked me questions in my hotel. But they did not think I had killed him at the time, because they let me go away all right, but you never can tell when the New York police will come after you. And if they did they might find out about the diamonds and Mrs. Carr's ring.

HE author of *Don't Call Me a Crook!* was a scoundrel, a thief, a drunkard and a womaniser. And an engineer to trade, a Scottish engineer at that, and traditionally Scotsmen and engineers go together. The above extract is from the opening page and, but for the verbal past tense, takes us into a conversational voice reminiscent of Damon Runyon, whose earliest collection of stories, *Guys and Dolls*, had appeared in 1932. Moore's memoir was first published in London in 1935 and contains a similar irony in his use of language. But the more into it we go the less of a similarity there is to Runyon. Moore's voice is streetwise, confident, and racy, but there is an edge to it, a toughness and sense of reality that rarely surfaces in Runyon's work.

The original edition carried the subtitle *My True Autobiography*. It is not that he considered most autobiography false but that he saw other possibilities. Moore was used to covering his tracks, and where better than autobiography?

In a recent novel[1] I wrote of a Scotsman domiciled in U.S.A. for a number of years. He is no Andrew Carnegie. Like many Americans he

1. *You have to be careful in the land of the free* (Orlando, FL: Harcourt, 2004).

has to dodge about earning a living as best he can. This can mean moving from place to place, the more temporary the relationship the better. Over the years I have encountered a few of my compatriots so engaged. It is a byword among exiled Scotsmen that if you are in a bar anywhere in the world and hear another Scottish accent you act deaf; if such a person is carrying the pipes and wearing a kilt you are also blind. The ones who approach you usually want something. It begins with a cuddle, then a drink, and ends in a fight. Variations are possible. It can begin with the fight, then the drink, and end with the cuddle. But usually it only happens with fellow Scotsmen. The rest of the world can relax.

But fair exchange is no robbery and one thing about these awkward Scotsmen, they take you to places the tourists never see.

When not working at his trade he lied and cheated his way "seven times around the world." "Lying" and "cheating" are not terms he would apply to his own behaviour. He admits to many "crimes" and it is in his memory that I trap the term in quotation marks.

Please don't call me a crook.

Okay Bob.

Except by his own account at least two of those crimes were homicide. He would probably dispute that on the grounds of disqualification, that the two victims were not white European. There is no escaping that Bob Moore's prejudices extend into racism and its logical extension, which is killing people, when working up the Yangtze Kiang in China. It surfaces earlier in his anti-Semitism while in Chicago trying to offload stolen diamonds. His prejudice ranges across most nationalities. During the early decades of the last century the vast majority of the white population was racist. It may be a fact but it is not an excuse. I could imagine Moore arguing that racism was neither here nor there, some people just made it hard for him, including the guys he shot.

Moore has few redeeming qualities. In Sweden at the age of 21 he cons a shopgirl out of her wages. In New York he seeks out the "nancyboys" in Times Square and robs one at the first opportunity. On a train to Chicago he hooks up with a woman, cons her out of a diamond ring, and pawns it, leaving her at the station skint, drunk, and incapable. In Buenos Aires he enters a relationship with an older lady that "was not what you would call a platonic arrangement," then scarpers north with her money and spends it in Atlantic City. In Glasgow he has an affair with a wealthy woman, spends all her dough, then dumps her. In Chicago he sends his wife back to Glasgow so he can get on with living his life.

There are points in the narrative where one has to ask why am I reading the writings of such a rogue? He would have robbed his granny and probably did. Yet not only did I read the work right to the end, I did so in a rush, then I wanted to find out more.

Bob Moore was born in Glasgow about 1898–99. Upon the outbreak of the 1914–18 war he enlisted, but was found to be too young at 16. His father was able to get him out. Later he re-enlists and joins the Royal Flying Corps. His hope was to wear a uniform and kill people. It was a bitter disappointment that he had to stay on an airfield in Boulogne greasing airplane engines. Eventually he was hit by a propellor and invalided out with a lump sum gratuity of £150. It had no lasting affect on his health. For the first time in three years he returned home to see his family in Glasgow.

But what of his family? He tells us next to nothing. He wrote this "true autobiography" at the age of 36 in the hope that it would earn him a fortune. That he had survived so long he put down to his "mother [who] made him eat a lot of soup" when he was a wee boy. He just wishes that it had not been homemade. If it had been a name brand he might have got his picture on the tin and made some dough. His family seems to have been of the "respectable" working class.

In those days Glasgow was an international port and centre of the shipbuilding industry. Like many another he went to sea. His work experience from the Royal Flying Corps allowed him to enter an engineering apprenticeship at an advanced level. Thus at the age of 21 he was a qualified engineer. He began his career as a junior engineer on a merchant ship trading between Glasgow and Sweden.

Some of the qualities of the man are apparent even here. He has no respect for age and none for any rank higher than his own. He is not fearless but impulsive, very dangerous when pushed. To use an old Glasgow phrase, Bob "goes ahead." In his first post he and the Chief Officer do not get on. When the Chief spins the crew a yarn about his war experiences Bob goes into a fit of giggles and makes a sarcastic comment. The Chief tosses a glass of milk at him. Bob replies with a big plate of potatoes. Later he grabs a heavy spanner and clatters the Chief across the skull with it. He nearly kills the man, which would have been a problem on board a ship because "there is not any place at all where you can get away and hide."

Before entering New York Harbour on his first trip to the States, a passenger asks him a favour: Will he take a certain package and deliver it to him in a certain hotel? Bob accepts the commission. The package contains a pile of diamonds and not drugs as he expected. Once ashore he vanishes to Chicago and sells the stuff for $10,500.

The U.S.A. has entered a time of social insanity, exacerbated—if not effected—by the imposition of Prohibition. These are crazy years but an immigrant youth can thrive on that, especially if one is prepossessing, with a taste for adventure, and quite unscrupulous.

He is never keen to divulge personal information. On occasion he even seems ashamed of himself, slightly. He rarely sends money home. A couple of times he gets it back, as for instance one time in London he goes skint and wires his father for the fare home. His family wants him to marry and settle down but he cannot manage this. Back in Glasgow he meets a girl and does marry her. He brings her out to the States but she returns home soon after. She is pregnant and has their child. He sends her a money present which she mistakes for a gesture towards reconciliation and returns to Chicago. It is with much relief that she finally returns to Glasgow. Marriage and families were not designed for guys like him.

Acts of heroism are not beyond him. These are personal rather than altruistic; the sort that drinking buddies perform on each other's behalf. He befriends a Dutchman aboard an oceangoing liner and shows him the ropes. The fellow happens to have a few thousand dollars in his pocket. He keeps Bob in booze. There is no sign of the hospitality ending. Bob stays with him when they go ashore in Canada. The Dutchman wants into the States but has the immigration quota against him. Bob takes him to Windsor, Ontario, a traditional crossing point.

It takes more than a week. The guy is incompetent. He keeps getting drunk and confusing the story, boasting to immigration officials that he is Dutch. Bob manages to avoid him getting murdered by cutthroat bootleggers and shot dead by police snipers across the U.S. border. Finally he sneaks him across the river and into Detroit. While breathing a sigh of relief, walking down the street to freedom, they are accosted by a cop. Fortunately they have no luggage, a dead giveaway. But Bob does have a half-full bottle of whisky. "[A] man's instinct to hang on to his whisky very often proves right in this life." It is his only property. He gives it to the cop who wishes them well for the future.

They head for "Hoboken in New Jersey where all the Hollanders stay and where there are a lot of speakeasies." His new pal is so grateful that Bob never has to work until the money runs out. When it does the Dutchman decides to bring his wife into the country. She has some money. He commisions Bob to perform the deed for a $1,000.

This he accomplishes in the most elegant manner. He travels alone

to Montreal but buys two return tickets. The ticket collector tears
half of one ticket. Later Bob tears half of the other. He meets with the
Dutch girl and stays with her a short while, coaching her in what to
do. She pretends to be his wife. They cross into the U.S.A. on the
remaining halves of the two return tickets and nobody is any the
wiser, they just assume she is his wife.

Moore is an exponent of irony. But there are occasions when his
use of ambiguity operates not for literary effect but to conceal reality.
He is not telling lies such that it might be discovered in a court of law.
He is just covering his back, protecting himself for future reference.
This is how people live on the edge. At a time in the future the burden
of proof is bound to lie with you. So you prepare for that eventuality,
wiping clean the traces. Very few names or dates appear where it
matters. Nobody will point a finger at Bob Moore.

In a Hoboken speakeasy—Kelly's Clam Broth House—two
wiseguys take him round a back alley and rob him. Later one of the
two is found gunned down. The cops come looking for Bob. The
murder weapon has been traced back to the Manhattan hotel where
he works as a shift engineer. Apparently he was one of the few
people with the key to the room where the gun was kept. What a
coincidence! He has no idea how it all happened but decides it is
best to skip town before the cops get him, whether for that or something else, including Mrs. Carr's diamond ring.

Soon after this he is in Boston where he runs into another scrape,
and is fired from one job then gets another as a housepainter.
However, he is not a member of the trade union; his work is "tarred
and feathered" and he is sent back to New York.

Now he lands his best ever job, chief engineer on a luxury yacht.
When people know he is "frae Glasga'" it is open sesame. That link
helps him throughout his working life. The luxury vessel is owned by
one of New York's foremost multimillionaires. There is a high
turnover in crew. But Bob sticks it out for an unheard of seven
months. On board luxury yachts everybody boozes and carouses,
including chief engineers. He gets as drunk as the rest.

The usual mutual hatred develops between him and higher grade
workers. But the only post higher than chief engineer is skipper. He
outlasts a few of them. One is a former "Russian naval officer who
served under the Czar." He wants Bob to work on deck when the
engine is idle. Bob reminds him that chief engineers do not perform
such lowly tasks. He does not rate the Russian's seamanship and to

annoy the man takes to carrying a life belt at all times. When one of the owner's sons blows up the engine Bob gets the skipper sacked.

The multimillionaire's old father is a skinflint who sacks one steward who buys lobsters instead of organising their theft from fishermen's pots. The two sons spend most of their life sailing up and down Long Island Sound, getting drunk on bootleg booze, bribing their way out of trouble, and picking up party girls for orgies. "I got up and went on deck and it was women's clothes from end to end . . . But not a sign of a woman . . . So I went down to the big cabin. They were all there, lying in heaps. That's how good a party it was."

A vague disapproval is apparent. "[They] used to bring me down rolls of notes to mind when they were oiled, and you could always peel off sixty or a hundred dollars. They never noticed any difference . . ." He has no liking for "the Boss's boys" and the feeling is mutual. The class antagonism complicates matters. They are contemptuous of him, and ridicule his uniform. The sons beat up two of the stewards. Moore, still in his 20s, was near enough the same age as the pair.

The family fires him but have to reemploy him because nobody else can operate the engines properly. This is no fluke. In the past when he gets fired off a job he scuppers the works in revenge. And there is always the chance he will be recalled to sort out the damage. So it proved on this occasion. They need him badly. Twenty sons of millionaires are all aboard, set for another wild party. Bob saves the day. He discovers an integral air pipe blocked by nothing less than the cork of a whisky bottle. Then he remembers that he "plugged" it himself the last time they fired him. He is applauded for his mechanical skills. Right enough, "You can't beat Scotch engineers."

Much of this episode in his life is recognisable from fictional descriptions of the "Roaring Twenties" in literature and the cinema. Moore's perspective differs through his firsthand experience from belowdecks. It is a crucial portrait of East Coast high society, complete with 15-year-old girls and high-court judges. "They were all crazy that night . . . By the time I had the dynamo going and all the lights on two more boatloads of them had come out. More men and Ziegfeld Follies girls. The first lot had been New York society girls. . . . Some of the men had names that you would know if I told you."

But that same night there was a fatality: a drunken girl dons one of Bob's spare uniforms, shouts "Whoopee!" and dives overboard. He goes in after her:

I rushed to the rail after her. It was quite black. You couldn't see anything, but I vaulted it and jumped well out. As I fell through the air I heard shouting break out behind me and guessed the rest on the yacht had seen. Then I struck that black water and in the shock I forgot everything else. Before I came up I felt the current catch me and suck at me. Then I was up, right aft, and there was a blob floating in front of me that I guessed was that girl. I couldn't see any face and she wasn't calling out or struggling . . . I made a grab and missed . . .

Amid the wild adventures, the bravura, the frequent criminality, and general mayhem that is the life of Bob Moore, his handling of the death of this young woman reveals something else, that his "true autobiography" is the work of a proper *writer*. It is to be regretted that it was his one and only literary production. From *Don't Call Me a Crook!* we gain a genuine insight into conditions of that period. Lawlessness is rampant. In Chicago a man is murdered for nothing more than blowing a raspberry at a passerby. He glimpses Al Capone passing in his "armoured car," with a machine gun on top and a couple of speed cops escorting him through the traffic.

At the same time Moore is treading the streets of Chicago Eugene V. Debs and other working-class activists are in prison. Moore knows nothing of that; he is trying to lead an ordinary life, a young working-class husband. He applies for a job as a caretaker, and joins a queue of a couple of thousand unemployed men. This does not give him any feelings of solidarity. He cons his way to the head of the queue, makes heavy use of his Scottish accent, and talks his way into the job. Later on, after his fallout with Heinz Billings and the Hoboken gangsters, Moore leaves his speakeasy job and queues for hours for a job at an all-night coffee stall.

He talks his way into that one too but inadvertently burns the place down. He takes a third engineer's post aboard a ship heading for China. Not only does he talk himself into the job he does the same for his current drinking buddy, an Englishman who is more dangerously crazy than himself. On their first night in Shanghai they are thrown out of their hotel for bringing two Chinese girls back to their room. Once they have drunk all their money Bob signs on aboard "a river boat carrying paraffin between Ichang and Chungking on the Yangtze Kiang." Although the boat is armour plated to safeguard against bandits he is more interested in the price of whisky, only 4s. 6d. a bottle. He discovers the Chief Engineer dead drunk on the floor, and eventually gets him revived: "You're frae Glasga'?" the Chief asks. He too is Glaswegian.

Moore's adventures and experiences in China are detailed, sometimes amusing but often difficult to take. Many foreign workers wallow in their ignorance and earn good wages for being blind to reality. Why is it that two working-class men like himself and the Chief Engineer only have to clap their "hands, and a lot of Chinamen came running"? Why are all these Europeans, Americans, and Japanese on the loose? He never questions the dreadful poverty of the people nor why this vast and beautiful country is in such a perilous state. The racism is staggering. "I did not know at this time that the way you must treat a Chinaman is to give him a kick in the pants, so I thought they were just like other human beings. But it seems you could not have any prestige in China if you treated a Chinaman like a human being . . ."

Moore rarely squirms at reality but does not suppress the information. He may not raise the questions but his attention to detail allows us to raise them. He is not blind to the suffering but cannot move beyond that horrible Colonial mentality. The period he spent in China came after the death of Sun Yat-sen and from the establishment of the National Government in 1928, under the leadership of Chiang Kai-shek. It was a time of turmoil, of civil war, and the rise of the socialist movement. The last thing he sees before leaving Hankow was

> . . . a procession—a procession of Chinamen in cages. The cages were not big enough to let a man kneel up straight, the only way he could manage was to crouch down with his head sticking forward; but even if there had been room he could not have moved from that position for each one had his hands tied to his heels. They were trussed worse than turkeys for market. The cages were mounted on poles and four men were carrying each cage. They must have suffered very severely for they had been days in these cages, and now when they were approaching their journey's end they did not receive any sympathy, but instead all the people in the streets crowded round and jeered. So I asked what these men had done since everyone was so unsympathetic, and I was told that they were guilty of being Communists. So evidently that is a very bad crime in China, but I think they are more to be pitied than blamed, for what can you think of a man who goes in for politics when all he will get out of it is being put in a cage?

A genuine literary classic did appear in the same year as Moore's autobiography. This was Tom Kromer's *Waiting for nothing*. A year later John Dos Passos published *The Big Money*, the third volume of his great *U.S.A.* trilogy. Early work had appeared from Erskine

Caldwell and William Saroyan; Ralph Ellison had just arrived in New York, already at work on his autobiographical notes. More would appear from such as Meridel Le Sueur and Tillie Olsen. These young American writers were nothing if not politically aware. Bob Moore comes nowhere in such a list but his work is also that of a young writer who is striving for something that includes the literary. The noticeable absence in his book is any political commitment.

Most immigrants remain distanced from the politics of the new country. There are different reasons for that. Some remained wedded to the politics of the old country. But in the case of Bob Moore, there is no indication of anything like that. Yet in the first quarter of last century his home city was a hive of political activity. At the point Moore enlisted in World War I there was a powerful antiwar movement within Glasgow's radical working class. Crucial figures on the scene included the revolutionary John Maclean and Arthur McManus, first chairman of the Communist Party of Great Britain.

McManus was a close friend of James Connolly, murdered by the British State in 1916 following the Easter Rising in Ireland. It is less widely known that Connolly was Scottish, born of Irish parents, and holds his own place in Scottish radical history. Connolly also lived in New Jersey for a period, working at the Singer plant in Elizabeth, and he was in contact with Daniel De Leon, furthering the cause of the Socialist Labor Party and the Wobblies.

In U.S. left wing circles the names of Maclean and McManus were known. When he was not languishing in British prisons Maclean corresponded with Eugene V. Debs and John Reed. His old friend James Larkin, the great Irish labour organiser, was then in the U.S.A., having gone to regain his health following the Dublin lockout of 1913. He helped produce the U.S. edition of *The Irish Worker* and included regular bulletins from radical Glasgow as well as from Ireland. Leon Trotsky wrote regularly for a U.S. radical journal and gave information on the treatment of Glasgow's antiwar activists. More information appeared in the *New York Call*. Max Eastman's sister, Crystal, traveled to Glasgow on behalf of *The Liberator* to report back on the situation. Equally news of the fate of U.S. socialists like Debs, Bill Haywood, and Tom Mooney not only reached Glasgow's left wing circles, but gave rise to agitation on their behalf.[2] Whether or not he is aware of the war being waged by

2. Some of the information given here is from James D. Young's *John Maclean: Clydeside Socialist* (Glasgow: Clydeside Press 1992); see also my Introduction to *Born up a Close: Memoirs of a Brigton Boy* by Hugh Savage (Glenduel, Scotland: Argyll Press, 2006).

either the U.S. or British authorities on radicals and socialists none of it appears in Bob Moore's "true autobiography."

If I had come upon this book as a young writer it would have had an affect on me. I have no doubt about that. Whether it would have influenced my writing, who knows? But young writers are impressionable.

How aware was he of other writers? He never refers to writers or magazines. The only books he mentions are *Private Spud Tamson* and penny dreadfuls. He reads newspapers, but the articles that get his attention pertain directly to his life: ship schedules, "Mrs. Hauptmann," and the Case of the Drowned Flapper. But people do not have to be readers or writers to produce autobiographies. Nowadays they employ "ghostwriters." He had an editor for his: Pat Spry. Nothing on Pat Spry appears on the Web. Was Pat short for Patricia or Patrick? The name has the feel of a pseudonym. But what about "Bob Moore" itself? Is that a pseudonym? Did he have anything to hide, apart from the stuff he confesses?

Don't Call Me a Crook! seems to have been Moore's one and only publication. Like Spry, there is not one entry on the Web concerning him. Other sites connected with literature and libraries offer no information. I checked out the largest reference library in Europe, which is located in Glasgow. But nothing. I was advised to check out records connected to the Merchant Navy, the book reviews of 1935, births, deaths, and marriages, and so on. I did not do any of that.

Has he covered his tracks too well? Maybe some intrepid researcher will want to take it on. The place to start if not the upper reaches of the Yangtze Kiang, or Hoboken, New Jersey, could be his hometown . . . or the Land Down Under . . . or a Japanese city known for its beef:

> If I make a lot of money out of writing my reminiscences I think I will go and settle on a farm in Australia, or, maybe, I will buy a house in Kobe in Japan, which is a very pretty place; . . . [and] the people in Kobe do not know how to read English, so they will not have seen anything to make them think I might be a crook . . . I could tell you things about Glasgow that would make your hair stand on end . . . [But] I do not like to hurt people's feelings when I have known them from my childhood; besides, I would not like to lose all the money for my reminiscences by being drawn into a court case.

JAMES KELMAN is the author of numerous novels, short stories, essays, and plays. He has taught creative writing at the University of Texas at Austin and San José State University. In 1994 he won the Booker Prize for *How late it was, how late*. Harcourt published his latest novel, *Kieron Smith, boy*, in the fall of 2008. Kelman was born in Glasgow, Scotland, and lives there most of the time.

ALSO FROM DISSIDENT BOOKS

NOTES on DEMOCRACY

by H. L. MENCKEN

A NEW EDITION

INTRODUCTION AND ANNOTATIONS BY MARION ELIZABETH RODGERS,
author of *Mencken: The American Iconoclast*

AFTERWORD BY TWO-TIME PULITZER PRIZE WINNER ANTHONY LEWIS

"The tone is beyond satire, almost caustic, like the guy
at the bar who sidles up to you with bad news—
the guy you can't help thinking has a point."
—*Los Angeles Times*

"With his **refreshing vehemence and impeccable political
incorrectness**, [Mencken] explores the root of the democratic
ideal, the notion that at the 'nether levels' of the social order
'lies a deep, illimitable reservoir of righteousness and wisdom,
unpolluted by the corruption of privilege.'"
—*The New York Observer*

"This is a book aimed at a certain type of skeptical and
cynical mind. It is like a very strong cheese:
only a few will like it, but those who do will crave it . . ."
—*The Seattle Times*

"**Written more than 80 years ago, Mencken's deeply cynical and
amusing book is remarkably relevant today.**"
—*The Globe and Mail* (Toronto)

HUMOR/POLITICS 978-0-9773788-1-4 $14.95 (U.S.)/$15.95 (CAN)

Available at Amazon.com, BarnesandNoble.com,
DissidentBooks.com, and good bookstores everywhere.